entrepreneurship

.com

Tim Burns

entrepreneurship.com

DEARBORN™
T R A D E
A **Kaplan Professional** Company

This publication is designed to provide accurate and authoritative information in regard to the subject matter covered. It is sold with the understanding that the publisher is not engaged in rendering legal, accounting, or other professional service. If legal advice or other expert assistance is required, the services of a competent professional person should be sought.

Acquisitions Editor: Mary B. Good
Senior Managing Editor: Jack Kiburz
Interior Design: Lucy Jenkins
Cover Design: Design Solutions
Typesetting: the dotted i

Library of Congress Cataloging-in-Publication Data

Burns, Tim.
    Entrepreneurship.com / Tim Burns.
      p.   cm.
    Includes index.
    ISBN 1-57410-136-6
    1. Business enterprises—Computer networks. 2. Electronic commerce.
    3. Internet marketing. 4. Entrepreneurship. I. Title.
  HD30.37 .B867 2000
    658.8'4—dc21
                                                00-010649

DEDICATION

This book is dedicated to the memory of my nephew, Joseph Michael Fritscher, God's Angel of Joy.

acknowledgments

Let me first acknowledge Mary Good, my editor at Dearborn Trade, for her guidance and expert editing skills as well as her enthusiasm for the project. Her involvement certainly helped make *entrepreneurship.com* a much better book. Let me also thank Sandy Thomas, senior editorial assistant at Dearborn, for her assistance. Thanks also to Jack Kiburz, senior managing editor, and Leslie Banks, publicist, at Dearborn for their assistance.

Thanks are also due to the Internet entrepreneurs who gave of their valuable time in sharing insights and "war stories." These include David Sipes and Taj Alavi of Branders.com; Craig Forman, Peter Poulos, and Donald Van de Mark of MyPrimeTime; Greg Meffert of NetEx; Soon Yu and Gina Lopuck of Gazoontite.com; Mark S. Lewis of eyeonet; Stuart Skorman of HungryMinds; Tom Cox of Golfballs.com; and David Lichtblau of Starmine.

I want to extend my appreciation to the members of the venture capital community. These include Moses Joseph of the Anila Fund; David Cowan of Bessemer Venture Partners; Steve Dow of Sevin Rosen Funds; Raj Atluru of Draper Fisher Jurvetson; and Brendon Kim of Altos Ventures. Let me also thank William Reichert of Garage.com.

Special appreciation to Pam Wegmann of Information Matters for her research and preparation of the resource guide. Other experts who helped make this a better book include Robbie Vitrano of Trumpet Advertising and John Deveney of Deveney Communication. Also special thanks to Jean Meyer for her editorial assistance and project support. Others who assisted include Mary Karl; Sarah Davies; Donald Owen, CPA; and Cheryl Frame.

contents

introduction

Times of great opportunity generally roll around every 100 years or so. At the turn of the previous century, it was industrial giants like Rockefeller and Carnegie who understood the opportunities created by the manufacturing age and were able to consolidate various industries to create enormous and sustainable wealth.

The beginning of this century is another time of great opportunity. The ushering in of the information age has created a particularly fertile climate for economic opportunity that has not been seen in more than a generation. Business commentators refer to this period of immense possibilities as the new economy. The Internet is one of the primary growth engines of the new economy and is helping to usher in a digital, interactive medium that transcends traditional boundaries to create a global community. This community changes the way people purchase goods and services, communicate with each other, learn, and obtain information. In fact, the opportunities today could even be greater than any that have *ever* existed in the past.

As you probably know, a few young entrepreneurs pioneered new economy business models and became billionaires. Although some of the value of their companies is based on exuberance, much of it is grounded in opportunity. Times of great change create immense opportunities. The movement into the information age has disrupted conventional economic models and fractured existing market structures. Academics call it *economic disequilibrium*. Investors call it an *unprecedented buying opportunity*. And entrepreneurs call it *gold*.

Businesses are being started and funded at a record pace as they try to stake their claim in the new economy. Never before have conditions been this ripe to start a major business. Never before has the strength of an idea been so powerful. This is truly the Age of the Entrepreneur.

Entrepreneurship.com is designed to guide you through the business and legal fundamentals of starting and running a business in the new economy.

It is based on my more than 15 years of counseling start-ups, many in the technology area, on both business and legal subjects. My own research and experience are supplemented with advice and interviews from leading Internet venture capitalists and business consultants as well as entrepreneurs.

This book is also useful for the existing brick-and-mortar business seeking to maximize its potential in the new economy. The transformation to a click-and-mortar business can vastly increase market reach and profit potential. Also known as "place and space," existing businesses seeking online possibilities can actually be preferable to pure Internet companies. With effective planning, they can leverage their "place" and synergistically cross market to increase their space. In transforming themselves into an e-business, existing businesses need to reevaluate their strategy and market opportunity through the eyes of a start-up.

However, to succeed in the new economy, you must first understand it. While it offers many opportunities, success can prove elusive without proper planning and execution. But planning in this new world can often be challenging, particularly in the face of a constantly changing environment. That is why I have developed the e-plan, which provides a flexible framework to develop your business model in today's dynamic economic climate. The e-plan also provides a ready blueprint to use in obtaining funding for your venture. Funding a new venture is often one of the biggest challenges facing the entrepreneur. Although the amount of the resources is great, so is the competition; venture capitalists are literally inundated with proposals. This book features input from leading venture capitalists on obtaining critical funds for your venture as well as discussion about the many additional sources of financing.

Note that the new economy is not without its risks and failures. To begin with, there is the tremendous competition just mentioned. The early success of Internet pioneers such as Yahoo!, Amazon.com, and eBay has created a frenzy of activity by other fledgling entrepreneurs. Start-ups are rushing to fill virtually every nook and cranny of the consumer market. Many are well funded, trying to corral that elusive goal of becoming a market leader. Their products range from pet food through hardware to cosmetics and from software through toys to groceries. These businesses, dubbed "e-tailers," are flooding the airwaves with advertising to establish brand identity, with some of them spending as much as 70 percent of their start-up funds on advertising. Many are questioning the amount of money spent on advertising as well as the overall effectiveness of the efforts. Storm clouds are gathering over the e-tailing sector and a major shakeout is predicted.

In addition, the investing market is growing increasingly antsy about the profitability of e-businesses. This represents a sharp departure from its former focus on promising prospects and market share. E-businesses today have to demonstrate that they can make money.

There are also some sobering lessons to be learned from the Industrial Revolution. At one time, there were 500 domestic automobile makers in the United States. However, by the end of the century, that number had been winnowed to 3. Will the same type of consolidation occur in the online world? Clearly not every me-too Internet business will ascend to market leadership. There will be some winners in this new economy but some losers as well.

So where does that leave you, the prospective entrepreneur? It still leaves you poised on the precipice of enormous opportunity, the once-in-a-lifetime variety. Entrepreneur Michael Dell cautions us to be selective with the opportunities that we pursue because we have only a few "laser bombs" in us. Consequently, it is important that you focus on the most compelling opportunity for you and then bring all of your resources to bear, like a laser bomb.

Entrepreneurship.com will guide you through this critical process. I begin with an understanding of the Internet economy and how it has transformed the traditional market chain. Next I present techniques for scouring and researching the market for the particular opportunity that you can develop into a sustainable business. Then I discuss a comprehensive market strategy that combines proven, traditional, and low-cost techniques of marketing management with the tremendous possibilities of direct Internet marketing. The financial metrics of your business model need to be addressed because earnings *do* matter. I discuss traditional financial performance indicators as a means for translating them into relevant financial metrics of the new economy. Finally, all of this is combined into a flexible format known as the *e-plan,* which facilitates quick revisions in the event of changes in the market and allows for easy presentation to potential investors and employees.

The book also discusses funding mechanisms, operational strategies, and Internet legal issues, and one chapter is for the brick-and-mortar business seeking to transform itself into a click-and-mortar business.

Amidst all the clamor and glamour of the new economy, the solidly built businesses will be the ones that succeed over time. In addition, it is not always the businesses with the most money that win but rather those nimble competitors who can best use their resources to outmaneuver others. The Internet provides a perfect battleground for such strategies as guerrilla marketing. Business success is not found in the latest management jargon but rather in the traditional business motto of customer satisfaction. For the first time, the customer is truly empowered, and the businesses that satisfies the customer will succeed.

Despite the intense competition, lucrative niches always exist in the economic landscape. In fact, many quiet fortunes are being made today and the next one could very well be yours. So whether you want to make a quiet fortune or appear on the cover of a national magazine, *entrepreneurship.com* will help you take advantage of the enormous opportunities in today's new economy.

WHO SHOULD READ THIS BOOK

This book is geared to anyone trying to claim a piece of the new economy and naturally applies to a brand-new business start-up trying to get off the ground. This book is also useful to existing businesses, the brick-and-mortar businesses that desire to expand into the new economy and become click-and-mortar businesses.

For either type of business, this book will guide you step-by-step with information on planning, funding, and executing your online business. It is often useful for existing businesses to take a fresh look at their industry in preparing their e-plan. Although the brick-and-mortar business obviously has experience in the market, take another look at your market through the eyes of a new economy start-up.

The book assumes that the reader already understands many of the fundamental concepts of the Internet, such as URL, browser, and search engine, and is generally familiar with navigating the Net. This is a how-to business book on the Internet as opposed to being a how-to Internet book. If you don't know the first thing about the Internet, I suggest that you first read a basic Internet book. In short, this book will discuss the business and legal aspects of e-business.

As mentioned earlier, you have a historic opportunity to achieve real economic gain and wealth as the economy moves into the information age. The Internet presents very exciting and interesting business opportunities. The purpose of *entrepreneurship.com* is to guide you through the necessary and important steps to be taken by the Internet entrepreneur, to serve as your treasure map, and to help plan and fund your Internet start-up. Good luck and happy treasure hunting.

Tim Burns
New Orleans, Louisiana
July 1, 2000

chapter 1

Introduction to Internet Entrepreneurship

❝When the operations of capitalism come to resemble those of the casino, ill fortune will be the lot of many.❞

John Maynard Keynes (1883–1946), economist

NOTHING BUT NET

To use a basketball term for a perfect shot, today's economy appears to be nothing but Net. In just a few short years, the Internet has graduated from the exclusive domain of the defense industry and academia to one of the most important developments of the information age—if not *the* most important development. Just as the steam engine and electricity helped to power an agrarian economy into the industrial age, the Internet is ushering the world economy into the information age. Many financial commentators are using the Internet as the official dividing line between the industrial age and the information age and are referring to Internet-related businesses as the new economy.

There is scarcely any discussion about business today that does not resonate with the relentless digital drumbeat of the Internet. Advertising airways are saturated with dot-com ads. Magazine racks are plastered with the happy faces of online success stories. No corporate strategy is complete without an e-business blueprint. Despite some dramatic fluctuations in the stock market, the investment community has not given up on new economy companies. Despite the ongoing Web shakeout, entrepreneurs still have great interest in somehow becoming involved in this online world, particularly as they watch some involved in Internet start-ups become millionaires and billionaires overnight.

Even Hollywood is getting into the act, using the Internet to transform *The Blair Witch Project*, a low-budget movie of debatable quality, into one of the most profitable films (from the standpoint of rate of return) in the history of Tinseltown.

The new heroes of the Internet have become cultural icons, their oft-repeated stories now legendary. What could be a more compelling illustration than *Time* magazine's tapping Jeff Bezos, the founder of Amazon.com, as its Man of the Year. With this distinction, the 35-year-old Bezos joined company with some rather influential figures—Mohandas Gandhi, Franklin Roosevelt , Martin Luther King, Jr., Pope John Paul II, Ronald Reagan, and Bill Clinton. More amazing was how quickly Bezos was able to achieve this honor. He did it in about the same amount of time Bill Clinton needed to serve a couple of his seven terms in the Arkansas statehouse before being elected president. In addition, Jeff Bezos was less than half the age of Ronald Reagan when selected Man of the Year. But this should not be that surprising as Amazon.com needed only 3 years and no stores to reach the same level of sales as Wal-Mart did in 10 years with 87 stores.

Some of the other Net notables include these:

- Steve Case, the chairman of America Online, who fended off attacks from Microsoft, larger online providers such as Prodigy and Compuserve, and an often skeptical industry to emerge as the largest online service. A crowning jewel of Case's career was his acquisition of Time Warner, which once turned him down for a job.
- Yahoo! founders David Filo and Gerry Yang, who turned a directory into one of the Internet's most powerful brands and respected business models.
- Netscape founder Jim Clark, the displaced head of Silicon Graphics, who teamed up with boy wonder programmer Mark Andreesen to form Netscape, which established the graphic Internet browser and revolutionized the Internet.

Rounding out the list of Net notables are those companies making it to the upper echelon in terms of consumer sales.* Some of these Net notables are also mentioned above.

Company	Annual Sales
eBay (online auction)	$1.1–1.3 billion
Amazon.com (consumer goods)	1.0–1.1 billion
Dell.com (computers)	500–600 million
Buy.com (consumer goods)	350–400 million
OnSale.com (consumer goods)	300–350 million
Gateway.com (computers)	250–300 million
Egghead.com (consulting services)	150–200 million
Barnesandnoble.com (books, music)	125–175 million
AOL.com (America Online)	100–150 million

*Reprinted by permission of the National Retail Federation.

HYPE OR HOPE?

The initial euphoria over Internet stocks created quite lofty valuations, transforming the stock market into a casino with investors wagering huge stakes in hopes of hitting the jackpot. In such a speculative climate, however, we are cautioned by economist John Maynard Keynes (in the quotation that begins this chapter) that "ill fortune will be the lot of many." Indeed, many Internet valuations have fallen considerably from their peak and a further shakeout is predicted, particularly in the e-tailing sector. Many investors have been burned and will continue to be burned. In granting generous valuations to Internet stocks, the market is "betting on the come," to borrow a phrase from craps. Just as gamblers place bets on the roll of the dice, investors are gambling on future performance.

Clearly, there will be winners and losers as estimations of future performance become clearer. Consider again the more than 500 automobile manufacturers in the United States in the early 1900s that were reduced to 3 by the end of the century. The shakeouts and consolidations are already under way in the Internet space. This initial wave of closures has claimed such high-profile Internet companies as Boo.com (apparel retailer), Toy-smart (toy retailer), violet.com (specialty retailer), and Craftshop.com (hobby, craft supplies). Some of these companies were very well funded; Boo.com received $135 million in seed capital and Toysmart had the backing of Disney.

Much of the Internet revolution is being propelled by money, with the West Coast driving the East Coast and the East Coast in turn driving the West Coast. The West Coast, more particularly the Silicon Valley area below San Francisco, is the heart of the venture capital community, which breathes money and life into start-ups. The East Coast, specifically New York and Wall Street, is the center of the investment banking community, which takes promising companies public. When Wall Street is bullish on a particular segment of the economy, such as biotechnology or Internet stocks, tremendous interest accompanied by funds from New York investment bankers and institutional investors abound. This in turn motivates Silicon Valley venture capitalists to pump more money into start-ups and creates more companies for Wall Street to take public—potentially a highly profitable cycle for all concerned. But when Wall Street turns bearish, this money spigot can dry up quite quickly.

During the past few years, this cycle has produced a historic amount of start-up capital for new businesses. According to the international accounting firm PricewaterhouseCoopers, 4,000 U.S. companies received a total of more than $35 billion in funding in 1999, an amount that constituted a considerable increase over the previous record of $14.2 billion set in 1998. And as I discuss in Chapter 15, venture capital is not the only source of start-up funding. A multitude of sources of capital to fund a start-up are out there, but the entrepreneur needs to be resourceful in obtaining funds.

The availability of money as well as the vast potential market for goods and services in the new economy has created tremendous hope for many entrepreneurs. Although investors have become more selective, there are still ample funds for good ideas. In addition, the Internet has created a whole new universe of commercial possibilities for new markets as well as existing products and services. Those businesses that can effectively harness the Internet's immense power will achieve considerable success. Despite stock market retreats and waves of bearishness, available opportunities in the new economy are still quite enticing and apply to start-ups as well as existing businesses that can effectively integrate the Internet into their operations.

Consequently, prospective entrepreneurs are attempting to start up businesses at record rates. Just check out any Kinko's 24-hour copy shop in the wee hours of the morning, particularly in areas with a high concentration of start-ups, like Austin, San Francisco, and New York. Invariably, you will find a determined group of people hard at work preparing business plans and trying to get their piece of the new economy. College students who are taking entrepreneurship courses are not writing business plans just for credit, but for real.

One of the beauties of the Internet is the fewer traditional barriers to market entry that often posed such formidable obstacles in the industrial age. There are no factories to build or huge investments to make in plant and equipment. Digital storefronts can be opened quickly and benefit from advertising at the lowest cost per exposure in the history of the world. Never before have ideas been so powerful and bestowed with so much financial weight. Never before have so many ideas been translated into funded businesses so quickly.

But beyond this frenzy of business activity is a stark reality: After all of the hype, the easy cash, the Internet buzzwords, and the heady valuations, an Internet business ultimately needs to be profitable. Otherwise, it will dry up as soon as the hype and cash do. A lasting Internet business is more than broad dreams, excited coffeehouse chatter, or vague ideas about transforming the world. It is a carefully planned model that can be sustained once all the excitement dies down. Even though an Internet business can be achieved by virtually anyone, anywhere, the prospect is not as easy as it looks.

For the aspiring Internet entrepreneur, there is both good news and bad news. First, the bad news.

Bad News

Most of the low-lying fruit is gone. Businesses patterned after many of the infant Internet businesses, such as selling books and trading stocks online (which seem so obvious in retrospect), are not particularly viable now. If you have an idea for selling certain goods and services online, chances are that at least a dozen other people have thought about the exact same thing. It is not uncommon for several business plans, often describing quite similar businesses, to be floating among venture capitalists simultaneously—reportedly at least half a dozen proposals to sell pet food, for example. But today "me-too" businesses are having a much more difficult time getting funded.

Silicon Valley venture capitalist Brendon Kim of Altos Ventures remarked how easy funding used to be for consumer-focused Internet start-ups. As late as mid-1999, start-ups with basic business models were being funded. For example, entrepreneurs could propose starting an online business selling a particular line of consumer goods and project that it could build adequate market share with funding of $30 million. Shazam! They would receive the $30 million to start the business. The fact that the entrepreneurs may have had little or no experience in the particular industry might not have made much of a difference if they could convince venture capitalists that they could pull it off. It was quite easy and quite amazing. Kim referred to the phenomenon as "business out of a box."

Those days are gone. Today, venture capital money for consumer businesses has virtually dried up. Consumer businesses are those that sell goods purchased for personal use primarily to end users or consumers, known as the business-to-consumer market, or B2C market. The B2C market is to be distinguished from the business-to-business market, or B2B market. Many of the B2C businesses are in the retailing sector, the e-tailers. The e-tailing sector is believed to be at considerable risk in upcoming months as start-ups begin to exhaust their cash.

Intense competition in the marketplace. Many of the early Internet businesses had the benefit of little competition. With the market to themselves, it was much easier to attract attention and become known in the marketplace. A large amount of their market awareness was driven by free media coverage from a curious and approving press corps. Not so any more. Today, there is tremendous competition among Internet businesses for market share and attention, particularly in the consumer market. Consider the following:

- It has been estimated that more than 1 million pages of Web content are being created daily.
- As of January 2000, nearly 14 million domain names were registered worldwide. This boils down to approximately 2.2 Internet domain names per 1,000 people worldwide or 25.2 domains per 1,000 people in the United States. However, not all of the domain names are in use; the majority are listed to cybersquatters who are hoping to later sell their name.
- To date, the top ten domain names in terms of sales are as follows:

Business.com	$7.5 million (sold for $100,000 in 1997)
AltaVista.com	3.3 million
Loans.com	3.0 million
Autos.com	2.2 million
Express.com	2.0 million
Fly.com	1.5 million
Bingo.com	1.1 million
WallStreet.com	1.0 million
ForSalebyOwner.com	0.8 million
Drugs.com	0.8 million

The large amounts of money that people are paying for domain names not only illustrate the intense competition in the marketplace but also the increased expense of entering the e-commerce world.

Increased barriers to entry. The barriers to market entry are typically the costs of establishing an Internet business. One of the advantages of the earlier Internet models was that Internet businesses could be launched for a fraction of the cost of creating their brick-and-mortar counterparts, but, according to Deutsche Banc Alex. Brown, the money barriers for establishing an e-tail site now are escalating. In fact, the cost of establishing a brand has risen tenfold in the past two years and is now $50 million.

The old model of build a better mousetrap, create some buzz, and they will come has fallen by the wayside. As indicated by Deutsche Banc, the cost of building a brand name has become a significant hurdle for a start-up, a hurdle compounded by the fact that not all the money spent on brand building is effective. Marketing pros estimate that about half of the money spent on advertising is wasted. The trick is figuring out which half. Yet Internet start-ups typically gamble 70 percent of their capital on brand advertising in the first year. The ones that miss the mark will probably not survive.

The emphasis on branding is a result of the realities of market leadership. Typically, the market leader captures 50 to 60 percent of a particular market; the next company captures 20 to 30 percent; and everyone else divides up the crumbs. This calculation applies to the Internet world as well, although the speed to market leadership there is compressed. Consider how quickly Amazon.com became the market leader in online book retailing, far outdistancing the better-established Barnes & Noble. Compare Amazon's rise with the many years required for Wal-Mart to dominate its category. This rush to establish a brand, and with it market leadership, is the reason so many dot-coms shelled out $2 million for a 30-second spot during the Super Bowl.

Not all attempts at reaching market leadership, however, are successful. One of the most bizarre Internet start-ups is Pixelon, based in San Juan Capistrano, California, which had ambitious plans to become an Internet network with thousands of content channels. To create a name for itself, it spent $12 million (one-third of its resources) on an extravagant launch party that it dubbed iBash. The party, held at the MGM Grand in Las Vegas, featured a wide menu of high-priced entertainers, such as Tony Bennett, the Dixie Chicks, LeAnn Rimes, the Who, and Kiss. The event created considerable buzz that quickly fizzled when, among other things, Pixelon was unable to transmit its party content online as promised. Investors also questioned the decision to spend so much on iBash. Although Pixelon clearly erred in overhyping its broadcast capabilities, its gamble on the party was perhaps more understandable. With so many dot-coms starting, companies have to generate buzz and recognition in the market; otherwise, they will be lost in the crowd. Some of the outrageous publicity gambles may win; others will lose. In this case, Pixelon lost and a new CEO was brought in to execute a less ambitious business model.

However, Pixelon's story does not end here. To further add to the company's woes, it was recently discovered that its founder, David Stanley (alias Michael Adam Fenne) was actually a fugitive scam artist on the state of Virginia's most-wanted list. In 1989, Stanley pleaded guilty to 55 counts of defrauding investors. What is amazing was that no one at Pixelon was aware of Stanley's past or even his real name. And more amazing is that he was able to talk investors out of $30 million. Although the company did obtain front page coverage in the prestigious *Industry Standard*, its sordid tale of greed, fraud, and stupidity has made Pixelon and its investors more infamous than famous. Pixelon recently filed for bankruptcy protection.

Caveat: Let me offer a caveat to some of my comments:

- The first rule about the Internet is that there are no rules. Although there is sometimes agreement on the conventional wisdom, many of the successful Internet businesses have been based on unconventional wisdom. Remember, no absolutes exist in the online world.
- Although venture capitalists are currently cold on the B2C model, that doesn't mean you can't get a B2C business funded. It is simply much harder than it was in 1999. Your business model has to be more compelling, and that assumes you're going to be seeking venture capital funding in the first place. (I discuss funding in more detail in Chapter 14.)
- Even though the costs of branding can be enormous, other ways are available to establish brand identity besides traditional marketing. I discuss guerrilla marketing in Chapter 9 and evaluate the ways to bootstrap marketing your venture. Proven marketing tools such as segmenting and positioning can help your venture capture the leadership position in a market niche. There can be lucrative opportunities in a market niche. As venture capitalist Steve Dow of Sevin Rosen Funds quips, to many people $1 million or $2 million a year in profits is still real money.

Good News

And now for the good news.

Continued growth of the Internet economy. Although some have predicted that the rate of growth for Internet usage is beginning to level off, the Internet economy continues to grow significantly. Consider the following:

- According to International Data Corporation (IDC), at the end of 1999, there were a total of 196 million Internet users worldwide. The forecast for 2003 is 502 million users. IDC did point out that because half of the Internet users live outside the United States, an accurate count is difficult. At the end of 1999, 13 percent of U.S. households were making regular purchases online. The forecast for 2003 is 40 percent.
- According to Forrester Research, an Internet research firm, business-to-business e-commerce is expected to grow from an estimated $406 billion in 2000 to $2.7 trillion in 2004.

Internet is here to stay. Despite stock market fluctuations, no one disputes that the Internet is here to stay. It has become a fundamental part of the business world, not a fad. As the statistics above indicate, the Internet is nowhere near its maturity. There is still plenty of fertile ground for entrepreneurs in the new economy. However, as I discuss later, the business model of the successful company needs to be fully developed and to address all necessary facets, including product or service selection, marketing strategy, and the financial aspects of the business. You cannot simply call yourself an e-business and expect the rest to fall into place.

Some venture capitalists, like Steve Dow, predict that the Internet will become so woven into the economic structure that the distinction between e-business and brick-and-mortar businesses will fade away. It is this melding together of traditional and Internet businesses that creates what former Intel CEO Andrew Grove refers to as click-and-mortar businesses, the heart of the new economy. Another term for a click-and-mortar business is space and place.

The key is to build a sustainable business. In my research and interviews for this book, I often came across the phrase *sustainable competitive advantage*. It seems that everyone is looking to invest in those businesses with a sustainable competitive advantage. This phrase is not part of the new economy but was written by management guru Peter Drucker some 40 years ago. It is one of many intersections between traditional business and the new economy—and perhaps the most important.

The ultimate survivors of the new economy will be those businesses constructed on the solid foundation of a fundamentally sound business model. These valid businesses will triumph over the ones that hyped themselves into high, but fleeting, valuations. The main task of this book is to help you fashion your idea or premise into a sustainable business model.

THE WILD WILD WEST

It is fitting that the Internet is being compared to the California gold rush of 1849, in which people headed west to seek their fortune. Not only is much of the activity of the new economy concentrated on the West Coast, but it is also a throwback to the Wild West. In its early days, the West was a wilderness with little law and order. Similarly, the Internet is an economic wilderness with no rules and certainly no law nor order.

The Internet is a wide-open economic battleground without rules or conventions. Companies enter the marketplace and often make up the rules as they go along. Congress and the federal regulatory agencies cast out a periodic lasso at the online world, trying to rein in some of the activity, but the Internet is more like a stampede than a traditional roundup. It is a domain where anything and everything goes, where upstarts challenge established companies on a daily basis. Every day is *High Noon* on the Internet.

In the ensuing struggle for survival, stronger predators will always be there to devour others by gnawing away at their market share with superior or even illegal weapons. The most publicized example, of course, is the Internet browser market that Microsoft methodically wrested from Netscape and that resulted in a federal judge's ruling that Microsoft's aggressive tactics violated antitrust laws.

Such uncharted territory produces tremendous danger as well as opportunity. Venturing to compete in the fast-moving and uncertain environment of the Internet requires a considerable degree of courage and boldness. One has to be bold to take risks, to compete with companies many times one's size, and to believe that one can keep up with the constant pace of change and innovation that characterizes the new economy. Remember, though, that boldness does not necessarily mean rashness. Although one needs to be daring, one needn't be reckless. Start-ups need to take chances, but they should not gamble impulsively.

Historic Opportunity for Economic Gain

With such a competitive, and even vicious, environment, one might wonder why bother to start an Internet business in the first place. One of the main reasons why the Internet is attracting so much interest is the historic opportunity for economic gain. The companies that ultimately succeed with an Internet business will do very well financially.

The last time such a condition existed was 100 years ago. According to MIT economist Lester C. Thurow, today may offer one of the best opportunities to obtain economic profit since the end of the 19th century. In his book, *Building Wealth,* Thurow argued that the movement from the industrial age to the information age has created considerable economic disequilibrium. And this disequilibrium creates the opportunity for considerable economic gain.

Think of the historic changes at the last turn of the century. Remember how entrepreneurs like Rockefeller, Ford, and Carnegie were able to build massive empires in the midst of the Industrial Revolution? The same situation prevails today amid the economic chaos of the information age. The shifting economy has created the opportunity for enormous wealth, some of which is already being seized by the early entrepreneurs of the Net. The market is simply betting that certain companies will be able to sustain their competitive advantage well into this century and achieve historic economic returns like the industrial giants of the past century.

There *is* some method in the stock market madness. And furthermore, some real economic opportunity out there. So take advantage of it.

SKILL SET OF THE INTERNET ENTREPRENEUR

To succeed in the online world, the Internet entrepreneur has to cultivate the necessary skill set. This skill set is grounded in four essential areas:

1. Compelling vision
2. Versatile planning
3. Driving passion
4. Confident execution

Compelling Vision

I was somewhat reluctant to use the V word—that is, *vision*—as it has become almost a cliché in business and personal development books. But the reason that it has become a cliché is that it is so important. All successful businesses were started by someone with a vision. As discussed earlier, the online world has become very competitive. Simple spinoffs of existing products or services usually produce nothing more than a mediocre me-too business and receive yawns from the investment banking community.

Vision occurs when ordinary people develop extraordinary ideas or insights. It could range from Bill Gates seeing a computer on every desk in the late 1970s to Steve Case seeing AOL as the world's portal to an online world. Vision is seeing the huge gaps in the marketplace or an opportunity to turn an existing supply chain on its head.

The visioning process is imagining how things could be and boldly posing the question, what if? But visioning is more than ordinary daydreaming. Although daydreaming is important and may contain the seeds of a vision, you must go a step further and impose order on the chaos. That involves bringing fantasy into reality. In the classic poem "Kubla Khan" by Samuel Taylor Coleridge, the author equates art to a "dome in air" that can never be adequately captured and expressed. Coleridge underscores his point by claiming that his poem, which came to him after a hashish-induced dream, is unfinished. The message is that pure art is never really completed. The vision of the Internet entrepreneur, however, cannot be an abstract dome in air. It needs to be translated into a working model. And that involves planning.

Versatile Planning

Success in the online world comes to the visionaries who can also plan. Sometimes in their rush to get funded and online, the eager venturer forgets all about planning, perceiving there's no time to plan. You simply have to make the time.

Some commentators insist that the Internet world changes so rapidly that any plan will probably be obsolete the moment the words hit the page.

Although there is some truth in this position, you need to adequately define and flesh out your business. From just the sheer pace of the new economy, the conventional business plan needs to be modified to allow for maximum flexibility and efficiency. I call this modified plan the *e-plan*, which is a business plan stripped to its bare essentials. Out is the bound 100-page business plan treatise and in is a plan that can be captured on a dozen Microsoft PowerPoint slides. Both involve the same thinking and analysis. What is different is the way each plan is presented. The e-plan slide presentation facilitates focus on the entire business and can be quickly adjusted in the event of changes in the marketplace. The PowerPoint slides also serve as a guide for presenting your model to potential investors and associates. Internet entrepreneurs find that they will be doing a lot more presenting than sending plans out to be read. The truth of the matter is that most long business plans are not read. Professional investors simply don't have the time.

The actual parts or slides of the plan are discussed in more detail in Chapter 4. The necessary areas that will be addressed include the executive summary, management team, business model, and financial projections.

Driving Passion

After your vision has been codified into a workable plan, it needs to be sustained by a driving passion. Internet start-ups must contend with a various assortment of roadblocks, pitfalls, disappointments, and surprises. Founders need to be absolutely passionate about their business in order to persevere in the face of the inevitable obstacles. And it is passion that makes the long hours bearable and helps one to actually look forward to another hectic day. Without a passion for your business, it is simply too much work.

Confident Execution

The final element of business planning is execution. Companies with a great vision and plan may stumble if they don't execute properly. With so many similar ideas rushing to market, it is the people who can quickly execute the plan that will separate the winners from the losers.

It is also important that the plan be executed confidently. There is so much competition in the marketplace for the attention of customers, for good employees, and for investors that all of them need reassurance. Confidence is that reassurance. The owners must project confidence in all aspects of their business. If they cannot inspire confidence, it will be difficult for them to lead and to get others to follow.

Visit almost any dot-com and you will find that employees and management are invariably piled up next to each other, banging away at their computer terminals. The energy level is thick in the air. But this energy has to be properly channeled and focused. That is where leadership comes into play—keeping the fires burning in your employees while keeping them focused on a sometimes moving target. Leadership is clarifying goals and then driving each team member to achieve his or her optimal performance while relishing his or her position as part of the team.

chapter **2**

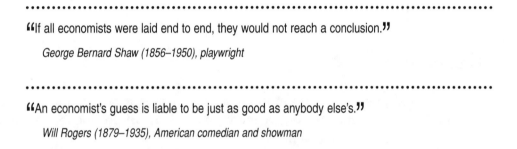

❝If all economists were laid end to end, they would not reach a conclusion.❞

George Bernard Shaw (1856–1950), playwright

❝An economist's guess is liable to be just as good as anybody else's.❞

Will Rogers (1879–1935), American comedian and showman

WHAT IS THE NEW ECONOMY?

Considerable discussion has taken place in business circles about the new economy. Before we discuss it ourselves, let's consider some fundamental economic models as well as some of the limitations of economic models in general. One anecdote from my college days seems to summarize these inherent limitations.

Story of the Stranded Economist

A physicist, an engineer, and an economist were marooned on a desert island. The only rations they could salvage from their ship's wreckage was a container of canned goods, but having no utensils, the three put their heads together to figure out how to open the can. The engineer suggested constructing an elaborate system of weights and pulleys that would eventually puncture the can. The physicist proposed positioning their eyeglasses a certain way so that light could be refracted into a laser that would bore a hole in the can. The economist was the last to speak and offered the following advice: "Assume we have a can opener."

That story, in a nutshell, summarizes some of the pitfalls of economics. Economic models are built on assumptions, which in many cases have to be generalized. By its nature as a social science, economics is an inexact science. As we enter the new economy, new models are being constructed to explain behavior and to predict courses of action. Although there is great logical appeal to these models, remember that they are built on assumptions only.

Old Economy

Economics is built around studying factors of production and markets. For purposes of the old economy, the factors of production are classified under four basic headings:

1. *Labor:* the time and effort that people devote to producing goods and services
2. *Land:* all the natural resources used to produce goods and services
3. *Machinery and equipment:* all the equipment, tools, and other manufactured goods used to produce other goods and services
4. *Entrepreneurial ability:* a special type of human resource that organizes the other three factors of production, makes business decisions, innovates, bears business risk, and is rewarded with profit

Figure 2.1 sets forth a particular firm's use of the four factors of production to produce its product. This model, which applied primarily to the manufacturing age, needs to be revised, however, for the new economy and the information age.

Figure 2.2 depicts the factors of production in the new economy. These factors of production include entrepreneurship and labor, which were also

FIGURE 2.1 Production Process—Old Economy

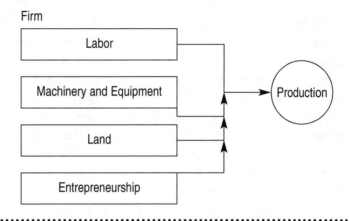

FIGURE 2.2 Production in the New Economy

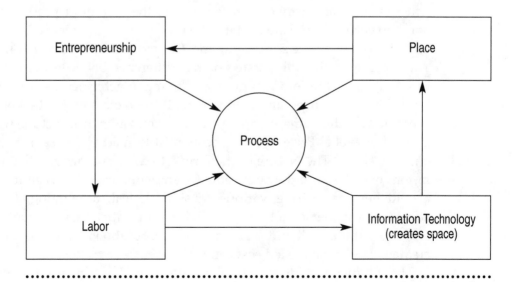

in the model for the old economy; however, the new economy model introduces two new factors of production information technology and place.

Information technology (IT). IT begins with a computer and includes all of the necessary software and hardware to create a company's presence in the online world and facilitate the conduct of e-business. IT enables a company to compete effectively in its chosen market "space," which will be discussed in more detail below. In addition, I discuss some of the specific components of IT in Chapter 11. IT is the new machinery and equipment of the information age, which is not to say that businesses in the new economy don't use physical machinery and equipment. Rather, machinery and equipment are not primary factors of production in the information age.

Place. Place includes the physical or brick-and-mortar presence of the business. It is distinguished from land in traditional economic models, which included natural resources that were often important factors of production. Place can range from a garage to a chain of retail outlets. As discussed previously, new economy businesses that can combine place and space enjoy many advantages.

In addition to introducing new factors of production, the economic model for the new economy also reflects the trend toward outsourcing certain functions and services. In Figure 2.1, the factors of production are lined up vertically and are contained within one firm. In Figure 2.2, the factors of production are spread out and not necessarily housed in one firm. These configurations illustrate another difference between the manufacturing age and the information age. The manufacturing age was characterized by large corporations in which all the factors of production were contained in the same company. This organizational structure was explained by Nobel Prize–winning economist Ronald H. Coase in a notable paper entitled "The Nature of the Firm." Coase hypothesized that corporations exist because they can reduce transaction costs between individuals. Rather than hiring various outside clerical, accounting, legal, or administrative personnel on an individual or entity basis, it made more sense to put them all under one roof. As corporations grew, this structure created considerable fixed costs and inefficiencies.

The Internet and other technology, however, have greatly reduced the transaction costs of contracting with outside vendors. As these transaction costs decreased, it became more economical for companies to focus on their core business and outsource the rest. (Outsourcing is discussed in more detail in Chapter 6.)

Another difference between the old economy and the new economy is in market analysis and efficiency. Market analysis consists of examining the forces of supply and demand in establishing the market. The market can be considered any arrangement that enables buyers and sellers to obtain information and do business with each other. The market for goods and services involves the exchange of goods and services for money. The market for factors or supplies concerns the purchase of factors of production. Markets link producers with consumers of goods and services. Sometimes the links are direct and sometimes they are indirect and involve many layers of producers of services and various traders. Markets generally work by consolidating a tremendous amount of information about the plans of buyers and sellers and summarizing this information in terms of price.

Many markets in the old economy are not particularly efficient, in which case the market is fragmented into various submarkets, where only a portion of potential buyers and sellers are linked together. In the new economy, the Internet can be used to consolidate the fragmented submarkets into one efficient marketplace or an exchange. The exchange can link together all of the buyers and sellers in a particular market. Before the advent of the Internet, few markets could be connected into an exchange other than the regulated stock or commodities exchanges. Today, consider the vast range of buyers and sellers on eBay, the online auction firm. Before there was an eBay, the market for selling personal goods was quite fragmented. With potential buyers and sellers spread all over the world, one would have had to advertise in every major newspaper to have the same reach. (I discuss searching inefficient markets for opportunities in Chapter 3.)

NEW ECONOMY

In addition to information age aspects of production factors and markets discussed above, other important aspects of the new economy are discussed in the following sections.

New Organizational Wealth

The new economy has resulted in a fundamental shift in the way companies are valued. The new organizational wealth no longer centers around physical capital but rather around intellectual capital. Much of a company's value is not in its plant and equipment but in its intangible assets. Such assets include the ideas and knowledge base of its key employees. Because much of a company's organizational wealth is found in particular employees, companies have to develop a unique way to manage and reward these individuals.

Space

The terms *market* or *market share* have given way to a new term: *space.* I'm not talking about travel beyond the atmosphere but rather to that portion of the marketplace or line of business in which a venture competes. The term *space* has transcended traditional market segments and can often eliminate their location limitations.

Figure 2.3 illustrates market segments per industry in the old economy. In the figure, products for a particular industry are represented on the horizontal axis and customers are represented on the vertical axis. Each rounded rectangle represents a particular industry segment. Note that for each industry there are defined products for defined customers. Some companies offer one or more products in each industry. Think of all the different product lines in the same industry in the consumer markets, ranging from beer to automobiles. Miller Brewing Company offers light beer, genuine draft beer, nonalcoholic beer, and Miller High Life. (I discuss market segmentation in more detail in Chapter 8.) Segmentation is dividing up a market into particular customer segments that are determined by targeting particular products to the needs of particular customers. First decide on the product and then the customer.

Consider segmenting the Internet industry. For example, your company might be an Internet service provider (ISP), and instead of individual consumers your customer base might be small businesses, which would be your business segment. For most start-ups in the old economy, the busi-

FIGURE 2.3   Market Segmentation (per industry)

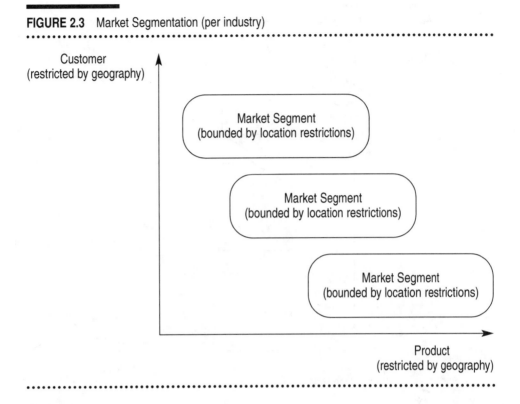

ness segment was restricted by geographical concerns and each customer segment had a defined market. To expand, one generally had to open operations in a different geographical area.

Figure 2.4 depicts the market segments that have been expanded into space for the new economy. In the third dimension of the diagram, space cuts across traditional market boundaries to give the product or service a truly global market reach. (See Chapter 3.) However, as I discuss in Chapter 8, this additional market reach is dependent on the value-added role that the particular business serves in the marketplace.

In evaluating new economy businesses, the term *scalable* is very important. Scalable businesses are those that can deliver their products or services across the space at only incremental marginal costs. This could be due to a robust IT infrastructure that allows them to profitably increase

FIGURE 2.4 Market Space

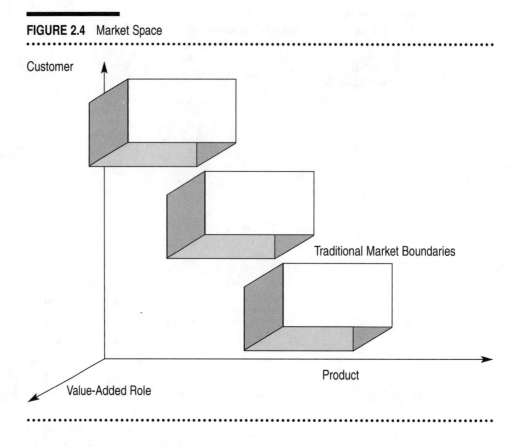

operations. The scalable Internet business allows expansion into different markets at incremental costs.

Compression

The Internet is compressing several traditional economic factors ranging from product life cycle to market structure. Time has become dramatically compressed in the new economy. Speed is now of paramount importance. Everything needs to be done more quickly—product launch, customer service, and all aspects of Internet operations, including product life cycle.

The term *product life cycle* refers to the natural cycle of a new product. New products in the old economy often enjoyed life cycles of several years before their markets matured. Witness the many models of automobiles that enjoyed a long tenure before being replaced by new models; some popular models sold well for many years with virtually no updating. However, product life cycles have shrunk dramatically in the online world. Important vocabulary words of the new economy are *newer, faster,* and *better.* Many joke that technology is obsolete the minute that it hits the market. That is probably true. The key to success with such a short product life cycle is to continually innovate to make your product newer, faster, or better and serve more needs. Your competition is certainly trying to continually improve.

In addition to time, the new economy is also compressing traditional market chains. In the old economy, the traditional market chain involved several layers and several different entities.

Figure 2.5 sets forth the typical flow of goods in the old economy:

- Supplier of raw materials to manufacturer
- Manufacturer to wholesaler
- Wholesaler to retailer
- Retailer to customer

FIGURE 2.5 Market Chain

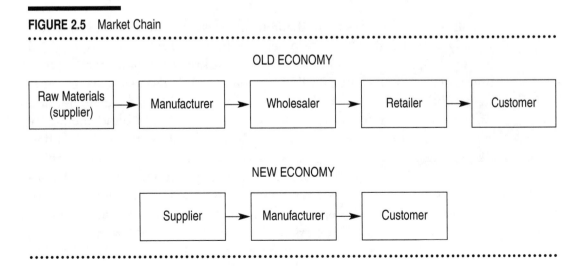

The Internet has facilitated the compression of this market chain in the new economy by removing several of the steps listed above. Note that in Figure 2.5 the marketing channels of wholesaler and retailer have been completely eliminated as businesses are transacting directly with consumers.

For example, Dell Computer Corporation gained an advantage in the computer industry, where margins are slim, by manufacturing and distributing computers directly to consumers, initially with a toll-free number. Although this practice seems standard today, it was quite innovative ten years ago. By compressing several of the layers in the traditional supply chain, Dell was able to expand its margins. Dell took this model a step further by using the Internet to allow customers to configure their computers online, thus minimizing the cost of employee time in the ordering process and creating a direct, efficient link between customers and the manufacturer. This also eliminated any of the inefficiencies in the supply chain, such as excess inventory. Dell enjoys the benefit of not having to build computers until an order is placed and payment received. Besides being efficient, cash flow is also maximized. Consequently, manufacturing capacity is at its optimum. Such a compressed, efficient market chain is something that businesses could only dream about not that long ago.

Customer Focus

Although businesses were theoretically designed to serve customers, it is only recently that the customer has become fully empowered (and knows it). Customer service is important, and the companies that succeed are those that create value for their customers. Today's customers are more demanding than ever, which raises the customer service bar higher and higher. In the old economy, powerful companies could build monopoly power and not have to worry that much about customers. Public utilities, like phone and power companies, could basically operate as they wanted to and the customer had little recourse. The indifference of the early industrial giants toward customer service was best personified by a remark that Henry Ford made regarding the color of his model T automobiles. Ford claimed that his customers could have any color they wanted as long as it was black. Although this remark was made in the early 1900s, the arrogance of the industrial giants prevailed well into the century. Detroit did not build durable cars until foreign car manufacturers began cutting significantly into the U.S. market.

It would be difficult to imagine businesses in the new economy taking an indifferent view toward customer service. They would not stay market leaders for long. With so much competition, there has never been a greater focus on the customer experience. One of the main reasons that companies like Amazon.com are so popular is that the customer experience is managed very carefully.

Companies that succeed recognize the enormous value of customers. Everyone laughed when America Online (AOL) showered the world with start-up disks. The investment community protested that the cost of customer acquisition was too high—in excess of $100 per customer. But Steve Case knew the value of customers. When AOL reached 20 million customers, people stopped laughing.

One of the advantages of the Internet is that it allows a business to become personal with its customers on a scale that has never been seen before. Naturally, the challenge is to not get too personal as privacy concerns are being expressed by consumers and addressed by federal regulators. One of the developments prompting this concern is "cookies," which are files planted in someone's computer by a Web site that allows the site to recognize a particular user and tailor product offerings to that user. However, problems arose when advertising networks accumulated this information about particular consumers and then tried to match the information with a database. (Privacy and its legal implications are discussed in Chapter 12.)

Marketing is all about winning one customer at a time and then keeping that customer. The phrase *stickiness* is now being used to gauge how well a business can acquire customers and keep them coming back. Sites like AOL and Yahoo are considered "sticky" sites because their users return frequently. During times of tremendous competition, it's easy for customers to switch to the next best thing, so the key is to keep the customer happy. The old adage stated that if you pleased one customer, that customer would tell someone else. But if you displeased a customer, *that* customer would tell ten people. On the Internet, you can multiply this by a factor of 100.

Many companies have been successful in using their customers to market for them. Consider the case of Hot Mail, which provided free e-mail and used its customers to help market to potential customers. Everyone who received a Hot Mail e-mail from a friend was encouraged to join Hot Mail too. The company was able to rapidly increase its customer base and was eventually bought at a premium by Microsoft. Venture capital firm Draper Fisher Jurvetson, which backed Hot Mail, developed this concept of "viral marketing."

Another issue that companies must contend with in the new economy is the propensity of customers to act on impulse. Companies have to be mindful to construct and offer services that customers can buy easily. Simply put, companies in the new economy have to delight their customers. It is no longer good enough to simply do what customers expect.

In today's fast-paced, competitive economy, customers gravitate to the deal that best satisfies their needs. This requires companies to build their whole model around customers and gain a reputation as a brand that solves customers' problems. The days of the emotional connection between buyer and seller are over. Customers seek out brands that they expect to solve their problems. As part of pleasing customers, consider the various aspects of the company that evaluate customers' experience. First and foremost is convenience. In today's fast-paced world, time is at a premium. Customers want one-stop shopping and want to be able to enter an order and have it filled quickly.

Prices are also an important part of the customer experience. Because of the convenience of the Internet, your prices always have to be competitive. Although you don't necessarily have to be the lowest-cost seller, you have to be *among* the lowest-cost sellers.

Strategic Alliances

In the new economy, there is an increased need for strategic alliances. To dominate a particular space in the amount of time required will usually overwhelm a single company. That is why the creation of various alliances and affiliate marketing programs can cause the whole to be greater than the sum of the parts. The market often judges companies on the strength of their alliances. In addition, companies can quickly pole-vault over their competitors with the right strategic alliances.

In an affiliate marketing program, your service is marketed by affiliate partners. Most of us are familiar with the affiliate marketing program sponsored by Amazon.com because Amazon has several hundred thousand affiliates with Amazon's banner ad on their sites. Such affiliate networks operate best when a good brand image of the company outside the network exists already and thus positions the affiliates to assist in marketing efforts. Some companies even encourage or assist other affiliates in marketing their programs. This use of affiliates takes advantage of the Internet and its ability to spread ideas and information quickly.

Value Creation

A topic closely related to effective marketing and customer relations is the ability of the Internet to create value that must be perceived positively by customers. If a business does nothing to add value, it is just another site cluttering the Internet.

Value is found in several forms. First are the valuable bundles of information and services—the approach taken by many online publishers, such as *The Wall Street Journal,* that charge subscribers for the online version of their publication. The better the information and services, the more a customer will pay. Even certain bundles of information and services at retail sites can be used to attract customer traffic because they are offering value to customers. In creating these bundles, it is important to not be overly general. It is the uniqueness of the information and uniqueness of the services that attract attention to the site.

An intriguing aspect of creating value lies with a distinctive part of the new economy called the experience economy. This part of the economy concerns companies that stage compelling experiences to save their products from becoming commodities. Generally, being labeled a commodity is the worst competitive position to be in for selling goods. When a good is thought of as a commodity, customers make their purchases solely on the basis of price, a comparatively weak position that generally results in low profit and slow growth. The key in the experience economy is to create a memorable experience for customers at each stage of the business.

An offline example of a coffee bean provides a good illustration of the experience economy. Companies that harvest coffee beans receive $1 a pound or 2¢ a cup for their product. When the manufacturer roasts the packages and in turn sells those beans to a grocery store, the price jumps to between 5 and 25¢ per cup. Served at a local diner, the price of the coffee is between 50¢ and $1 a cup. Now enters Starbucks, which makes the ordering, creation, and consumption of coffee a memorable experience. For the experience, consumers pay between $2 and $5 a cup.

Although one obviously can't deliver the complete Starbucks experience online, the more memorable the experience you create for customers, the more they will be willing to pay. For example, Amazon always provides an excellent book-browsing experience. The site is content rich, easy to navigate, and contains helpful suggestions that are individualized to each user. The site provides an illustration of the cover art for most books that can even be enlarged. Amazon combines all the advantages of the book-buying experience with a considerable amount of useful information.

TEN FALLACIES OF INTERNET ENTREPRENEURSHIP

Now that we have reviewed some of the important factors of the new economy, let's look at some Internet entrepreneurship fallacies followed by an examination of a reality-based Internet model.

1. Go public and then worry about making money. The stock market's exuberance over the new economy has resulted in many companies going public before their business models were refined. This permitted many "not ready for prime time" companies to begin trading in the public market. Some such as Noosch, an online printing company, filed to go public not only without any income but even without any revenue. Apparently, Noosch gave away all of its services in the previous year.

The investment fervor has died down considerably, and now companies have to be based on a profitable business model before being funded at an initial level, much less as a public company.

2. Use the hamburger model in building your Internet business. In other words, start an Internet business so that you can quickly flip it. Although selling your business can be a key exit strategy, it is not necessarily as easy as it looks. To command a good selling price, you must first create value beyond a catchy name and idea. Otherwise, what you have is simply not worth that much. It is important to look beyond the hamburger model and aim at constructing a sustainable and profitable business. The easy money days of the Internet are long gone.

3. Put up your site and they will come. This myth seems so intuitive and obvious that I almost didn't include it, but too many Internet entrepreneurs still believe it. Typically, people are so anxious to get something up and running that they neglect giving any thought to their business model. Although speed is important in the Internet world, sites must be marketed properly to be successful. If viral marketing is going to be used to promote the site, then a careful model must be developed for it to work. A site has to be launched with some coordination. In many cases, constructing the site is the easy part; attracting paying customers is the difficult part.

4. Go after everyone. The Internet is all about large markets, and, in fact, venture capital firms will generally not even consider your business unless you have a potential market of at least $1 billion. This doesn't mean, however, that your market has to include everyone. There are many tightly drawn markets, particularly world markets, that exceed $1 billion, so determine what the core market of your business is. The business that tries to be everything to everyone will generally not succeed.

The start-up company needs to focus on an underserved segment of the market where it can deliver an outstanding result. The next chapter presents the framework of scouring the market for a viable space. The key is to isolate a market need that you can fulfill better than anyone else. Such market needs include tightly drawn niches that often translate into large markets on the Internet.

5. Advertise lavishly to develop a brand name. This fallacy also has to be disproved, for brand identities are important. In fact, one of the primary aims of marketing is to develop a brand name that creates positive images in the customer's mind. When we consider the compressed Internet world, a powerful brand could constitute an insurmountable advantage.

As mentioned in Chapter 1, some Internet start-ups are currently spending as much as 70 percent of their money on trying to create a known brand name. Branding is much more than dumping tons of money into traditional advertising (see Chapters 8 and 9). It is an integrated marketing strategy that culminates in an outstanding customer experience.

6. Go with glitzy sites. We have all had experiences with sites that overwhelm viewers with their graphics. They may be fun to look at, but a site that is too glitzy and cluttered could sound the death knell for the business. The first issue in site design is practicality. Although bandwidth is constantly increasing, excess graphics may create a very slow site. Although this seems to be common sense, many established companies have poorly constructed sites that are difficult to navigate. Remember that the site needs to be geared to your customers. Customers should be able to navigate the site easily and, more important, be able to make purchases easily. Amazon.com developed and patented a one-click purchasing method for its site, whereby registered users are able to purchase an item with a single click.

I remember visiting the site of a popular sunglasses manufacturer. Instead of being customer friendly, the site reminded me of a cross between a horror movie and the game Dungeons and Dragons. It was only through a determined effort that I was able to get the information I needed. I persisted because I already owned a pair of the manufacturer's sunglasses that needed repair. I mailed my sunglasses to the manufacturer and shouldn't have been surprised when they shipped them, by mistake, to someone else. Although the company did give me a free pair, they were a lesser quality. Needless to say, I never bought anything from that company again.

7. Web traffic is everything. Here is another myth that needs to be contradicted. Although Web traffic is *almost* everything, it is not completely everything. Sales are everything. Even for popular portals, the Web traffic that they harness must be converted into sales and revenue at some point. Companies need to capitalize on traffic with revenues from advertising and the sale of goods or services, and a site that is generating a lot of traffic but few paying customers for itself or its advertisers needs to reexamine its business model.

8. Use bizarre ads. Many people equate the new economy with the new trends in alternative advertising and expression. There is nothing wrong with your advertising being innovative or hip because it could help your company become known. But do know where to draw the line. Bizarre ads don't always work, particularly when they don't describe your product. Sometimes the ads that win awards are not always the ones that produce the most sales. Again, remember who your customers are and how you can influence them to visit your site and buy your products and services.

Despite heavy Internet advertising in the 1999 Christmas season, a survey by Active Research indicated that 22 percent of the shoppers surveyed were unable to cite any specific Internet advertisement. Beyond.com attracted a media buzz when it featured a naked stay-at-home worker who patronized the retailer. Faced with slack sales, however, the company withdrew from retailing to focus instead on building online stores for other businesses.

Another example of bizarre ads was the one for Outpost.com, a computer selling site. The company hired the same ad agency (which had a reputation for memorable ads) that did the famous Little Caesar's "Pizza Pizza" spot. Some of the items designed for Outpost.com featured a gerbil being shot from a cannon and wolves attacking a high school marching band. Although the multi-million-dollar ad campaign generated a lot of buzz for Outpost, nobody really knew what the company did. Consequently, much of the advertising was wasted.

9. Plan everything before doing anything. This is the opposite extreme of not planning at all and involves overplanning and tinkering with your business model until it is just right. Obviously, because time is so critical on the Internet, once you have developed your basic model, it is important to launch it as soon as possible.

An important caveat to a quick launch, however, is to never promise more than you can deliver. It is one thing to tinker with your marketing or your site layout, but it's another to promise a service and then fail to deliver. This failure could be extremely detrimental to your business and require spending considerable resources to recover.

10. Money for Internet start-ups is easy to raise. Despite continuing interest in Internet businesses, raising money is still a considerable hurdle. Venture capitalists fund only a small portion of the proposals they receive. Venture capitalist Steve Dow admits that many good businesses go unfunded because they don't meet the venture capital criteria of large potential market and quick exit strategy. This doesn't mean they aren't viable businesses, but they need to get their money from other sources. Traditionally, financing start-ups is one of a venture's biggest challenges. Internet entrepreneurs have to be both creative and aggressive in their search for Internet capital.

I have incorporated in this book many suggestions from venture capitalists to assist you in fashioning a business plan, or e-plan, that will give you the most impact in the venture capital community. Businesses that receive venture capital need fundamentally sound business models, excellent management teams, and good answers for venture capitalists' questions about the viability of their businesses. In addition, networking is a critical part of raising money. You stand a much better chance of obtaining the full attention of venture capitalists if you have been introduced by someone they know and trust. The trick is obtaining that introduction.

As I discuss in Chapter 16, venture capital is not the only source of money for the Internet start-up. There are numerous sources of capital to finance your business. Many Internet entrepreneurs, even established ones, sometimes have to dip into their own resources to fund businesses.

THE REALITY-BASED INTERNET BUSINESS MODEL

The reality-based Internet business model incorporates those aspects of the new economy that are important for survival and avoids the Internet myths listed above. I asked David Cowan of Bessemer Venture Partners and a cofounder of the software encryption company Verisign about models of Internet companies in which he is interested in investing. His answer: "[I'm interested in investing in] The business which aims to transform a legacy industry using the Internet as a platform for information exchange and market making, ultimately to rationalize the supply chain."

In other words, use the Internet as a bridge to connect buyers and sellers in fragmented markets. In this manner, the Internet provides a platform for optimal exchange and maximizes value to consumers. Many may recognize this description as a valuable prototype for the conventional B2B value chain model, but listed below are additional Internet business models.

E-tailers. This is the initial and most obvious example of e-commerce in which goods are sold to the Web consumer, also known as the business-to-consumer, or B2C, model. Achieving a strong brand identity is important in order to dominate your space. Besides the e-tailer, other models include the e-mall, which is a collection of e-tailers. Some of the early competitors in this area that are best known include Amazon.com, furniture.com, and drugstore.com. Although the venture community is not currently enamored with the B2C model, that doesn't mean there aren't opportunities in this market. In addition, the conventional wisdom could always change.

Content portals. Content portals can be thought of as gateways to the Internet. Many portals are high-traffic sites that were able to obtain considerable early recognition on the Web. They include Yahoo! and Excite@Home, which offer a directory of Web sites and search engine capabilities as well as such information as news, weather, e-mail, and stock quotes. Both of these sites started with advertising as the sole source of revenue but later became more involved with the sale of goods and services.

Infomediary. This model is closely related to content portals and organizes information between buyers and sellers to add value to a particular transaction. Examples of infomediaries include travel aggregators, such as Expedia and Realtor.com, which assists homebuyers.

Process improvement. This model applies to an application service provider (ASP) that assists in a company's process improvement, such as purchasing and procurement. Examples include Ariba, which offers B2B business commerce software, and vJungle, which streamlines small business processes.

Communities. Communities are fairly similar to portals in that each serves to accumulate a particular audience based on their content appeal to that audience. Many of these communities receive revenue in the form of advertising. Communities also may receive commissions based on sales at their site. Examples include Geocities, ivillage, and other places where people gather.

Auctions/exchange. The auction model serves to bring together buyers and sellers. Among these are eBay and Priceline.com.

Value chain. This model involves services that help to integrate or provide value to the traditional value chain. Healtheon/WebMD is trying to unite the forces within the medical community to put all medical providers and health care information in one place and provide a one-stop solution. In addition, this model involves the creation of value up the chain through the integration of services and information. Also, E-Loan is taking a similar strategy in the area of home mortgages. E-Loan allows borrowers to search among more than 50,000 products from 70 lenders. The value-added services provided include a comparison of a mortgage's loan terms and rates, as well as recommendations to customers based on their debt objectives, risk profile, hold period, and other financial criteria.

chapter 3

The Fundamentals of Opportunity Recognition: Selecting Your Space

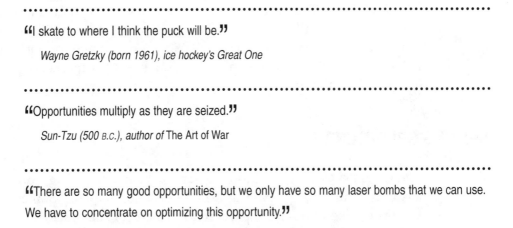

"I skate to where I think the puck will be."

Wayne Gretzky (born 1961), ice hockey's Great One

"Opportunities multiply as they are seized."

Sun-Tzu (500 B.C.), author of The Art of War

"There are so many good opportunities, but we only have so many laser bombs that we can use. We have to concentrate on optimizing this opportunity."

Michael Dell (born 1964), computer pioneer and founder of Dell Computer Corporation

OPPORTUNITY RECOGNITION

The main challenge for the entrepreneur in the new economy is to select a promising business to pursue. Although there are tremendous opportunities, it is advisable to focus your attention on a particular one because, as Michael Dell suggests, we have only so many laser bombs. In other words, don't be tempted by multiple opportunities or good ideas. Instead, concentrate your efforts on the particular market where you believe that you can make a significant impact. This is the core of opportunity recognition:

finding the right thing to do. Particular opportunities can also be characterized as gaps or needs in the marketplace. Nearly every venture capitalist I spoke with mentioned that the Internet businesses with the best chance of survival are those that fill a defined need in the marketplace.

A need or gap in the marketplace occurs whenever pain exists. Pain can come in many forms: perhaps it is difficult to find certain products; service may be unreliable; information may be hard to obtain. Pain is a compelling indicator of opportunity because you don't have to persuade consumers that they really need your particular good or service. They already know that because they are feeling pain.

Once you have isolated a particular market need, the next step is to refine the need and narrow your particular market opportunity. This involves an in-depth understanding of the market environment, including its competitive challenges. Some of this understanding will be derived from your initial analysis of the market in your search for opportunities. It will be further refined based on your research of your market opportunity discussed in Chapter 7.

SEEKING OPPORTUNITY

Where is the pain? As mentioned above, the most fertile ground for opportunity is in areas of pain in a particular marketplace. Sometimes the pain is not always obvious, particularly when consumers are not familiar with any alternative. However, once consumers' pain is relieved with a superior alternative, they can become quickly addicted.

Consider the book-buying experience. Although the pain associated with buying books might not have been obvious to many, venture capitalist David Cowan, managing director of Bessemer Venture Partners, makes the following case. For the consumer desiring to buy a book, the process was not as easy as it looked, even in the large superstores. Consider the customer who prefers to read reviews of a particular book before buying it. Such reviews are generally not available in the bookstore but would appear in various newspapers or periodicals that the customer might subscribe to. Having read the review, the customer would then have to go to the store to try to find the book. If the book was not in the section where the customer thought it would be, a visit to the information desk would be necessary. Such visits often yield mixed results, depending on how busy the particular store was and the competence of its employees. At this point, generally three things would happen. One was that you were told that the store carried the book and were directed to it. Another was that the store did not carry the book and it would have to be ordered. The third was that the store carried the book, but they were either out of it or it couldn't be located. In the last two instances, the book would have to be ordered and the customer would have to wait seven to ten days and then return to the store and purchase the book.

And you wonder why Amazon.com is so successful in the book-selling market! Look at all the pain it relieved with its one-stop source for titles, reviews from professionals as well as consumers, and 24-hour ordering for delivery to your home, with most books being shipped after 24 hours.

There are other markets where the pain is obvious—for example, fragmented markets where information can be difficult to obtain and transacting business is complicated. Consider the residential construction industry. If you've ever been involved in the construction or major remodeling of a house, you know that it can be an arduous endeavor. Generally, the construction of a new home or major remodeling takes between 3 and 12 months. One of the main causes for delay is that the homebuilder or contractor orders a broad range of materials from numerous suppliers, including building material, appliances, accessories, and home furnishings. The fragmented nature of the residential construction industry has created a complex distribution network for building materials and products, which are transferred several times through the supply chain. A supplier (retailer) either buys directly from a manufacturer and then sells to a homebuilder or buys from a national/regional supplier (wholesaler), who previously has purchased the materials from the manufacturer. This is known as a fragmented supply chain and is illustrated in Figure 3.1.

The supply chain is important to the timeliness of delivery of building materials and products from multiple sources to the job site, directly impacting the cost and timing of completing the home. In addition, the materials are generally ordered through a paper-based process that requires the manual preparation and tracking of purchase orders and consequently leads to many mistakes. Receiving either the wrong materials or late materials can completely throw off the timing of completing construction.

FIGURE 3.1 Fragmented Supply Chain

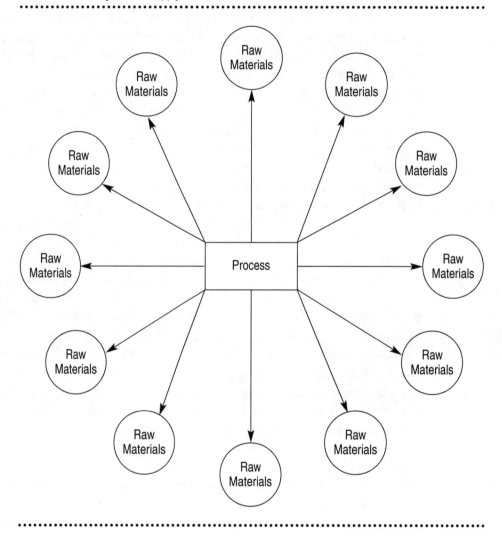

The solution is to streamline the supply chain with Internet-based procurement. One company in the residential construction space that recently went public is BuildNet Inc. Its solution to the inefficient supply chain is an Internet-based exchange that enhances the efficiency of the homebuilding process. Rather than ordering through multiple layers, homebuilders use the exchange to control the ordering and delivery of building materials. This improves planning by replacing the manual, paper-based communications and fulfillment process with an Internet exchange. The integrated exchange model is illustrated in Figure 3.2.

FIGURE 3.2   Integrated Exchange Model

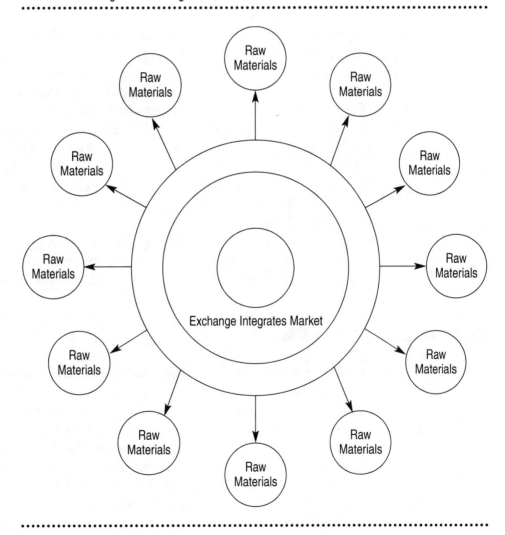

Where are the needs? Another way to seek market opportunities is to look for needs. Market needs are closely related to pain for needs in the marketplace can create a degree of pain. Another way to search for opportunity is to ask: Where are the gaps? Internet businesses that find the gaps and needs in the marketplace and fill them will succeed.

MARKET OPPORTUNITY METHODOLOGY

Various methods for determining needs and opportunities in the marketplace are available. The determination can sometimes be derived from previous experience in a particular industry. Experience provides a broad understanding and familiarity with a market and its characteristics as well as its gaps and opportunities. But don't necessarily eliminate an industry just because you have no experience in it. Jeff Bezos reportedly developed the idea for Amazon by writing down a list of ten products that could be sold over the Internet and then decided on books. He had no previous experience in the book-selling industry. Scott Cook, who had no computer or technology background, developed Quicken after his wife complained about balancing her checkbook.

Some business ideas can be flashes of insight based on your own experience. Others have to be researched. And still others you may stumble on. A few of the methods of scouring for market opportunity are discussed next.

Researching Particular Markets

Many markets, particularly those in the B2B space, can be served only by specialized content, knowledge, and contacts. According to venture capitalist Jim Smith of Mohr, Davidow Ventures, his firm generally requires that the companies it funds have experience in their particular B2B market. This is not so much from the standpoint of information because he expects all entrepreneurs to be experts in their respective markets. Rather, it is the particular contacts in the industry that are valued and can provide a competitive advantage. Consequently, if you already have experience and contacts in a particular market, you can leverage them to reenter that market online. The advantages are that you already have an understanding of the general marketplace and knowledge of its needs and gaps. This inside knowledge plus your contact base can be instrumental in helping you design a business that will compete effectively in a particular space.

Another way to begin a business is to begin researching particular markets for unmet needs. Although I discuss research in more detail in Chapter 7, you can begin by considering various markets and how the Internet can transform a particular market. This obviously requires understanding various markets as well as understanding the market chain. Once you have a good understanding of the market chain, you can begin previewing the particular market for opportunities. If you don't have such experience, it could be helpful to partner with someone who does.

Analyzing a Marketplace

It is important to understand the market and its chain to determine the particular part of the chain to focus your business on. The market chain describes the various stages in the economy where raw products, services, and equipment come together in a particular process and are then distributed to customers. The market chain in the new economy was discussed in Chapter 2. Its four component parts are as follows:

1. *Business process:* This is the actual process, such as manufacturing or information processing, that creates the particular good or service. This business process often involves the use of raw materials, equipment, or services as factors of production.

   For the computer manufacturer, for example, the business process is the assembly of the computers. The raw materials include the component parts of the computer, such as the case, microprocessor, storage drive, and other parts. The equipment is the manufacturing tools and the service is the labor necessary to assemble the computer.

   For a knowledge worker, such as an attorney, the process is a bit different. The raw materials are the research or reference materials. The equipment consists of computers and other office machinery, whereas the services are more knowledge based.

2. *Products or services:* These are particular products or services created by the business process. For the computer manufacturer, the final product is obviously the computer. For the attorney, the legal work is the final work product, whether a brief, contract, or other form of legal document.
3. *Distribution channels:* These include the various channels that are used to deliver or distribute goods and services to the customer. Computers can be sold through direct marketing or through retail or wholesale outlets. Legal services are generally sold directly to the consumer.
4. *Customers:* These are the ultimate end users of particular products.

Analyzing the market chain of a particular business is one manner in which the opportunities in the market can be discovered. Review the market chain for inefficiencies or problems or for methods that the Internet can improve. One Internet business focused on the legal market is Loislaw. The company is an online database of research and reference material geared to attorneys. The part of the supply chain that the company is focused on concerns a primary raw material for the legal production process, namely legal research. Loislaw is designed to replace the traditional legal library, which often imposes substantial costs as well as storage requirements on an attorney. In addition, bound materials have to be periodically updated with pocket parts to remain current. Legal research was often a cumbersome and expensive process. Loislaw addressed this pain in the marketplace by creating an online database that organized reference materials and permitted easy access. In addition, the database can be accessed from anywhere, so there is no need to carry books home from the law library to do research. Loislaw illustrates how the Internet can enhance the production process of legal services by enhancing raw materials.

Southwest Airlines provides an excellent example of the way the Internet can enhance the distribution part of the market chain. Prior to the Internet, airline tickets were generally ordered and distributed by phone. Customers either contacted the airline directly or used intermediaries such as travel agencies. The process could sometimes be complicated and require several phone calls to determine prices as well as available seating. The Internet provides Southwest customers with the same information as travel agents and airline employees. This direct access to price and availability makes ticket distribution much more efficient and saves the airline considerable labor costs. The Internet-ordering process has also helped to eliminate mistakes. Customers who purchase online receive discounted prices and share in the airline's cost savings. Presently, 27 percent of Southwest's tickets are booked online.

Focusing on an Industry

One way to approach starting an Internet business is to focus on a particular industry. Many market opportunities are often industry specific and choosing a particular industry allows you to focus your business on those parts of the market chain where you can offer unique value. An online business is viable wherever it can create real economic efficiencies along the market chain. For example, the start-up Healtheon/WebMD is using its integration of medical data as a value-added component that is roughly equivalent to a production process. It is able to take all the materials and raw data from medical records and convert them into a usable format. This added value in upgrading the data for easier use can further entrench the company in the marketplace and solidify its distribution network.

In other cases, the opportunities for companies hinge on their being able to carefully scour and segment the market. Particularly in the vast Internet domain, you have to select a particular segment to which you direct marketing resources.

Particular industries are broken down into the shared North American Industrial Classification System (NAICS) code. The NAICS code replaced the Standard Industrial Code (SIC) classification for different industries. Some of the industries are the following:

- Agriculture
- Forestry
- Mining
- Construction
- Manufacturing
- Transportation

- Communications
- Electric and gas utilities
- Sanitary services
- Wholesale trade
- Retail trade
- Finance
- Insurance

Using the NAICS code provides guidance for doing further research on various industries.

Look Beyond the Business Jargon

In researching this book, I came across various models describing successful businesses in the new economy. Many of these models employ such business jargon as *disintermediation* and *disaggregation*. These and similar terms set forth valid principles. Disintermediation involves the elimination of a layer or function that exists between two layers or functions. In the market chain, disintermediation might involve eliminating the wholesale or retail layer or process of the market. Disaggregation is the opposite of aggregation and involves the separation of a mass into its component parts.

There is nothing wrong with using business jargon to describe certain aspects of business, but it's also important to look beyond the jargon in choosing a particular market opportunity. After you cut through the jargon and the models of Internet business, your success hinges on one particular attribute: customer satisfaction. The critical ingredient of a sustainable business in the new economy is the ability to attract, retain, and continually satisfy customers. Businesses that succeed at this will prosper and those that don't will fail.

Customers are the lifeblood of a business. The reason businesses seek to fulfill a compelling market opportunity is to attract customers. The entire focus of a business model should be customer preferences. Will potential customers perceive the business as valuable to them? Customers, of course, don't simply gravitate to new businesses on their own, which is why a carefully planned marketing program needs to be developed. (See Chapters 7, 8, and 9 for more on marketing.)

Attracting customers is only part of the battle; the next challenge is to retain them. A sticky site—one with strong customer loyalty as noted in Chapter 2—receives repeat business from its customers and is less likely to lose business to competitors. As discussed earlier, America Online and Yahoo are considered sticky sites. Customer loyalty is built up through site content, the types of products or the community of interest offered. The key is to keep your customers continually satisfied by exceeding their expectations.

Although it may seem that various theories for Internet businesses abound, there is actually only one—attracting, retaining, and continually satisfying customers.

Examples of Recent and Noteworthy Internet Start-Ups

Following are some examples of recent Internet start-ups that sought out the pain, the needs, or the gaps in the marketplace.

Branders.com. Branders.com is a recent start-up headquartered in Foster City, California; David Sipes is the vice president of business development and a cofounder of the company. His work experience includes stints at PricewaterhouseCoopers and Pepsi, and, most recently, he has been a principal at Booz Allen & Hamilton. An energetic young man with a passion for hard rock music and snowboarding, Sipes has an extensive background in business-to-business marketing. When the Internet revolution hit, Sipes knew that he wanted to be a part of it but wasn't certain where to start. He started first with his contact base from his previous positions, which put him in touch with venture capitalists and other entrepreneurs.

He then began to review the online marketplace in search of opportunities. Initially, he considered pet supplies but concluded that this category wasn't sufficiently economically attractive; then he considered the automotive industry. Eventually, conversations with friends and associates led him to the promotional products industry.

Promotional products are items such as hats, coffee mugs, banners, and other items featuring the logo of a particular company or organization. As their name suggests, promotional products are generally used for advertising or promotional purposes, frequently given as gifts to customers. The types of products range all over the board from fairly inexpensive to expensive items such as high-quality pens or briefcases. Typically, the people ordering promotional products are sales and marketing professionals, specifically trade show managers, event coordinators, and marketing managers.

Selecting a promotional product often involves several meetings with a particular vendor. There are many choices of products, colors, and textures as well as the logo design and appearance of the product. Faxing models back and forth doesn't provide buyers with a complete picture of the product. One of the main problems with the offline purchasing system, in fact, is that buyers aren't able to see a product before they buy. In addition, the process takes too much time—an average of 21 days. Customers of Branders.com, on the other hand, can complete their purchases in less than ten minutes.

When you consider the industry from the standpoint of the above paragraph, the economies and gaps are obvious. Promotional products are a fragmented market and the purchasing experience can be time consuming. Enter Branders.com, in which customers (buyers) can click their way to selecting the most appropriate promotional item for their needs and budget. The site of Branders.com allows customers to easily search for products on the basis of price and then review all variations of the product in real time. Customers can compare raised letterhead to flat letterhead and see every variation of the product. This capacity for real-time evaluation allows customers to quickly and accurately review their product before ordering. In short, Branders.com offers many competitive advantages in its space. In fact, the competitive advantages are so obvious that Sipes found himself constantly approached by venture capitalists at every stage of the financing process and consequently was able to secure financing on excellent terms.

Some of the advantages of Branders.com include the following:

- Provides a one-stop shop for customizing merchandise
- Aids in product selection with advanced, customized search
- Allows buyers to customize their products online and in real time
- Reduces fulfillment activities
- Improves corporate identity management

Before launching its site, Branders.com conducted a comprehensive survey to determine consumer preferences in the promotional product market. It wanted to know what was most important to potential clients and organize its site around consumer utility. Branders.com is based on filling a need for consumers of promotional products in a superior manner, which is why its business model is so compelling.

StarMine.com. This Internet start-up is based in San Francisco and is currently housed between an automotive shop and a flower market on the outskirts of the downtown financial district. StarMine.com is based on a software product that was developed by its founder and president, Joe Gatto, whose background is in decision and risk analysis. It is Gatto's expertise in subjective probability and forecasting that led to his inquiring into the variance in earnings estimates of stock market analysts.

Financial services firms, such as stock brokerages and investment banks, assign stock market analysts to particular companies to review and report on their operations. An important function of analysts is to predict the earnings of particular companies. These earnings estimates are then aggregated into a consensus for a particular stock and are often used by investors to evaluate particular stocks. In evaluating the consensus, Gatto discovered that it placed an equal weight on the estimate of each analyst, regardless of the date the estimate was made or the track record of the analyst. Analysts with bad track records were weighted equally with analysts with good track records. In addition, more recent estimates were not weighted any differently than older estimates; for example, a more recent estimate would encompass the latest factors affecting the earnings of the particular company.

Gatto developed a technology that automatically generates more intelligent estimates because of its timeliness, historical accuracy, and other metrics for each contributing analyst. Gatto claims that StarMine estimates significantly outperform the analysts' consensus in predicting the future earnings of a company. The technology allows the user to weigh or adjust the consensus estimate by such factors as

- how recent the estimate is;
- how accurate an analyst has been in the past;

- the experience of on analyst in tracking the particular company;
- the analyst's brokerage firm; and
- whether an analyst has been recognized in *Institutional Investor,* which ranks the performance of particular stock market analysts.

According to David Lichtblau, the vice president of marketing for Star-Mine, the company fills an important need for investors and analysts who want to obtain better information from analysts' earnings estimates. The StarMine technology provides information about which analyst to listen to and which one to ignore. With 2,000 new earnings estimates generated daily, it is important to distinguish between the good estimates and the poor estimates. StarMine fills this need of supplying more complete and precise information about earnings estimates.

myprimetime.com. MyPrimeTime, Inc., is housed behind the Old Mint building in San Francisco. Its office space is a refurbished shell of a building complete with brick walls and earthquake support beams. The company was founded by three journalists who sought to create a community among baby boomers (those between the ages of 35 and 54). The goal for myprimetime.com is to create a space of editorial content and actionable information to help boomers improve their life.

According to Donald Van de Mark, a cofounder, vice president, and editorial director of MyPrimeTime, the market opportunity seized by My-PrimeTime was in focusing its content on the boomer generation. Boomers are often overlooked by many industries that either cater to youth or target the growing elderly population. Sandwiched in between, boomers face opportunities and risks their parents never dreamed of. From swelling stock portfolios to relatives living into their nineties, the baby boom generation needs finely edited, highly personalized coaching to maximize their life.

Turbotrip.com. Turbotrip.com (formerly Roomfinders.com) started as an 800 telephone service that provided hotel room rates and availability in New Orleans. At the time, there was no central registry of rates and availability for hotels in New Orleans. Guests trying to book rooms directly were forced to call each hotel separately, an expensive and aggravating game.

During the infancy of the Internet, Turbotrip began posting listings online, charging hotels $1 per month to list a hotel on its site. Customers would read the postings and then send e-mails to request information. Of course, this had to be followed up by phone.

In 1998, the company refined its service to permit rooms to be booked online. Presently, someone can visit turbotrip and check availability and rates for rooms in over 60 cities and then book rooms directly online. The key advantage is the one-stop shopping and convenience of the service. In addition, turbotrip offers rooms for the same price hotels do.

Netex.com. This company, founded by software engineer Greg Meffert, was originally started as Imaging Technology Solutions. Its first product, Zydeco, was designed to interact with imaging software to manage documents. Initially, the company consulted with corporations and used its software product to manage a client's documents. Next, the company sought to distribute its product on a retail level as shrink-wrapped software.

The product quickly reached sales of 50,000, but the company began experiencing growing pains as well as problems in the retail market. Amid the turbulence, Meffert noticed that Zydeco's easy e-mail feature was a big hit with customers. It allowed them to quickly e-mail documents to others. Meffert then shifted focus to the e-mail component of Zydeco as well as the Internet market. He developed a product that allowed people to send encrypted e-mails in lieu of the more expensive express mail.

In the cases listed above, many people were able to determine their business through previous work experience, a spin-off of an existing product, a flash of brilliance, or even through a process of elimination. The following is a review of a few questions to help you develop an Internet business:

- Where are some needs and gaps in the market?
- How could I help fill this need?
- What part of the market chain should I focus on in making a unique contribution or difference?

As mentioned earlier, focus is important to the Internet entrepreneur. Focus on the market. Focus on the customer. Focus on that portion of the market where you can provide the most value to the customer. Preparing your e-plan will lead to a sharper focus on the Internet economy. As mentioned earlier, it is naive to think that no one else is trying to exploit your particular opportunity. The truth is that many competitors are working on the same idea, requiring you to focus on what you do and be constantly thinking of the steps that you can take to give value to the customer.

If you are going to become an intermediary, you probably need to choose a highly fragmented market. Centralized markets can serve that function themselves. This happened recently when General Motors, Ford, and DaimlerChrysler announced they would combine forces to create a single Internet marketplace in which they would perform all of their buying.

TRENDS IN THE INTERNET MARKET

Current trends in the new economy can also help guide you in identifying an opportunity in the marketplace. Let's examine these trends next.

Convergence

The term *convergence* applies to the coming together, the uniting, of the various means of communication as well as of reception. It applies basically to the computer, the telephone, and television. All of these products are struggling to be the portal from which consumers receive information and content and which they also use to communicate with others. As part of the convergence revolution, you see cable companies and telephone companies offering Internet access. In addition, you see a race between the traditional entertainment industry and online portals for entertainment content.

Evidence of this model of convergence is all over the relevant marketplace. Convergence was the driving force behind the acquisition of Time Warner by America Online (AOL). Reportedly, one of the reasons that Time Warner let itself be acquired is that it had been unsuccessful with its Internet strategy. Soon the entertainment industry is going to have competition from Internet portals providing content. The synergies are also obvious as AOL wanted the rich entertainment content of Time Warner.

Other evidence of this convergence model is the acquisition of many cable companies by such Internet players as Microsoft and AOL. Again, the bottom line is the convergence of all the mediums and the race to be the one that controls the customer. In addition, the telephone industry is converging with the Internet as more and more people use the Internet for communication.

Remote Access

Another trend in the online world is remote access. At a recent meeting of the annual conference of the Cellular Telecommunication Industry Association in New Orleans, all of the major Internet players were out in force. Speaking at the convention were Jeff Bezos, Steve Case, and Bill Gates. Many of the major Internet players are rushing to embrace a technology called the wireless application protocol, or WAP. The major Internet players are signing different types of joint venture deals with the communication and mobile phone industry. They are looking toward the day in the near future when Web-connected devices made by the cellular telephone industry will be more prevalent than PCs. That is why Steve Case launched AOL Anywhere. There is a rush among many of the existing large Web portals to dominate the space. With AOL Anywhere, customers can send instant messages to their buddy lists. In addition, Microsoft rolled out a new version of MSN mobile that gives its subscribers access to Hotmail and the travel site Expedia. Oracle launched a portal that allows users to access e-mail and flight times.

Wireless is predicted to be a profound growth area of the Internet. According to the Gartner Group, 40 percent of all e-commerce will be wireless in four years. In addition, by 2003, more than 18 million browser-enabled cell phones and 12 million Internet-enabled handheld computers will be used to conduct mobile commerce. Needless to say, new companies have popped up to compete in this marketplace. One of these is Viafone.

Viafone. This Redwood, California, company started in 1999 and recently received venture capital funds. Viafone provides a turnkey and customizable application service provider (ASP) that provides online merchants a compelling presence across all leading wireless devices. The company powers the mobile commerce presence of retailers behind the scenes and tightly integrates it with merchants' existing e-commerce structure. The mobile commerce AST solution enables customers to

- obtain an Internet price quote for a product from a brick-and-mortar retailer;
- purchase a book or CD from their favorite online source; and
- receive time-sensitive and personalized product offers on their cellular telephone as they drive near a local retailer.

4

The E-plan: The Internet Entrepreneur's Treasure Map

....

"Plans are nothing; planning is everything."

Dwight D. Eisenhower (1890–1969), 34th American president

....

"Life is what happens while you are making other plans."

John Lennon (1940–1980), Beatle

PLANNING IN A REAL-TIME ECONOMY

Is There Time to Plan?

Business commentators are generally divided on the ability to effectively plan in the new economy. Some opine that the pace of change is so rapid that it is impossible to plan for the future. Others, however, insist that planning is necessary. Successful companies during this competitive era are preparing very clear business plans that develop the vision of their intended destination. Their blueprint or business plan, however, must allow them the flexibility to respond when the unexpected occurs.

Consider some ancient wisdom amid the new economy: "If you fail to plan, you plan to fail." Planning is necessary to develop your vision, but it needs to be flexible. As a result, I am advocating a variation of the traditional business plan that I call the e-plan. The e-plan helps you capture your vision while providing a flexible platform for responding to the inevitable changes and shifts in the economy. The new economy is no place for the 100-page business plan that flushes out every conceivable detail. This exercise is not about earning a gold star on your business plan from a difficult teacher or some picky banker. Rather, it is about capturing your vision in a flexible format that facilitates the execution of your business model—that is the essence of the e-plan.

In addition, there is a general correlation between planning and financing. This correlation is an inverse relationship between the development stage of a particular business model and the financing cost in terms of equity relinquished. In other words, the less developed a business model, the more expensive the financing in terms of proportionate equity given up. This makes sense because there is more risk involved. Generally, companies relinquish a greater share of equity at early stages of financing than at later stages, when the business model might be more established.

THE E-PLAN

As mentioned earlier, extensive business plans were often aimed at traditional lenders, who wanted to be sure that no stone was left unturned. Chances are that in today's economy, many of the old stones will disappear and be replaced by new ones by the time a conventional business plan is finished. I was never a fan of the business plan treatise. I usually recommended to clients that business plans should be concise and range about 20 pages. Supplementary information, such as product circulars and marketing materials, can be included in an appendix, but the narrative part of the plan should be a maximum of 20 pages. The object is not to unearth every conceivable detail but to think through your business model. Few plans are read in their entirety by potential investors, and the new economy, furthermore, requires an even more concise way of formulating a business model.

This new format, the e-plan, is designed to help all the users of the business plan, which includes the entrepreneur as well as potential investors and employees. It is streamlined both for speed of digestion and ease of use.

The e-plan consists of an executive summary and approximately a dozen PowerPoint slides. Each slide addresses an important component of your business model. I consider the e-plan to be more of a compass than a map. It is designed to guide you in the right direction but is flexible enough to accommodate shifts and changes in the marketplace. As these changes occur, the e-plan can be used to produce a corresponding shift in strategy.

Some of the advantages of the e-plan format are its overview, flexibility, and presentation.

Overview. The executive summary and the slide format provide a quick overview of all important components of your business model and provide a comprehensive understanding of the model. The e-plan serves as a ready reference for the big picture.

Flexibility. The slide format provides you with the ability to change directions quickly. As changes occur in the marketplace, your big picture can be changed accordingly.

Presentation. The slide format also facilitates the presentation of your business to potential investors and employees. Chances are that more people will be hearing your presentation as opposed to reading your plan. The slide format provides a focal point. The slides can be presented with an LCD projector or simply printed out. David Cowan of Bessemer Venture Partners mentioned that he would prefer having the slides e-mailed to him and have the entrepreneur walk him through the business model to facilitate his grasping the necessary fundamentals in the minimal amount of time.

If the intended recipient of the slides does not have PowerPoint or a presentation software, the slides can then be saved in outline form.

OVERVIEW OF THE E-PLAN

Executive Summary

This one- or two-page document is the single most important part of your plan. In a nutshell, it summarizes your particular market opportunity and the solution to a problem that your business offers. As mentioned earlier, busy investors often don't have the time to read the complete business plan, particularly when they are qualifying potential businesses. They usually rely on the executive summary to provide a snapshot of your business model. Although I go into more detail about preparing your executive summary in the next chapter, one way to look at the summary is to think of it as the story of your business. What need does your business fulfill? How can you best summarize your business in 60 seconds or less? What is your vision?

One way to consider the executive summary is known as the "elevator pitch." Imagine yourself in an elevator with a potential investor or customer. The elevator has started up from the ground and you have 35 floors or 90 seconds (including stops) to persuade the investor to fund your venture. You give it your best shot. That is the executive summary—your best shot.

Slide 1: Name of Company. Suffice it to say that the name of any Internet business is extremely important. Various issues related to the name of your company will be discussed in more detail in the next chapter. As you might have already found out, selecting a domain name these days is no simple matter. As indicated in Chapter 1, choice domain names are being bought and sold for heavy premiums. With the domain name so important, it is obviously something to which you need to give considerable thought. Start immediately searching for one if you don't have a name already.

Slide 2: Mission Statement. The mission statement is an abbreviated form of the executive summary. In one or two sentences, what does your company stand for? We look more closely at the mission statement in the next chapter.

Slide 3: Management Team. The management team is of particular concern to investors. Note that I used the word *team*. Writer John Donne proclaimed that "no man is an island." In addition, no entrepreneur is an island either. The entrepreneurs that can attract the right people are the ones that ultimately succeed. The management team is the backbone of the company. A founder that cannot attract a quality management team will have trouble attracting good employees as well as customers.

Slide 4: Market. This slide will analyze the size of the potential market as well as its growth rate. One of the primary advantages of the Internet is that the target markets are so huge. As I discuss in Chapter 7, the size of the market is determined by your research.

Slide 5: Industry. Industry concerns a discussion of the structure of the particular industry that you are targeting. Who are the buyers and the sellers? Who are the suppliers? What is the market chain of the industry? How would you diagram it? Is the industry in a growth mode? I examine industry research in Chapter 7.

Slide 6: Pain: Market Opportunity. This slide considers the pain or the opportunity in the market. Where is that part of the market broken or inefficient? How does it create an opportunity for you? Where is a problem that your business will solve? The best business opportunities are based on the most compelling needs of the marketplace. This often applies to a highly fragmented industry or an industry with an inefficient market chain. I discuss refining your business model around the pain in the market in Chapter 8.

Slide 7: Solution. What is your solution to the problem or pain in the marketplace? What is your answer to the disintermediation or the need in the marketplace? How does your product or service benefit the marketplace? Why is your solution unique from others? Do you have a competitive advantage that can be sustained? Is your solution scalable, allowing it to be implemented on a large scale? The solution is also discussed in Chapter 8.

Slide 8: Marketing Plan. This slide presents an overview of your marketing plan. How are you going to attract customers? Are there viral marketing possibilities that you can exploit? As discussed earlier, viral marketing is a strategy in which customers do much of the marketing for you. What unique marketing advantages do you have? What important alliances can you develop? I discuss preparing your marketing strategy in Chapter 9.

Slide 9: Financial Projections. This portion of the plan involves the projection of revenues and expenses from the business. Although many investors discount projections, they can play an important role in examining the financial portion of the business model. The most useful projections are developed around a meaningful unit of measure, or metric. For example, revenues and expenses could be analyzed and expressed on a per customer basis. What is your acquisition cost per customer? What is its worth in terms of lifetime revenue? How many customers do you need to break even?

Your projections should detail your use of start-up funds, which include initial capital expenses and working capital needs until the business reaches breakeven. Accounting and the preparation of financial projections are presented in Chapter 10.

Slide 10: Valuation Analysis. This final slide can be thought of as a segue between where your presentation ends and negotiations begin. Build the case for the valuation of your company based on your business model. Choose the most relevant metrics to compare your business with one trading publicly. This could be used when talking to potential investors or employees. Valuation is discussed in Chapter 16.

Backup Materials

Although the e-plan is designed for efficient presentation, it still requires the same analysis as a conventional business plan. The main difference is in the economy of presentation. As mentioned earlier, the e-plan does not concern itself with presenting all conceivable issues related to the business. Not all issues can be determined in advance in the new economy. Venture capitalist David Cowan says that he is often put off by a business plan that is too detailed. He wonders why the entrepreneur is not busy trying to attract customers as opposed to brushing up on the plan.

Despite its abbreviated appearance, however, the e-plan involves many of the same exercises as the written business plan. Market research is required to determine the size of the market as well as the opportunity. In addition, it is also important to develop coordinated marketing strategies. The business model still has to be constructed based on projected revenues and expenses. The point is that there is still considerable work to do, but the e-plan is designed to facilitate finishing the work as quickly as possible so that you can get started attracting customers before someone else does. It is helpful to keep your background information—size of your market, marketing strategies, projected revenues and expenses—organized in the event you wish to supplement the e-plan.

Investors come in all shapes and sizes and may request additional information. The e-plan can be used to hook their interest, and background information can be used to respond to their questions. If a potential investor wants a conventional plan, the extra work is justified if the investor is significant enough. In this case, the e-plan slides can simply be elaborated. It might be a good idea to write out a plan not to exceed 20 pages; this written plan could be summarized into an e-plan or the e-plan expanded to a written plan. As discussed earlier, business planning is an ongoing and dynamic process. As you receive more input and information, you revise the plan accordingly.

Presenting a business plan is much like getting a book published. There are guidelines but no hard and fast rules for getting published. For example, an unpublished fiction writer would probably have to submit an entire manuscript to be taken seriously, but a compelling proposal from a new writer could be snapped up immediately even without a manuscript. The novel *The Horse Whisperer* received a record advance even though it was only partially completed. The author, Nicolas Evans, faxed what he had to an agent and received a publishing contract and a movie deal almost immediately. Similarly, a very compelling idea could receive funding with a minimal presentation. Another idea, however, could require a more detailed presentation. Like book publishing, there are general guidelines but no hard and fast rules about business plan preparation because of the many uses for the business plan.

USES OF THE E-PLAN

The main audience for your e-plan is you. First and foremost, the e-plan is a way of quickly capturing your vision and putting it in a format for execution. The plan has to make sense to you and guide you in propelling your vision into reality.

The next audience for your business plan is potential investors. Investors today simply don't have the time to wade through long plans. A short, direct format serves their purpose better. Moses Joseph of Anila Corporation relayed that knowledge of the market is much more important than a written business plan. He mentioned that he can tell whether a person really knows the market within five minutes of talking to him or her. In Joseph's opinion, the value is not so much the written plan but rather the discipline of the planning process itself. This process forces you to fully examine the particular market opportunity and confront certain critical issues associated with your venture. It is very important for entrepreneurs to completely and fully understand their market.

The next audience for your business plan is your potential employees, suppliers, and affiliates. For this use, a good business plan can show them that your business is for real and that you have given it considerable thought.

E-plan Helpful to Brick-and-Mortar Businesses

The e-plan can also be a useful mechanism for existing businesses to take advantage of the new economy. The existing business could reevaluate its operations and market in light of the new economy. What new markets can be entered? How could the business be expanded in existing markets? What additional opportunities are created by the Internet and how could they be taken advantage of? The e-plan could serve as a blueprint to convert your existing business into an e-business.

As mentioned earlier, the existing business has many advantages in converting into an e-business. These advantages include knowledge of the market and its customer base; and the e-plan could assist you in taking a fresh look at the market and planning your e-business from the ground up. However, conversion also has disadvantages, including contemporary structures and relationships that might have to be disrupted to take full advantage of the Internet.

ADVANTAGES OF PLANNING

If you are not already convinced of the advantages of planning, consider the following sections.

Planning as a capital-raising tool. As previously discussed, the business plan is your ticket to get past the door and initiate a conversation about funding. There are certain instances when a unique product or technology justifies a substantial investment at face value, although this is more the exception than the rule.

Planning as a recruiting tool. The e-plan can be a powerful selling document for attracting key executives. As I mentioned, you will probably present your plan orally more often than in writing. A compelling plan that captures the interest and imagination of potential employees and executives is a powerful recruiting tool. Competition for talent is at a premium. Even though people working for start-ups are generally risk takers, they also want to take their best risk. The well-prepared business plan, which sets forth a compelling market opportunity fortified by proper research, is a strong tool for persuading a potential executive to take a chance with you.

Planning as a marketing tool. Carefully structured, the plan can be used to market your business. Between its careful research, scalable business model, and a compelling oral presentation, the e-plan should present your vision to potential customers or strategic partners. This vision can serve as an effective marketing tool to sell your company to those with whom you seek to do business.

Planning as a qualifier. The e-plan can qualify a start-up that is attempting to affiliate with a larger and more established corporation. Although large corporations are foolish to ignore start-ups, the e-plan can result in a larger entity taking a start-up more seriously.

Caveat: An important warning at this stage, which will be discussed in more detail in a discussion of legal issues in Chapter 12, is that you must protect your intellectual property. In distributing the business plan, you should try to obtain a confidentiality agreement with anyone who has access to your plan. Although venture capitalists will not generally sign confidentiality agreements, obtain the signatures wherever you can.

Planning forces discipline. The plan forces entrepreneurs to think through their entire venture. It makes you address the important and critical components of your business model. Some parts of the plan will clearly be more difficult to formulate than others. Generally, the issues that are difficult to plan could also cause problems in the operational stage. However, during the planning stage you have a better opportunity to think the issues through before having to address them.

In addition, the plan will help to point out any gaps in your model. Don't get caught off guard in an interview with investors or potential employees. Your contacts and time are simply too precious to waste with a poorly planned presentation. Generally, you only receive one shot to make your pitch. This is not to say the plan will guarantee coverage of every contingency, but at least it will help you focus on the important parts.

Planning corroborates value. The plan serves as an important corroboration to the value of your particular business by gathering together the necessary backup information. As I discuss later in the financing section, the joy of receiving financing needs to be tempered with the reality of the terms. It is advisable to establish the best case for valuation at each stage of funding. The better the valuation, the more of the company you will be able to keep. I heard Jim Clark speak recently, and he still appears angry about relinquishing 40 percent of Silicon Graphics for $800,000. That left him with 1 percent of the company when it went public in contrast with many of his friends who still owned 10 to 15 percent of their companies. Although it was a costly lesson, Clark did learn from the experience. When he approached venture capitalists for funding Netscape, he was able to retain a much greater ownership percentage. You want to make the best case for valuation the first time; unlike Clark, you may not get a second chance.

Planning inspires confidence. Another advantage of the plan is that it inspires the confidence of employees, boards of directors, and shareholders. These key stakeholders are important to the overall success of the business. It is comforting for them to know that the business principals have established a definite direction for the business and are proceeding toward their vision. Remember, though, that the business plan is a dynamic document. It will continue to change as market opportunities change.

Planning as a goal. To reach any goal, you need a target. Although the goal of your business might be to dominate a particular space, you must set out that vision as well as the steps that you are going to take to implement it. One of the beauties of business planning is that it taps into the power of goal setting. A valid goal needs to be *specific, written, measurable,* and *achievable.*

Never underestimate the impact of writing something down. Even in a real-time economy, putting something in writing can be thought of as the first major step toward its accomplishment. Why do you think that New Year's resolutions and to-do lists are so popular? I mentioned earlier that the Internet business is more than just excited chatter. Clearly, the opportunities offered by the Internet are generating tremendous buzz among would-be entrepreneurs. For many, their ambition does not rise above the prattle and they change their business models every day, developing in essence a business du jour. Committing something to paper can be a little scary because it requires you to take some action. Consequently, committing a dream to paper is the first step toward its accomplishment.

Being specific imposes definite parameters on your dreams and begins to lay the foundation for your business and your success. One of the main advantages of the Internet is its vastness, but this advantage can also be your downfall if you fail to define your market space. It is often helpful to understand and target your market, particularly in the B2B space. Even Amazon.com, the world's bookstore, knew who their initial target market was—the segment of individuals who buy books.

Setting forth the goals of your enterprise, particularly financial goals, often instills a dose of reality into the business. More important, this reality gives you a measuring stick with which to judge the results of your business. If you are targeting a certain revenue, net income goals, or customer acquisition goals, being able to measure these goals lets you know how much on target the enterprise is. Establishing measurable results lets you quantify the amount of initial funding your venture will require.

Although the goals set forth in the plan need to be ambitious, they must also be achievable. A guideline for achievable goals are those just out of reach but not out of sight. Therefore, instill a dose of practicality into your plan and establish achievable goals.

Planning assists financial management. Clearly, the venture that is better planned will be better managed. If managers have certain goals in mind, it is easier for them to direct the proper resources toward achieving those goals. The business plan can be a key management tool as it forces you to define the future direction for the company in terms of measurable results. The plan also allows time for reflection and serves to "prioritize" the issues that must be addressed to achieve the corporate goals. In addition, the plan also directs the effective allocation of time for each manager and employee and can, therefore, form the nucleus of your operating structure. The plan also allows you to be proactive rather than reactive and able to anticipate the right opportunities. The plan provides a benchmark with which to measure progress and gets everyone moving in the same direction.

Planning as a reference. Another use of the business plan is as a handy reference for important data and statistics. In today's economy, there is no shortage of information or data. The key is to process data into usable information that is available when you need it. In addition, where else will you record important insights about the business?

chapter 5

First Things First: Your Executive Summary, Name, and Mission Statement

"Mission and philosophy is the key starting point in business. A business is not defined by its name, statutes, or articles of incorporation. It is defined by the business mission. Only a clear definition of the mission and purpose of the organization makes possible clear and realistic business objectives.**"**

Peter Drucker (born 1909), father of modern management

"All the news that's fit to print.**"**

Adolph Ochs (1858–1935), New York Times *mission*

In this chapter, we'll examine the initial parts of the e-plan, which include the executive summary and mission statement of your business. We'll also consider the name of your business—generally your domain name—which is the first slide of your e-plan. The name of your business is important not only from an identity and image standpoint but also from the standpoint of locating the business on the Internet.

EXECUTIVE SUMMARY

Tell Your Story

The first part of your e-plan is the executive summary. One way to view the executive summary is as your story. What is your story? If a potential investor or key employee asked you about your business, what would you say? As mentioned earlier, the chances are that others will hear your story more frequently than they will read it. Despite this, the executive summary is still the most important part of your e-plan because it is the most likely to be read. The key is to be able to hook the reader into looking further into your business. Simply put, the executive summary is your opportunity to capture someone's attention in the competitive new economy. You might not have another chance, so make the most of it.

The executive summary can be a potent way of conveying your dream and painting your vision. It is important in attracting investors as well as potential employees and customers. Many companies provide an executive summary or tell their story on their Web site.

As a general rule of thumb, the executive summary should not be more than one to two pages and should contain all relevant information about your business. Think of your executive summary as a narrative overview of the e-plan. Accordingly, it should address the following issues:

- Mission statement (discussed in more detail below)
- Management team (discussed in Chapter 6)
- Size of market (discussed in Chapter 7)
- Description of the industry (discussed in Chapter 7)
- Market opportunity—where is the pain? (discussed in Chapter 3)
- Your solution (discussed in Chapter 3)
- Marketing plan overview (discussed in Chapter 9)
- Business model: key financial data (discussed in Chapter 11)

Obviously, the e-plan involves addressing the high points of your business venture in a short piece. The challenge is to convey the information in a concise, complete, and confident fashion. The executive summary or story should portray your vision in a credible manner.

Following are some guidelines in preparing your executive summary.

Be straightforward. Tell your story in a straightforward manner that covers the salient and necessary points. Avoid hype. Although the possibilities posed by your business may be exciting, maintain an objective and narrative tone. Let the facts speak for themselves. You don't need to muffle your passion and commitment. Just don't go overboard.

Tell the whole story. Although brevity is important, you still need to touch on all the important points. How large is your potential marketplace? What need are you going to fill? What is unique about your solution to the pain in the marketplace?

Don't be bashful. If your goal is to be a market leader, then say so. If your goal is to change the fundamental way that business is transacted, point that out. If the market opportunity is enormous, document it. Reach for the stars, but develop your discussion logically and back up your assertions.

Write forcefully. Write in a concise manner that makes the most of your words and ensures you make an impact. Just as the bootstrap entrepreneur seeks to stretch funding as far as it will go, this same frugal process applies to words. Say the most in the least amount of words. Attention span is a precious commodity in the new economy; simply say what you mean. The real key to effective and concise writing is rewriting. First get your thoughts down and then rewrite them. People often have difficulty figuring out where to start. Don't worry about where to start—just get started. Write your story down in the best way possible and then keep rewriting it until it conveys the most with the least amount of words. Solicit feedback from friends and associates. Rewrite again, addressing the feedback, until the plan conveys the desired points most effectively. During the editing process, remove all redundant ideas and words. Another helpful step is to read it out loud, which often allows you to hear your conclusions and decide whether they sound plausible.

Examples of Noteworthy Mission Statements

The following excerpt tells the story of a well-known Internet company. See if you can recognize it.

The Internet offers for the first time the opportunity to create a compelling global marketplace for person-to-person trading—the exchange of goods between individuals. This trading has traditionally been conducted through trading forums, such as classified advertisements, collectibles shows, garage sales and flea markets, or through intermediaries, such as auction houses and local dealer shops. These markets are highly inefficient because: (i) their fragmented, regional nature makes it difficult and expensive for buyers and sellers to meet, exchange information and complete transactions; (ii) they offer a limited variety and breadth of goods; (iii) they often have high transaction costs from intermediaries; and (iv) they are information inefficient, as buyers and sellers lack a reliable and convenient means of setting prices for sales or purchases.

Despite these inefficiencies, the company believes that the market for traditional person-to-person trading in the U.S. through auctions and classified ads exceeded $50 billion in goods sold in 1997. An Internet-based centralized trading place can overcome the inefficiencies associated with traditional person-to-person trading by facilitating buyers and sellers meeting, listing items for sale, exchanging information, interacting with each other and, ultimately, consummating transactions. Through such a trading place, buyers can access a significantly broader selection of goods to purchase and sellers have the opportunity to sell their goods efficiently to a broader base of buyers. As a result, a significant market opportunity exists for an Internet-based centralized trading place that applies the unique attributes of the Internet to facilitate person-to-person trading.

Who is this Web leader? If you guessed eBay, you are correct. This "story" was excerpted from eBay's registration statement that was filed with the Securities and Exchange Commission.

Buildnet Inc. The next example of a company's plan is from Buildnet, a leading B2B marketplace for the residential construction industry. This excerpt, too, is taken from its registration statement filed with the Securities and Exchange Commission.

Business-to-business e-commerce is expected to grow rapidly as the widespread adoption of intranets and the acceptance of the Internet has created a business communications platform that offers the potential for companies to streamline complex processes, lower costs and improve productivity. Business-to-business e-commerce is expected to grow from an estimated $406 billion in 2000 to $2.7 trillion in 2004, according to Forrester Research. The residential construction industry is one of the largest sectors of the U.S. economy. According to the U.S. Census Bureau, the value of residential construction in the United States in 1997 was approximately $238 billion. Also, according to the Census Bureau, there were approximately 1.3 million single-family housing starts in 1999. We believe that this industry has characteristics that create an attractive opportunity for business-to-business e-commerce, including large numbers of buyers and sellers, a high degree of fragmentation among buyers and sellers, significant dependence on information exchange and large transaction volume. . . .

We have designed the BuildNet Exchange to provide secure Internet-based procurement, e-commerce and information services for homebuilders, suppliers and manufacturers. We believe that the BuildNet Exchange addresses many of the supply chain inefficiencies that adversely impact the residential construction industry. The supplier and homebuilder segments of the residential construction industry are highly fragmented and driven by regional and local demand. Participants lack accurate and timely information on product requirements, building materials are transferred multiple times through the supply chain and most procurement processes are paper-based and labor-intensive. The BuildNet Exchange allows users to confirm pricing and product specifications, place purchase orders and add both product and order information automatically to builders' and suppliers' management systems. In addition, manufacturers can place product information and catalogs on the BuildNet Exchange for access by home-builders and suppliers.

We believe that the BuildNet Exchange will provide significant benefits to homebuilders, suppliers and manufacturers. Home-builders will be able to automate and streamline their procurement process and improve their production planning efficiency. Suppliers will be able to improve inventory management and enjoy greater lead times for providing value-added services. Manufacturers will be able to provide updated and cost-effective online product information to buyers and increase the efficiency of their marketing efforts.

Our objective is to be the business-to-business e-commerce solution for the residential construction industry. Key elements of our strategy to achieve our objective include the following:

1. Roll out the BuildNet Exchange commercially.
2. Leverage strategic relationships.
3. Generate multiple revenue streams.
4. Connect manufacturers to the BuildNet Exchange.
5. Build brand recognition.
6. Expand e-commerce solutions into complementary markets.
7. Pursue strategic acquisitions and relationships.

●●●

"What's in a Name?"

William Shakespeare, playwright (1564–1616)

SLIDE 1: COMPANY NAME

The first slide of the e-plan is the name of your company. To answer Shakespeare's question, "What's in a name?" there's plenty these days. Consider the $7.5 million that was paid for the business.com URL or the $3 million that was paid for the loans.com URL. Clearly, names of companies, more particularly their domain names, are more valuable than ever. There is a mad rush to obtain domain names, and many of them are already taken.

Consequently, you don't want to wait until the last minute to select your domain name, which is usually also the registered name of the company.

Much of the conventional wisdom goes out the door when choosing a domain name. One of the reasons that domain names have become such a hot commodity relates to the unregulated nature of the Web. InterNIC, now Network Solutions (which was acquired by Verisign), was given the authority to grant names, which they did with impartiality to anyone with $70. You didn't have to prove you had a business or even a site before reserving your name. This open structure led to the snapping up of names to be later sold for a profit, a practice known as cybersquatting. In late 1999, Congress passed a law challenging this practice, but those protected by the law are generally those who have existing trademarks (see Chapter 12).

Big profits are being made from the sale of domain names. The largest sums are being paid for common domain names like business.com and loans.com. Such names are too generic for trademark protection and are therefore not covered by the new act. But before you run out and pay top dollar for a domain name, consider the following guidelines for choosing a name: simplicity, preferability of a dot-com name, and conventional wisdom.

Simplicity. Just as your executive summary should be simple and straightforward, the same reasoning applies to your name. It should be short and easy to spell. I once had a client who became excited about the availability of the name ambidextrous.com. He thought that all the words in the dictionary had been taken at the time, but apparently the word *ambidextrous* had not. I pointed out that the reason for its availability was probably because no one could spell it.

I recently heard a radio advertisement for the online pharmacy Savondrugs.com, which is affiliated with Albertson's grocery store chain. The ad reminded me of a spelling drill—more emphasis was placed on the convoluted spelling than on describing the pharmacy's products. I felt that the name was perhaps more cumbersome than useful.

The preferability of dot-com names. Despite discussions about increasing the number of suffix options for uniform resource locators (URLs), the dot-com suffix is still the choicest address for Internet real estate. The dot-com suffix signifies a commercial entity and is considered far superior to other suffixes such as dot-net, which stands for network. With so many of the dot-com names already scooped up, some are resorting to dot-net, even though their company is a commercial enterprise.

One service, RealNames, is attempting to replace the use of a long, complicated Web address with Internet keywords. For an annual charge of $100, a customer can register its company name with RealNames and obtain an Internet keyword. The keyword would work directly with Microsoft Internet Explorer in transporting people to your site. Simply type your keyword into the browser address window, and you will be sent to the particular site. The keyword, which is generally the company name, is meant to simplify the domain name process, in particular the use of suffixes and prefixes. For example, instead of typing <www.thebluffs-b-and-b.com/> into the address window, you would only have to type in The Bluffs B&B.

Unlike regular domain names, Internet keywords that are too generic can't be registered. For example, you couldn't register *learn* or *auto* as Internet keywords. Instead, the keyword names need to be specific, such as Learning Center or Autobytel.

Perhaps if the Web moves in the direction of keywords, there will be less of a premium on short generic names. In the meantime, sites such as Greatdomains.com allow you to bid on names. Some can be obtained inexpensively while others require a more serious financial commitment.

For example, when Branders.com was settling on a name, it discovered that its intended domain name branders.com was being used by a rock band in Alabama. Through the grapevine, Branders heard that the band was preparing to go to college. Company officials kept e-mailing band members to ask whether they would be interested in switching their name to brander.com, which the start-up had secured. The e-mails went unanswered until one of the company's officers called one of the local Internet service providers in the band's small town. He was told that the group had received the e-mails but wanted to sell the name instead, although the group was too embarrassed to ask for money. Branders.com proposed $500. The group considered the proposal and then countered. There were three in the group, and they wanted to split the proceeds equally, so $600 was their figure.

It is useful to consider whether a company should use dot-com in its official company name. In other words, should it market itself as company.com?

One train of thought is that the use of dot-com in the company name reinforces its cyberspace address and clearly identifies the company as part of the new economy. Another train of thought is that the use of dot-com could date the company in a few years when being a dot-com is no big deal.

The use of dot-com in the company name will probably appear redundant at some point, as every business will then be a dot-com to a certain extent. The trick is figuring out when. Some industry leaders, such as eBay and AOL, don't lean heavily on their dot-com suffix. Others, such as Amazon.com, take a different approach. I suggest that you consider how the dot-com "feels" and "sounds" as part of the company. If it feels and sounds right, use it; you can always drop it later. However, if it strikes you as repetitive, then leave it off.

Conventional wisdom. Generally, you want to avoid the conventional wisdom in selecting a domain name. The conventional wisdom is to pick a name that describes the service you provide, but consider some of the leaders of the Internet economy that don't have names inherently describing what they do: eBay, Amazon.com, and Yahoo.

Instead, these companies are governed by the rule that says to pick a name that is unique and memorable. Choose a name that creates a personality. It is doubtful that the names listed above would have commanded a large premium in the open market; premiums are being paid for the obvious names. As the new economy has shown from time to time, it is often the things that are not obvious and unique that are winners. Whether the large dollars being paid for descriptive names will be money well spent is still to be determined. Lately, it is the unique names that have succeeded so far.

Many companies have developed unique names by either choosing descriptive words or combining words in a certain manner. Although much of the English language has depleted registered names, there are still many different types of word combinations, such as fogdog and Razorfish, that have established a clear Internet identity.

Other advice includes putting words together in a distinctive way. Think of a combination that is easy to remember to create an image. Examples include Agilent Technology and Verisign.

SLIDE 2: MISSION STATEMENT

The mission statement is a shortened form of the executive summary. It highlights in a paragraph the executive summary of your particular business. In one or more statements, what is your business about? This is the essence of what your business is and should be geared to in the marketplace.

Examples of Noteworthy Mission Statements

The following are examples of mission statements from various companies. Some of them may be too long to fit on one PowerPoint slide. In that case, you could either edit the statement to fit one slide or use two slides to present your mission statement. Generally, the shorter the mission statement, the better.

America Online, Inc. The following mission statement of America Online was taken from a registration statement filed with the Securities and Exchange Commission:

The Company's mission is to lead the development of a new interactive medium that transcends traditional boundaries between people and places to change the way people obtain information, communicate with one another, buy products and services, and learn.

StarMine. The mission statement of StarMine was taken from its Web site:

StarMine provides software tools and services to objectively measure the performance of stock market analysts, improve on the "consensus" in predicting earnings and stock price movements, and easily visualize and manipulate analyst data to build superior trading models. StarMine maintains a complete historical and current database of analyst-by-analyst estimates and recommendations from I/B/E/S and others dating back to 1983. StarMine offers its advanced research tools to institutional investors, brokerage firm research departments, and individual investors over the Internet.

MyPrimeTime. The mission statement of MyPrimeTime was excerpted from its Web site:

Welcome to myprimetime.com! In five areas: Family, Money, Health, Work and Play, we give you stories, tools, shopping, even inspiration to help you live the life you've always wanted.

Whether you're just learning about stocks and mutual funds, starting your own business, searching for better sex or planning the vacation of a lifetime, myprimetime.com! is designed to help. . . . Our target audience is baby boomers—not just because there are nearly 80 million of us with trillions of dollars and no real home on the Web but because at midlife it's natural to reassess who we are and where we're going. Because we're living longer, healthier lives, baby boomers need tools and information to make decisions in order to create the worlds we've dreamed of. This is our mission.

chapter 6

Choosing Your Team

NO ENTREPRENEUR IS AN ISLAND

Slide 3 of your e-plan focuses on the human components of your business and involves putting together your team. Note that your team not only includes management, but also includes employees and professional advisors. Other members may include suppliers, affiliates, partners, and any other stakeholder in your business. The key is to surround yourself with the people you need.

The myth of the entrepreneur laboring alone in his or her basement to refine the perfect product or business process is generally just that, a myth. Succeeding in business is all about people. Entrepreneurs need to convince others to buy into their business. If you can't attract a good team to your business, how can you be expected to attract customers? Success in business is all about attracting people to your idea.

Stop and consider all of the great businesses that were not founded alone. Microsoft was started by Bill Gates and Paul Allen. Later, Steve Ballmers surfaced as a critical, yet somewhat anonymous, part of the Microsoft machinery. Hewlett-Packard was founded by the two Palo Alto engineers for whom the company is named. Yahoo! was started by David Filo and Jerry Yang. The founding of Netscape involved the bridging of several generations when Silicon Valley veteran Jim Clark teamed up with a recent college graduate named Mark Andreesen. A new business can be greatly assisted by a functioning and cohesive team from the outset.

THE CORE TEAM

For the start-up, the core team is critical from both a funding and an operational standpoint. Although investors technically fund the business, they are really investing in its principals. What else is there at the time besides an idea? There is usually no existing structure or ongoing business. Whatever happens in the business is what the principals make happen. The investors are as concerned about the choice of the core team as they are the selection of the business model. In fact, the core team could be even more important. Because ideas are plentiful, execution is the real key to the new economy. It is the core team that executes the business model and makes it happen.

Cover Your Bases

Another way to look at assembling the core team is to consider whether you have all your bases covered. Have all the important stations in your business been manned? Depending on your resources, the functions described in the sections that follow could be filled by several individuals. Alternatively for the bootstrapping start-up, one individual might fill more than one of the positions. Some duties can also be fulfilled on an outsourced basis or by professional advisors, but they are critical functions, and it is important that they are properly addressed. As noted below, many of the early dot-com failures can be directly traced to poor execution in one or more of these critical functions.

It is also important that all of the departments of the business work together to maximize their effectiveness. For example, the technical attributes of the e-business architecture have to be coordinated with the planning and efforts of the marketing department. The cost of the architecture has to stay within budget and fit within the financial framework.

What then are the core functions?

Executive. The executive is the individual(s) who will run the company and implement its strategic vision. Administrative talents are important to this management task. Previous experience in running a company or start-up is a tremendous plus in the eyes of investors. It is not uncommon for the founders to "hand off" to a more experienced administrator. Because much of the new economy is uncharted territory, management must be able to react quickly to developments or changes in the marketplace.

Marketing. The marketing function is extremely important for the company. In some cases, the chief marketing executive receives more compensation than the president. Perhaps this distinction is fitting in such a consumer-focused and competitive marketplace. In addition to company employees, the marketing function can also be expanded to include strategic affiliations. Alternatively, someone else could be given that responsibility separately.

Marketing is a complex and involved process (see Chapters 7, 8, and 9). The Internet has enabled new marketing channels to be established and has extended traditional marketing methods. However, all must be effectively coordinated in an overall marketing strategy that maximizes the benefits of the Internet. Otherwise, you could get swallowed up in the competition.

Financial. The financial function is also important. Contrary to popular belief, cash doesn't grow on trees for the Internet start-up; this was once almost true, but those days have passed. Resilient companies can survive many things in the competitive business world but not running out of cash. Good financial management can be particularly difficult in the new economy. Companies are pressured to achieve market leadership, and once bountiful funding can dry up at a moment's notice, which forces new ventures into a perilous high-wire act of balancing company growth with available resources. One false move could mean the end.

Consequently, able financial management requires stabilizing both the sources and uses of cash. Financial managers, along with other executives, must be aggressive and innovative in seeking out funds. In addition, they have to be not only prudent but tightfisted in spending money.

Technical. The person or persons in charge of the technical aspects of the business can be either a vice president of engineering or a chief technical officer. Their duties include the technical aspects of the business, encompassing the company's Web site as well as its e-business architecture. Obviously, your Internet presence and e-commerce interchange are critical to a new economy company. As noted in Chapter 2, e-business architecture has replaced traditional plant and equipment. Just as the manufacturing business is dependent on smooth plant operations, the information business is reliant on its information technology (IT) platform.

Dot-Com Obituaries

Although the Internet business landscape is relatively new, it is nonetheless littered with the first wave of dot-com failures. Many of these early failures can be traced to shortcomings in one or more of the functions just described.

boo.com. The collapse of upscale fashion e-tailer boo.com Group Ltd. became Europe's first big dot-com failure and a spectacular belly flop at that. The company burned $135 million of funding in only six months. Reportedly contributing to the company's demise was a pattern of lavish overspending on such items as multiple offices and frequent travel. Ernst Malmsted, the company's Swedish cofounder, blamed the failure on the lack of financial controls. In an interview with the *Financial Times*, he stated, "We wanted everything to be perfect. My mistake has been not to have a counterpart who was a strong financial controller." There were technical problems as well. The company delayed the launch of its Web site for a number of months. When the site eventually opened, it proved difficult to navigate and reportedly irritated shoppers. There was even the belief that the company's business plan was fundamentally flawed from the outset, allowing spending too much too soon for too little. Although the company's monthly revenue had increased to approximately $650,000, its costs were just too much.

ePatients. The demise of ePatients illustrates a potential pitfall when inexperienced entrepreneurs rely too heavily on an outside chief executive. The company was started by two idealistic Stanford medical students, Sean Lin and Meetpaul Singh, who had the dream of forming an online community for the seriously ill. Each had relatives who faced life-threatening illnesses. Both of the medical students observed that patients communicating with other patients with the same disease provided critical emotional support. This support assisted in their fight against the illness and actually prolonged their life. Later, one of the students happened on an independent study by a Stanford professor that reported that patients with an acute form of breast cancer who participated in a support group lived twice as long as those who didn't participate. Thus, the idea for ePatients was hatched, an online community that would connect hundreds of thousands of ill patients and serve as a clearinghouse for the latest medical breakthroughs.

At first, things fell quickly into place. The students raised angel financing from a respected cardiologist, who put them in touch with a medical executive who had a successful track record with medical device companies. The executive took the students by the hand to his attorney and venture capitalists, and the two young entrepreneurs seemed to be well on their way. However, the seeds of their defeat were sown in their early success.

The executive was eventually named CEO of ePatients and the company began hiring employees. Friction soon began to develop between the CEO and the company founders. The main points of contention pertained to company ownership and control as well as the financing terms of the venture capitalists. The problems quickly escalated and culminated in the dismissal of the CEO and the rejection of the financing terms. The company imploded soon afterwards. Perhaps this unfortunate ending could have been avoided had the two medical students studied the business world more before starting a company.

Toysmart. Toysmart was an Internet start-up dedicated to selling non-violent, enriching toys to children online. The online toy retailer was backed by the Walt Disney Company, which also held a majority stake. With an infusion of $25 million in cash and $20 million in advertising credits on properties it owned, Disney initially appeared as Toysmart's savior. A mere nine months later, however, Disney turned from savior to grim reaper when it pulled the plug on Toysmart. Christmas sales had been disappointing, Web traffic was not meeting expectations, and Toysmart was running out of money. The company later declared bankruptcy.

From a financial standpoint, Toysmart illustrates the potential problems that can occur when Internet entrepreneurs are dependent on larger companies for financing. Like Disney, larger companies may have limited patience for unprofitable subsidiaries. In addition, there was Toysmart's inability to achieve an acceptable return on its marketing expenditures in terms of sales and traffic. Simply put, Toysmart was unable to successfully leverage its relationship with Disney in the nine months it was given. Whether more time, cash, and attention from Disney would have made any difference can only be a matter of speculation.

LEADERSHIP

In the following sections I present certain recommended practices for selecting appropriate personnel for your venture, whether employees, consultants, or advisors. One factor that is important in attracting the right people is leadership, a popular topic in business circles today. Various theories about this important but elusive quality are often advanced in management literature. What are the key attributes of leaders? Can leadership traits be developed or does one have to be born a leader? How do leaders generate a compelling vision? When you sift through the various theories, one quality stands out: true leaders have followers. In fact, a leader is defined as "someone who shows the way."

Entrepreneurs should be able to inspire others to follow them with their passion, belief, and commitment to their vision. People are naturally drawn to winners. You may not be the most articulate or charismatic person, but if you have a burning goal that you are passionate about, you can become an effective leader. Your e-plan can help you show the way and establish the necessary framework for your vision.

Remember to communicate your vision to others in a confident fashion. A compelling vision attracts followers. Don't be reluctant to show your enthusiasm, but be authentic and convincing. Most of us can sense when others really believe in what they say and do. The new economy presents enormous opportunities—and there is plenty to be excited about. But be prepared for the tough questions, or your enthusiasm will be reduced to hype.

All great leaders have a grand vision. In some cases, they seek to change the world for the better. In other cases, they try to avoid catastrophe. During the height of World War II, a famous vision for Britain's finest hour was provided by Sir Winston Churchill:

> Hitler knows he will break us on this island or lose the war. If we can stand up to him, all Europe may be free, and the life of the world may move forward into broad, sunlit uplands. But if we fail, the whole world, including the United States, including all we have known and cared for, will sink into the abyss of a new Dark Age, made more sinister and perhaps more protracted by the lights of perverted science. Let us therefore brace ourselves to our duties and so bear ourselves that if the British Empire and its Commonwealth last for a thousand years, men will still say, "This was their finest hour."

Churchill, perhaps the greatest leader of the 20th century, was successful in leading his country to resist the Nazi menace and played an important role in the outcome of World War II. At the time, England was being ravaged by nightly air raids, and many leading figures were urging surrender. But it was Churchill's vision and his ability to lead that saved his country and perhaps the world.

Although your vision will undoubtedly not be of this historic magnitude, it can nonetheless be significant. Starting and sustaining a successful business in the competitive new economy is no small achievement. It's easy to display leadership when the business is running well. However, your leadership is tested when you encounter the inevitable bumps in the road. During such times you must adhere to your vision, sustain your fervor, and project confidence. That is the true show of leadership. (Chapter 13 reviews performance strategies of the entrepreneur, which include persevering in the face of adversity.)

One Internet entrepreneur who persevered in the face of adversity was Greg Meffert, the founder of Internet start-up NetEx. NetEx is a leading provider of document encryption software for e-mail delivery. It originally started as Imaging Technology Solutions (ITS) and was engaged in document imaging and management. Meffert co-owned ITS with two outside investors. One day, the two investors unexpectedly confronted Meffert with an ultimatum to sell out to them and leave the company. Although Meffert supervised the programming staff, the investors controlled the cash. Initially, Meffert felt he had no alternative but to leave quietly. While explaining the situation to the technology staff, however, he was surprised by their adverse reaction to his departure and their resolute expressions of loyalty to him. Although Meffert explained that he had no money to pay them, they assured him that he would figure it out somehow.

Although Meffert is reserved by nature, he had earned the unwavering loyalty of his programming staff. Without realizing it, Meffert had become their leader and they were ready to follow. It was up to him to show the way. As it turned out, the outside investors wanted $100,000 to walk. Just when Meffert thought that he couldn't raise the money, a major document management order from the U.S. government for $200,000 rolled in off a fax machine. Meffert quickly snatched it up before the outside investors, who were still hanging around the office, discovered it. Using the order as collateral, he borrowed the necessary $100,000 and bought out the outside investors.

EMPLOYEES

An important challenge for the start-up is being able to attract the right employees for they can make or break a business. Sometimes key employees are found accidentally. When Scott Adams started Intuit, the maker of Quicken, he had no employees or technical experience. As previously noted, the idea for Quicken was triggered when Adam's wife complained about balancing her checkbook—the genesis of Quicken software. Because Adams worked in consumer marketing, he needed to find someone to program the software. He ventured to the Stanford University campus and asked the first person he saw where to post notices for programmers. That particular student agreed to do the program and became an important member of the Intuit team.

But not all key employees are found this easily. Finding and recruiting employees involves considerable work and a concentrated effort. Let's review some general considerations and qualities when you're hiring employees.

Trustworthiness. One of the most important characteristics of employees is their trustworthiness. Trade secrets are of paramount importance in the new economy. Even basic information about a company's business model can be an important proprietary advantage, and its disclosure could cause considerable damage in the marketplace. Although you can protect your information with a confidentiality agreement, the damage done by a rogue employee can sometimes reach beyond the practical remedies of the legal system. In other words, a victory in court, often years down the road, could end up being a small consolation prize should your business be derailed by a breach of trust. And this scenario assumes that you have the money to litigate in the first place. Instead, seek to avoid such controversy in the first place and hire trustworthy employees.

It is therefore wise—actually necessary—to check references and confirm the veracity of applicants. Someone who misrepresents himself to an employer is more likely to do other dishonest things down the road. Consequently, be vigilant in monitoring employee truthfulness during the hiring process.

Reliability. From the standpoint of employees, reliability means always doing what they promise to do. A company can build an empire around a small group of reliable employees. An employee's reliability can often be tested under the crushing demands of the new economy, yet employees must still be responsible for the tasks they agree to perform.

Early in my career, I was facing increasing burdens at work. A sympathetic supervisor inquired whether I needed any help. I replied that I thought I could handle everything. He curtly replied that if I assumed responsibility for certain tasks, I had better handle them. In other words, good intentions don't count when critical deadlines are missed. Therefore, emphasize reliability to your prospective employees.

Fit. Another item to consider when selecting employees is their ability to fit in with the company and its culture. One of the most important things in a successful organization is a winning culture. Even though it is the founder's job to establish the culture from the top, the right employees can help to sustain a winning culture and carry out the vision.

Commitment. Employees need to be committed to the organization. If employees are simply looking out for themselves in the short run, you are likely to lose them whenever a better offer comes along or the business happens to fall on difficult times. Commitment makes a tremendous difference.

One way to test employee commitment is to consider whether the applicant shares a strong passion for your mission. The founders of StarMine have a definite strategy in testing commitment and interest in their venture. StarMine, discussed in Chapter 3, is built on a proprietary software that tracks the performance of stock market analysts. The company's principals prefer their hires to have a strong interest in the stock market. They are fully aware how competitive the marketplace is for employees, particularly skilled technical employees. Therefore, they figure that applicants with a true passion for the stock market will be more committed employees.

HIRING PRACTICES

Although a detailed discussion of hiring practices is beyond the scope of this book, a few suggestions for your hiring practices may be helpful:

- *Decide on your recruiting methodology.* Will applicants be recruited through referrals? Will you use an outside recruiter? Will you use the job-listing sites on the Internet such as monster.com?
- *Establish critical performance attributes of the job and then measure candidates against these attributes.* This process involves breaking a job down

to certain performance attributes. What are the most important functions of the job? Although there may be several related areas for the job, isolate the most important functions. Then evaluate the particular candidate by his or her compliance with the critical functions.

- *Screen applicants.* The next step is to screen the applicants based on the selected performance attributes. For example, StarMine could screen based on the applicant's interest in the stock market. The screening tool could either be used during the interview process or in conjunction with an application or questionnaire. Traditional questionnaires or applications are notoriously bad. Instead, gather information about employees through a training and experience checklist and accomplishment record. The checklist consists of performance capabilities, which are used to assess an applicant. An accomplishment record can be something as simple as requesting a paragraph about an applicant's accomplishments.

- *Develop an effective interview strategy.* The unstructured interview is usually the norm for the interview process, but unstructured interviews are usually a poor predictor of performance because the review is often subjective. The solution is to impose some structure on the interview. Such structure could include standardized interview questions. One of the legendary standardized interview questions that Microsoft used to query potential candidates concerned the number of gas stations in the United States. It was not so much the answer that the interviewers were interested in but rather the thought process demonstrated by the applicant. For those who responded that they had no idea, the interview was effectively over; if they couldn't make a reasonable attempt to answer the question, they did not possess the problem-solving capability needed for Microsoft.

  The structured interview should consist of other such job-related questions. Based on the questions, determine whether the applicant could fulfill the requirements of the job. A standardized rating scale also assists in making the evaluation.

- *References. The Wall Street Journal* recently reported the alarming number of candidates who are misrepresenting both their educational as well as previous work experience. Therefore, always check background information and references of applicants.

OUTSOURCING

The next step in building your team focuses on the talent you are obtaining through outsourcing. According to a recent survey, nearly all companies have outsourced at least one activity. Generally, the main reasons for outsourcing include reducing costs, saving time, and improving quality.

Just as the hiring of employees should be planned, the same applies to outsourcing. A company would normally want to avoid outsourcing its core functions or competencies. Instead, the company would weigh the costs and benefits of outsourcing certain noncore parts of its operations. The main business activities that are typically outsourced include general and administrative, human resources, information systems, transportation, and distribution and marketing. The trend toward outsourcing began when companies started paring their workforces in the early 1990s. The term *virtual corporation* was coined to describe progressive companies that were outsourcing certain noncore functions. Then, as the connectivity of the Internet revolution took hold, communication and transaction costs were vastly reduced. The Internet allowed companies to communicate with outside vendors inexpensively and efficiently. This helped accelerate the outsourcing trend and made the once progressive virtual corporation commonplace.

Despite the ease of outside communication, a company needs to weigh the benefits and costs in determining which activities should be outsourced. Compare the cost, time, and quality of outsourcing a function versus handling it in-house. Sometimes speed can be the most important factor. Companies wishing to quickly ratchet up their operations simply don't have the time to build an infrastructure. In this case, outsourcing is the most feasible alternative. Although time could be critical, outsourcing, like the e-plan, requires planning time. An employee or a team inside the company should be in charge of outsourcing activities.

After a determination is made to outsource, the next step is to focus on the particular needs of the arrangement. Establish the parameters and priorities of the outsourcing engagement from the outset. Solicit proposals from various vendors and rank them according to quality, scope of services, and cost. Finally, select the particular vendor and negotiate the terms of the engagement. Remember, however, that, like employees, vendors providing outsourcing activities need to be managed.

PROFESSIONAL ADVISORS

Another important source of personnel for your business is your technical advisors. The intricacies involved in running a business are very serious. Business and tax laws and other regulatory requirements have grown increasingly complex. Although money is often a scarce resource for the start-up, time can be an even scarcer resource, so it is important to obtain the proper technical advice. The main professional advisors for your business include your e-business consultant, attorney, and CPA.

E-Business Consultants

Depending on the level of technical expertise within the company, the information technology (IT) component of your business can either be totally or partially outsourced. There are many providers of e-business solutions, ranging from large and established consulting firms to Internet freelancers. Their images vary from the traditional corporate buttoned-down look to spiked hair and nose rings. All of your consultants can be housed under one roof or they can form a loose, but connected, federation of professional skills.

Although individual appearances of consultants may vary, they all provide the same essential services, which is the conduct of e-business. The components of IT infrastructure include Web site design, Web site maintenance, and e-business architecture (see Chapter 11 for more details about IT). IT elements enable your company to establish an online presence, transact business over the Internet, and maximize your use of this powerful medium to attract and retain customers.

The costs of e-business consulting services vary dramatically depending on their scope and the provider. Your company may choose to outsource the entire function. Many start-ups, however, cannot afford to hire a large firm, such as a Cisco, to provide a total e-business solutions package. Many smaller consulting firms that provide essential IT services at a considerably reduced cost are now popping up. Alternatively, between its consultants and its in-house capabilities, the company could assemble its own IT network. Many ways are available for a company to construct its e-business architecture.

Although costs are obviously an important factor, performance is even more important. Customers expect nothing less than perfection in today's competitive environment. Your site has to be able to deliver on its promises and provide an outstanding customer experience. Anything less and your business could be history.

Hiring an Attorney

At the risk of incurring the wrath of the American Bar Association, I will share with you a little secret: There are plenty of lawyers around. In fact, the United States has more lawyers per capita than anywhere else in the world. Without discussing the social issues, the excess supply of lawyers can benefit you as a consumer of legal services. But although there are many lawyers, there are far fewer good ones. In my career, I have worked for a small law firm, a medium-sized firm, and the legal section of a Fortune 100 company, where I came into contact with many outside lawyers. During my career, I discovered there are good and bad lawyers at firms of all sizes. Your challenge is to find a lawyer to serve as your primary counsel as well as business advisor. Issues to consider include the topics of the following sections.

Professional competence. The first issue to consider in hiring your attorney is professional competence. The complexity of the new economy requires an expansive legal focus. Areas of competency now include technology and Internet law as well as traditional business law (see Chapter 12). Technology and Internet law include intellectual property, privacy, and e-commerce legal matters. Business law includes such areas as taxation, choice of a business entity, and the appropriate financing structure. More complex business transactions include mergers, acquisitions, and public offerings of securities.

Ideally, your attorney should have a background in corporate and technology matters and be familiar with the business and legal issues faced by start-ups. Don't expect your attorney to be an expert in all the areas discussed above but the attorney should have access to a particular expertise. Law is becoming increasingly specialized and many of the areas discussed above constitute different practice specialties. Larger firms generally have separate sections to address various areas; smaller or boutique firms may address one or only a few of the areas.

Personal attributes. In addition to professional competence, your attorney should have certain personal attributes that facilitate a good working relationship. These attributes include dedication, accessibility, and flexibility.

Your attorney should be dedicated to you and your business and have your needs at heart. He or she needs to devote the proper attention to your legal matters. For example, if you choose a larger firm, will you have the attention of your primary lawyer or will you be fobbed off on a bright, but green, associate? One strategy is to go with a big firm but obtain a commitment of personal attention from the lawyer you want. Another strategy is to pick a lead lawyer at a smaller firm who can farm out specialties to different firms. Some advantages of spreading your work to different firms is that it keeps the firms on their toes.

Finally, your lawyer should be flexible and easy to work with. All good lawyers are going to be busy but should be willing to juggle their schedules when critical issues arise.

Some additional tips for hiring your attorney:

- Research the market. Ask for referrals from friends and associates. Call your local bar association to find the names of attorneys who specialize in technology and business.
- Once you have located a few prospects, contact them about possible representation. Meet with the attorney and request references from other clients. Don't hire any lawyer you don't feel comfortable with.
- If you are new in business or have limited resources, request a discount in initial fees in exchange for the potential prospect of long-term representation. If you don't ask, you won't receive. Many lawyers are willing to cut a promising start-up some slack. But be reasonable with your requests. In addition, some attorneys will even accept an equity interest in their clients in lieu of legal fees. Although this arrangement has been lucrative for some lawyers, such as the Venture Law Group in Palo Alto, it is not for everyone. From your standpoint, it may be cheaper in the long run to pay cash for services rather than

give up equity. Many of the initial legal needs of a start-up, such as incorporation and basic contract matters, are not that complicated and should not be overly expensive. From the lawyer's standpoint, remember an attorney is not a venture capitalist with access to outside dollars. Legal counsels have to pay their overhead like everyone else. Consequently, your counsel could be inclined to pay more attention to a client who at least pays nominal fees as opposed to one where the payoff is far more uncertain and distant.

- Respect your attorney's time, particularly if you have requested a discount. Realize that attorneys' time is their product. Only call your attorney when you really need to talk. Learn to anticipate deadlines: nothing is more of an imposition on a professional than having to do something at the last minute, particularly when the crisis could have been avoided. Although emergencies happen to everyone, learn to anticipate deadlines and allot your attorney the necessary time to complete the needed task.

Hiring a Certified Public Accountant

Your CPA too can be an important asset to your business. Many of the suggestions for hiring an attorney also apply to your CPA. Like the legal profession, the accounting profession is very competitive. Generally, your CPA should be an important business advisor in addition to performing your financial accounting and tax services.

Some tips for hiring the right CPA:

- Make inquiries about prospective CPAs. Obtain referrals from friends or associates. Contact your local or state organization of CPAs to obtain information. You should also interview prospective accountants and ask for referrals.
- Hire your CPA as a business advisor. The American Institute of Certified Public Accountants is spearheading a drive for its members to become full-service business advisors instead of simply offering tax or audit services. For the smaller start-up, the CPA could function as an in-house chief financial officer (CFO) handling the wide array of

financial and management needs facing your business. Many of the larger accounting firms also offer information technology services and have sections that specialize in e-business. Other things being equal, there could be a decided advantage in having your financial and IT duties handled under the same roof.

- Seek out a CPA who has experience with technology companies and companies engaged in e-business.
- Respect your CPA's time also. Like attorneys, accountants are highly trained and charge for their time.

LEVERAGE YOUR ADVISORS

Your advisors are often able to provide benefits to your business beyond their professional expertise. As a client, you may benefit from your advisors' professional standing and contacts. In other words, you may be able to leverage the professional relationship. Your attorney, for example, may be able to put you in touch with key individuals, such as investors or prospective employees. Your CPA may be able to introduce you to bankers or other financing sources.

In fact, the reputation of prospective professional advisors could be a factor in your choice. However, don't choose reputation at the expense of professional competence, loyalty, or other personal attributes. In addition, don't expect your professional advisors to feel obligated to supply referrals. Remember that you are hiring their expertise, not their Rolodex. It is helpful to first establish a relationship and then request introductions after a certain comfort level has been reached. Don't be shy in asking your advisors for an introduction. But do so selectively.

chapter 7

Marketing Fundamentals: Researching Your Market and Industry

"War is 90 percent information."

Napoleon Bonaparte

This chapter, along with Chapters 8 and 9, is intended to assist you in preparing the marketing portions of your e-plan. Specifically, this chapter on market research should help you with Slide 4 of the e-plan, which discusses market analysis, and Slide 5, which addresses industry analysis. The other marketing slides are Slide 6, which presents your market solution, and Slide 7, which is your marketing plan. (Microsoft PowerPoint slides are explained in Chapter 1 and expanded in Chapter 4.)

It is important to fully research and understand your market before you can accurately focus on the pain or need in the marketplace that gives rise to a particular business opportunity.

WHAT IS THE PURPOSE OF MARKETING?

Many ideas about the purpose of marketing are bantered about these days, including generating brand awareness, entertaining your audience, and creating an image. But the real purpose of marketing is to attract and retain customers and sell more of your product or service to more customers more often. In other words, the purpose of marketing is to help the company improve its bottom line and increase profits.

Some Internet companies forget this purpose in their rush to attract attention to themselves. Marketing is more than just building brand awareness. It's building customer use and reliance. Some Internet ads have used such advertising gimmicks as gerbils being shot out of a cannon and naked online shoppers, but it's difficult to see how such ads increase sales. The purpose of advertising is to induce customers to buy. Many award-winning ad campaigns for brick-and-mortar companies did not increase sales. The famous 1980's spot of the tough Pittsburgh Steeler defensive lineman Mean Joe Greene being offered a Coca-Cola by a young admiring fan ended with Greene tossing the young man his football jersey. Although the spot created considerable buzz and won awards, the ad reportedly did not increase the sales of Coca-Cola and was pulled. In the 1990s, there was the massive ad campaign for Nissan motors that featured rock music, toy automobiles, and dolls. Nissan's ads, too, were engaging and award winning, but they didn't sell more cars.

Effective marketing can determine whether an Internet start-up survives. As the new economy continues to evolve, the challenges to attract customers will only become greater. It is those companies that can develop coordinated and integrated marketing plans that will be the ones who ultimately survive. Nonetheless, the reaction of many Internet start-ups to this marketing challenge has been to dump as much as 70 percent of their budget into advertising in an attempt to develop a brand name. Many have already run out of cash and the Web shakeout is under way. Marketing is much more than advertising. It is more than developing awareness. Marketing involves focused and strategic planning toward a desired destination. In an age of customer empowerment, marketing is a coordinated communication strategy with potential customers that convinces them to try and then continue to use your particular product or service.

It is important to understand the competitive advantage and superior value that you offer the marketplace and how to communicate that value to the customer. Rather than using the shotgun blast or the mass-market approach, you want to develop a strategy that focuses like a laser on your target market. Target marketing is much more effective and creates a greater likelihood of success. The key to developing the laser gun approach is to fully understand the marketplace, what customers truly value, and how you can position yourself in their minds.

The companies that get it will be the ones who make it. Although marketing is often thought to be a soft academic discipline, it can actually be quite quantitative. In addition to the disciplines of finance and accounting, marketing is an unusual blend of information and data as well as instinct and art.

Marketing Primer

The key to effective marketing is to develop a marketing strategy, which is an overall plan to market a product or service that includes selecting and analyzing a target market and creating a promotional mix. The six basic steps to effective marketing are described below.

1. Research. The first step is to research the particular opportunity you uncovered that is based on pain or need in the marketplace. The goal of research is to gain an in-depth understanding of the industry, its customers, and its competitors. The research process helps to refine your understanding of the opportunity and create a business model that takes advantage of the opportunity. Generally, your research is likely to uncover several target markets or segments, in which particular products could be offered to particular customers because buyers normally differ in their preferences and needs.

2. Target particular segments of the market. After reviewing the market, your venture should target particular market segments, which are product(s) that the venture can offer to particular customer(s). Another way to describe market segments is space. Once your company decides on its particular market segment, it will then have to position its product(s) in the eyes of its target customers.

Targeting may seem a contradictory exercise in the new economy. After all, isn't one of the advantages of the Internet its ability to capture vast markets? Of course it is. However, most market segments will be plenty vast.

3. Decide on the promotional mix. The promotional mix includes the various forms of promotional activities that are used to communicate with customers and potential customers. Promotional activities include public relations, advertising, sales promotion, and direct marketing.

4. Implement your marketing strategy. You need a coordinated effort to implement your marketing strategy, which includes positioning and promoting your product to the target market.

5. Evaluate your results. The company needs to determine the results of its marketing strategy or its return on investment with respect to its market expenditures.

6. Manage the consumer relationship. Getting consumers in the door or to your site is only half the battle. Retaining customers is a particular challenge in a competitive environment. The company should emphasize its customer service and carefully manage the customer experience.

MARKET RESEARCH: DO YOUR HOMEWORK

After you have formulated your business concept, the next step is to do your homework—that is, research both your market and your industry. This research is a critical step in the planning process that can refine and improve your original business concept. What you learn from your homework is often the foundation on which your business is built. Your research helps you understand and target the market or markets for your venture. It can flush out the subtleties and hidden opportunities in the market and position you to take full advantage of those opportunities. In a highly competitive marketplace, it is often the little things—the differential advantages—that can add up to a sustainable competitive advantage. The sustainable competitive advantage is defined as a business

- that offers a consistent difference in product or service attributes;
- that is a direct consequence of a capability gap; and
- that can be sustained over time.

The sustainable competitive advantage must be based on delivering superior value to customers. The differences in your product or service attributes and those of competitors must be a key buying criterion for customers. However, sustaining a competitive advantage over time is difficult. One way to do it is to continually improve your product and your customer satisfaction, which makes it difficult for even the most observant competitor to keep up. By the time a competitor has duplicated your product or service, you are offering even more superior value to customers. Your market research can provide an understanding of the market that will enable you to stay ahead of your competitors. You get ahead and stay ahead. Your goal, as explained in this and the chapters that follow, is to develop an instinct for researching your markets and then applying this knowledge to refining your business to a market segment in which you can provide superior value.

For example, marketing research for an online consumer retail shop would be very different from that for an international business-to-business surplus machinery auction site. These respective businesses have different models and their success is driven by different factors. One is competing in a broad B2C marketplace, while the other is focused on a more defined B2B market space. The point is to develop an instinct for such differences and plan your research accordingly.

OVERVIEW OF THE RESEARCH PROCESS

Researching your business model requires you to keep up with two areas. The first is your subject industry, such as art, shoes, or content, which is your business model industry (or industries if you sell multiple types of products). In addition, you need to keep pace with the Internet and IT industries because these make up the area in which you have chosen to conduct business and which will permeate all functional areas of your company.

Business Model Industry

Remember our earlier discussion on filling the gap or fixing the pain in the marketplace? In bringing any product to market, the business has to offer either something new or better that fulfills the need or desire. Another opportunity might lie in some new or underserved market. Consequently, in formulating and refining your business concept, it is important to reliably establish that your business meets the buyer need or desire. Simply put, you need to show that (1) there are enough buyers for your product or service, and (2) you can capture a share of that market significant enough to reach a breakeven point and eventually make a profit.

The term *profit* is the latest Internet buzzword, and the stock and investment community is turning against the e-businesses that have yet to turn a profit. In order for your business to be viable and sustainable, eventual profit is not an if; it's a when. Therefore, your e-plan must project the point at which your business will turn the profit-making corner. (I discuss projections in Chapter 11.) Your venture has to make such a projection based on solid data gained from adequately researching customers' needs in your industry area.

Research includes the options available to customers, a polite way of describing your competition. At this point you have chosen your business concept and developed a basic idea for a sustainable competitive advantage. Now you are ready to conduct research and determine the potential viability of your envisioned advantage and how it meets the need of your target market.

If you decide to hire someone to do your research, you need to ask a few questions before retaining a contract research company or researcher. I'll review those questions later in this chapter after discussing how to do research yourself.

Caveats. If you decide to do your own research, a few caveats are in order before you plunge into an ocean of information.

- Don't rely solely on the Internet for researching your Internet venture!

Considering the topic of this book, that may seem a contradictory or ironic statement. But if you rely on the Internet as your only information source for your venture, you'll be making a critical mistake. You'll overlook the majority of available information. This doesn't mean you shouldn't use the Internet as one of your research sources. Indeed you should, both for primary and secondary information. But a great deal of information is in print form only, in electronic and online commercial databases only, and, most important, in experts' heads only. Relying solely on the Net precludes information from other sources of data.

- Don't get smothered by information!

As you know, the sources of available information, particularly on the Internet, are nearly infinite, so it's easy to become overwhelmed. It helps to have an overall understanding of your research needs and then develop a plan to systematically gather information. In other words, generate an overview of the key areas of information you need before venturing into details and reaching conclusions. Depending on how many concentrated blocks of time you can devote to your market research, expect to spend several full days gathering and analyzing information in order to refine your business concept. Organize the research into logical sections before you begin. Then set aside time to go after it.

If you don't have the time to do the research yourself, you can always hire someone to do it for you. But it must be done, whether you do it yourself or hire a research professional. Current information is a necessity in today's rapidly changing economy.

The research process can be tedious and you sometimes feel you're spinning your wheels. But those valuable golden nuggets of information exist, and you can uncover them if you search in a systematic fashion.

- Research with a purpose.

It's helpful to have a definite purpose in mind when you start your research. What information is relevant to your business model? Don't be tempted by tangential information that doesn't relate to your key information needs. But do expect that you will also uncover the unexpected and that your research course may change depending on what you find. It is advisable to follow the new information because it may prompt you to change your mind about how you're going to approach your business model.

• Value the research experience.

This might be a stretch, but you can actually learn to appreciate the exercise of researching your entrepreneurial dream. Outside research often brings back unpleasant memories of scurrying around school libraries looking for information for term papers. But always remember that the data you uncover could contain the seeds of your sustainable competitive advantage. As you unearth information, you may eventually experience the rush of discovering a hidden trend or need in an industry, making light bulbs go off in your head and ideas flow.

You'll also learn to appreciate the value of research. Research reduces the risks of making bad decisions and increases the chances of making solid business decisions that will affect just how successful your business will be.

Another tip in researching the marketplace is to make a research librarian your best friend. Securing help from a good research librarian can dramatically decrease your learning curve and help you get started on the right foot. Don't expect the librarian to do your research for you, but it doesn't hurt to be nice. Research librarians can save you hours of fruitless fishing.

• Read between the lines.

Often you won't find the exact data you are looking for, so you need to read between the lines and interpret the data you do find. The technical term for this process is referred to as *interpolation*. Because your budget and your time for research are probably limited, you'll sometimes have to do the best you can with what you have. Often, there are no exact answers, and even market research companies have to make educated guesses. In addition, the new economy contains many uncertainties as well as frequent changes in direction. Sometimes you simply have to draw the best conclusion you can with the data you have.

That is one reason that your business model has to be flexible so that as the market changes, you can change also. One of the advantages of using the Internet in your marketing (discussed in Chapter 9) is that it facilitates your quickly changing and adapting a different model or approach to reaching your target market.

In addition, don't become frustrated if you can't find the exact data that you need. The key is to become so familiar with the industry or markets that you can make the interpolations you need. One of the advantages of fact gathering during the research process is to obtain a feel for the market. This intuition and understanding provide you a filtering mechanism for market data and reactions that can help you make informed judgment calls.

The Two Types of Research Data

Even with the vast array of information available, there are really only two kinds of information: primary and secondary.

Primary data are new information that is being collected for the first time. The word *primary* indicates that the data take measurements from a new point in time, from a new point of view, or from a different set of sources than before. Primary research creates a new set of data that has not heretofore existed. For example, the United States Census Bureau, in its surveys of the U.S. population, conducts and compiles primary research on the population every ten years. Primary information includes surveys, focus groups, and statistics compiled by the government or information-gathering agencies. Statistics are usually derived from primary research and are often the raw data from which you can directly derive conclusions. Primary data may also include information derived from interviews with consultants and from personnel in companies and associations, friends inside your business, friends outside your business, the grapevine, and suppliers. Never forget customers as the most valuable source of information.

Secondary information is information that already exists and could also have been compiled and filtered from various sources; an example is newspaper stories. Secondary information includes books, government studies, business journal articles, newsletters, wire stories, and information gleaned from online services and the Internet. Secondary information exists in tremendous quantities and at a great variety of levels. Eighty to 90 percent of the time, most of what you want to know is already out there. It's usually yours for the taking—*if* you have the time and *if* you can find it.

When using information from secondary sources, be attuned to potential biases and know that it may contain errors. The best way to guard against misleading information is to find the same information in a separate source. The goal of information researchers is to discover and verify as much as possible the primary and secondary information that applies to their product or service.

Secondary Information Research Methods

You will use three basic methods to conduct your secondary market research: (1) manual research; (2) telephone research; and (3) electronic research.

Manual research. As I noted earlier, Internet search engines are not always the first place to start when conducting research. The Internet can often be quite an unwieldy medium to use to conduct research. Information is not always well organized online. Instead, it might be preferable to start with manual sources, namely books, periodicals, databases, and similar resources. Many of these manual sources are online also, but you need to develop some familiarity with the main research tools.

A good place to start is either a university library or the main branch of the public library. Manual research provides an excellent overview of available resources and can lead to other sources. Eventually, you'll want to log on to a computer terminal, but that is a topic for the next section.

A good place to start your manual research is with the reference librarian. Discuss with the reference librarian the type of research you are interested in, and he or she will probably suggest both manual and online sources. Some useful manual sources include the *Encyclopedia of Associations,* which helps you find associations that you couldn't find on the Web. Remember that associations are an excellent source of information about particular industries. Another good reference is the *Small Business Source Book.* Each of these publications provides additional sources, such as contact information for trade associations, industry data, and references to articles and trade publications.

While in the library, you can also find information about your industry in various business periodicals. There are numerous periodicals that concentrate on particular industries and contain good information as well as war stories. Articles that appear in periodicals are sometimes written by other members of the industry as well as by consultants. Often browsing through industry periodicals provides useful information about a particular industry that you cannot find online. While many major business publications have full editions online, most trade periodicals don't.

General business periodicals also have a great deal of useful information about your industry as well as overall business issues, devoting considerable attention in fact to the new economy. General business publications include *The Wall Street Journal, Business Week, Fortune,* and *Forbes. Newsweek* even publishes a supplement called *eLife.* Publications specifically geared to the start-up include *Inc.* magazine as well as *Entrepreneur.* Two new publications specifically geared to the Internet economy are *The Industry Standard* and *Business 2.0.* Another magazine, *Red Herring,* addresses financing aspects of the new economy. All of these periodicals have online editions with search capabilities.

Electronic and online research. There is a difference between these two methods, both of which use the PC. Electronic research refers to CD-ROM products that are loaded on file servers or PCs in a library. They include encyclopedias on CD, but for our purposes I'm referring to static CD-ROM databases such as ABI/Inform and periodical indices, which are updated periodically.

Online research relies on a live database connected through a dial-up or other communication line. Commercial services include subscription database online services such as Dow Jones Interactive, Nexis, and Dialog, and are constantly updated throughout the day and night. The services provide full text of organized and highly developed multiple databases with highly sophisticated search engines and logic. Of course, they charge varying fees in keeping with the value they provide and never fail to turn up relevant data. They are the professional researcher's tool—particularly efficient for searching in a short time.

On your second trip to the library, you have a clearer focus for your research. Utilize the CD-ROM or online databases that contain either bibliographic references to, or selected full-text articles from, a small variety of magazines, newspapers, or newsletters One example that your library may have is ABI Inform, which contains indexes, abstracts, and full text articles from trade, research, and business journals. Again ask the reference librarian for guidance if you are unfamiliar with these sources. Conduct keyword searches with ABI Inform or another of the library's periodicals, indexes, or full text databases.

Because you are going to be a dot-com company, you, of course, need to research the Web, especially for the competition. You can also use the Internet to see what basic industry or market segment information is available. When you research the competition, notice how they present their business. Expand on others' good ideas but respect their copyrighted material. Although a new area, copyright laws are being applied to this new electronic medium. Maintain your focus and stay on the paths that pertain directly to what you need to know.

If all of this research seems overwhelming, don't be alarmed. That's natural. Remember, you can always hire someone to conduct the research for you for a reasonable amount of money. But whether you do it yourself or hire it out, it must be done; otherwise, you are making your business decisions in the dark.

Telephone research. One of your best research tools is the simplest: the telephone. You will use it to interview experts and elicit their knowledge. You can use your telephone to find industry experts in government offices and analysts in brokerage firms. You can use it to get to associations and experts quoted in the articles you found.

When you do your telephone research, remember the basic rules of telephone etiquette. The person on the other end of the line is doing you a favor and sharing his or her valuable time with you. Be warm and friendly, but professional. Keep the tone upbeat. Be prepared with your five to seven insightful questions, and take notes as the experts answer. Before you get off the phone, ask if there is anyone else you should talk to. And be sure to send a thank-you note.

You should also use your telephone to research your competition. And you could expand your research to other parts of the globe. Fertile business models may be located outside the United States, although they would generally require more resources to explore as well as an understanding of a foreign culture and language.

GENERAL RESEARCH STRATEGY

The three main areas or components that you need to research are: (1) your particular industry; (2) the market (your customers); and (3) the competition. It is important to research these areas not only at the inception of your start-up but to remain current with them on an ongoing basis. As you know, change in the e-business arena is constant and rapid, so you need to keep up with new information on a continual (probably daily) basis.

The overriding goal behind researching these three areas, commonly lumped under the title of market research, is to make an educated estimate that will prove or disprove your market potential for a successful e-commerce business. The primary question to be addressed is the existence of an adequate market for your business. Referring to the discussion of building your e-business around the pain or needs in the marketplace in Chapter 3, your research should address whether the pain or needs are compelling enough to create a viable market for your product. How large is this potential market? Can you isolate a particular segment or space in the market to offer a viable product or service? Where are the gaps in the market? Where are the needs? Are there other competitors in the market? What opportunities exist in the marketplace to position your product or service against others?

You want to develop a thorough understanding of consumer preferences in the industry. What specific needs do consumers have? How do you go about alleviating the pain in the marketplace? What attributes would distinguish your product or service from others? What are the subtleties in the market?

Finally, you need an understanding of your competitors. Are other companies trying to address similar needs? How can you distinguish yourself from them?

Researching the Industry

Research by traditional brick-and-mortar companies usually didn't go past the particular industry. However, the online market is quite different. You not only need to know the industry specific to the product or service but you also need to research the e-commerce industry. Although there are nuances in transacting business on the Web related to a particular industry, there are some common trends that will affect all businesses regardless of what they sell. In Chapter 3, I discussed a few of these definable trends in the Internet market, which included convergence of technologies and the trend toward wireless communications. Another trend in the market is industry consolidation, in which considerable consolidation as well as mergers and acquisitions of the information technology and e-commerce companies is predicted. This could have the effect of rapidly filling particular markets.

Another factor to be considered is the continuing uncertainty regarding taxation of products sold on the Web. There is a heated and ongoing debate over whether to tax products sold on the Internet. And if a tax is imposed, how would such a tax be structured, considering the complicated multitude of municipal and state taxing schemes? There is a moratorium on such taxes until October 2001, so until then industry and government delegates will continue to struggle with the question of structuring Internet taxes with currently no consensus on the horizon. This freedom from sales taxes constitutes some of the cost advantages of e-tailers over brick-and-mortar stores. How would your operations be impacted if sales taxes were imposed in the future?

The next step is to consider how your business concept will be impacted by industry factors and trends. More important, how can you position your business to take advantage of these trends?

Consider other trends that are evident in the e-commerce industry but not noted above. Devour as much current material as is necessary to get a grasp on this topic Read articles, research Web sites and pages on the topic, interview people who specialize in marketing on the Net, and interview other Internet companies. Many periodical sources contain articles every week on e-commerce and e-business. Find them and read them. Consider all the sources where you might find information, and make a list of them. Think Internet but also library and telephone, even though you are researching e-commerce and e-business.

The other area you need to research is the particular market that you are entering. Although you will be an Internet company, you need to focus on the industry that is served by your business model. It is important to get an overall feel of the type of industry that you work in, to understand its market niches, and to determine where you fit in. You want to be able to make an assessment of the condition of the industry. Where is it in its life cycle? Is it expanding, in a growth phase, or mature? Is the industry in a declining or an advancing position? What is its growth history? What are the forecasts for the industry? What is the usual profit margin? Is the industry already saturated with competitors? Internet competition? Are there any government regulations that affect it, now or in the foreseeable future? As an added complication, the condition of the industry may differ depending on geographic location and related events. The health of the industry in your area may be different from the industry on a national or global level.

Where does one get information on industries? Start by researching published literature, periodicals, and news publications on your topic. See what you can find on the Web first, but the best state-of-the-art method for finding relevant articles is to search the industrial strength commercial information services such as Dow Jones Interactive, Lexis-Nexis, and Dialog. If your local library doesn't offer a fee-based service to search these kinds of databases, and you don't want to subscribe to these services, contact the Association of Independent Information Professionals. It can refer you to several independent researchers who make a living helping with such types of research projects. As an alternative, you can use the CD-ROM databases at your library (ask the librarian for help if you need it); they pale in comparison with the aforementioned online services but are useful nonetheless. Read everything relevant that you find.

The two next best places to go are industry associations and the national government. Industry associations exist for the purpose of promoting their trade groups so they are usually willing to share data on their industry, including quantitative numbers you can insert into your business plan, such as historical growth, forecasted growth, total annual dollar volumes, and unit volumes either produced or sold. Many associations have Web sites, but don't expect them to make all of their in-house information available on the Web. In fact, most of what they house in their internal, private libraries is not posted on the Web. Many associations publish periodicals and journals specializing in the industry and these monthly or quarterly publications contain information-rich articles. Additionally, associations often store in-house white papers and reports that have been delivered at conferences and conventions.

After you have exhausted an association's Web site (if it has one and if you found it) for what you want, call it on the telephone. See what additional information you can get from its resource center. At a later date, after you have done a good portion of your homework and can ask more in-depth focused questions, you will want to call back and interview an expert or two at the association to derive their insights as well. Incidentally, do expect to have to pay for some or all of the information associations will provide for you. Although we are in the information age, information is not always free.

Next, tap into the national government. The U.S. government tracks a large variety of industries usually within the Department of Commerce. Call the public information office in the Washington, D.C., area to get started on your journey through the government's bureaucratic maze. Be patient and persistent and eventually you will find an analyst who tracks your industry day in and day out.

Other sources for industry information are analysts at brokerage firms. They specialize in industries and often its companies. Be sure you have researched the literature before calling brokerage firm analysts. You will probably have difficulty getting hold of one, so be prepared with intelligent questions.

After you obtain an overall feel for your industry, the next step is to focus your analysis on the particulars of the industry as they relate to your concept. Obtain an understanding of the trends in your industry and the various tactics of successful businesses in the industry. In dividing the industry into its component parts, you are looking for the interaction of industry participants with suppliers, customers, competitors, and related entities.

As discussed before, it is helpful to consider an industry in terms of its market chain or value chain, which is depicted in Figure 7.1. Use your industry research to understand all the various nooks and crannies of the market chain. That should help you solidify your understanding of the industry.

Researching Your Customer Market(s)

The next step in your research process is to become well acquainted with your customer. The phrase *know your customer* is the most important have any studies on customer demand and/or requirements for your company's product.

When you have finished your reading homework, track down some experts to hear what they have to say. Interview dot-com company executives in parallel, but noncompeting, product or service areas.

Two excellent methods for learning about your markets and how and why they buy online is to conduct surveys or focus groups of online audiences. A survey is quantitative research in which a representative sampling of the customer audience is polled for its often multiple-choice responses to numerous questions. A focus group is qualitative research in which a small representative group of consumers is led through a carefully crafted series of open discussion questions. Focus groups allow more digging into the customer's psyche and explanations of buying decisions than do surveys.

A recent development in these research methodologies is related to the whole Internet revolution. Research projects have moved online and will continue to evolve as technology evolves. Significant numbers of Internet-based respondents have been recruited by major research firms for on-hand panels for research projects. Willing communities of online participants have been built. Surveys have moved online with 3-D virtual reality capabilities where respondents are able to rotate, zoom in on, and manipulate three-dimensional products.

Focus groups can be viewed via interactive live broadcasts so the company commissioning the research avoids travel expenses and thereby realizes cost savings of e-commerce and communication automation. In particular, these online groups can be of great value by providing feedback on the online buying experience. Just keep in mind that if your market includes the offline community whom you are trying to lure online, you cannot limit your research to the online community.

A word of warning: When it comes to online research, privacy is going to be a highly sensitive and important issue. It's obvious that our Congress and European countries have a limited threshold for tolerating online consumer privacy violations. In October 1999, the Children's Online Privacy Protection Act went into effect in the United States. Policed by the Federal Trade Commission, it requires all Web sites to obtain parental permission for children under 13 to collect, use, or disclose data collected from the children. This can be an important issue for sites aimed at younger children.

FIGURE 7.1   Market Chain

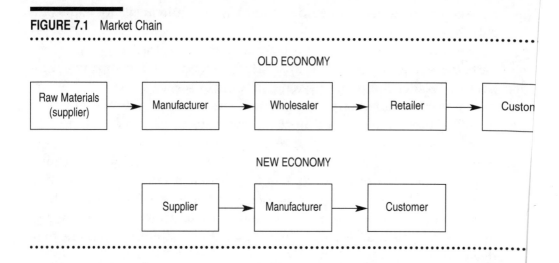

one in marketing. It requires that you identify, quantify, and under
your particular customers, for the better you understand your custo
the more competitive your business will be.

Who are your customers? In what quantity do they exist? Whe
your customers? (This may be particularly important to an e-busine
business site for its distribution plan.) What particular need are you
to fill? If your customers are derived from one industry or a few id
able industries, then what is the profile of that target industry or indu
What encourages your customers to buy? Is there a decision that tr
a variety of buying decisions? (For example, if I decide to go on a
vacation, then that decision triggers all kinds of buying decisions, s
land or air travel, airline or rental car, hotel, clothing or equipmer
chases, etc.) Why do your customers make the buying decisions th
Can you build a profile? How might their buying methods differ tom

There are a number of ways you can get information on your po
customers. First, conduct manual research at the library to see what
you can find that discuss your target market. Newspapers often c
good and timely articles on motivational factors influencing purch
a particular good or service. The most comprehensive source for n
pers are the commercial online sources named above. In additio
again use associations and their trade journal publications to see

A newly formed online marketing research association has drafted a code of ethics in this area. Among the practices it considers unethical are sending unsolicited e-mails to recruit respondents, using or providing e-mail addresses after a survey is done to sell products, or using Spambots to collect personal information without the respondent's consent.

Finally, the last kind of information you need to collect about your customers is ongoing information. You need to constantly know who your customers are, how they came to your site, and if you have, or are building, their loyalty. This last category of customer research must be built into your daily processes and operations. You can do this by installing software programs that capture all aspects of sales and customer data—data you can slice and dice every which way for creating reports that let you respond to market shifts. If you build the gathering of the data into the process, labor costs should be minimal.

Researching the Competition

The final area to focus research efforts on is your competition. Who are the competitors in your particular space and how do you compare with them? In considering potential competitors, you often have to look beyond who might be your direct competitors at the time. Note that the lines between different market spaces are quickly becoming blurred. Noncompetitors could invade your space very quickly. For example, when Amazon.com and CDNow first started, their products were books and CDs, respectively. Both were successful Internet pioneers that peaceably coexisted in their respective market spaces. It is doubtful that CDNow considered Amazon.com a competitor in the early days. Of course, we all know what happened. Amazon.com began selling CDs and the fortunes of CDNow, once a promising company, declined dramatically. Consequently, you have to take an expansive view and consider *potential* competitors when evaluating your competition.

You have to also consider indirect competitors—companies that might not be competing in your particular space but whose goods could serve as substitutes for yours. Also, you want to evaluate your particular competitors in relation to your product or service. How do they rank with you in terms of such variables as price, quality, selection, and customer service?

You can search for competitors at the library based on your shared NAICS code (North American Industrial Classification System, formerly the SIC [Standard Industrial Classification] Code). Every industry is assigned a primary code and potentially secondary codes for less prominent lines of business. You can create lists. Look on the Internet. Search the search engines. Check the associations' Web sites and call if a site doesn't post the main industry players. Dig until you stop finding new ones.

One helpful way to visualize the competition is by setting up a competitive matrix profile, as shown in Figure 7.2. The diagram allows you to map out all of the competitors in your particular industry and profile each one on the basis of various factors. Note that the profile also includes indirect or even potential competitors that you might be aware of.

FIGURE 7.2   Competitive Matrix Profile

Competitive Factor	Business 1	Business 2	Business 3	Business 4
Direct or Indirect competitor				
Price				
Quality				
Internet Presence				
Additional Services				
Business Condition (steady, increasing, decreasing)				
Strength/Weakness				
Selection				

8

Segmentation, Targeting, and Positioning: Isolating the Opportunity and Refining Your Business Model

....

"The customer only wants to know what the product or service will do for him tomorrow. All he is interested in are his own values, his own wants, his own reality. For this reason alone, any serious attempt to state what our business is must start with the customer, his realities, his situation, his behavior, his expectations, and his values.**"**

Peter Drucker (born 1909), father of modern management

The previous chapter examined market research, which is an important step in understanding your particular industry, your competition, and your customer. In the competitive new economy, the businesses that really know their customer and then effectively serve their customer are the ones that succeed. Ideally, your research helped you understand the competitive dynamics of the particular industry as well as locate market opportunities. In addition, your research should help you determine any subtleties in consumer preference that could be the basis for a competitive advantage.

This chapter considers the next step in the marketing process, which is to narrow or target your market. This step involves targeting both the particular product or service that you will offer as well as the particular customers that you will offer it to. Those parts of the market are known as your segment or space, a concept that was introduced in Chapter 2. Your aim is to determine the particular space that you can most effectively compete in by offering unique value with the ultimate goal of dominating your particular space.

THE TARGETING PROCESS: SHOT GUN VERSUS LASER GUN

The opposite of target marketing is mass marketing. Whereas target marketing is the laser gun approach, mass marketing can be thought of as the shotgun approach. Mass marketing was a particularly popular model in the industrial economy, when goods were mass manufactured for the largest possible market. Even today, some of the B2C Internet businesses are offering their products to the largest possible market. However, mass marketing requires that considerable resources be spent on advertising and other promotional activities because of the vastness of the consumer base. Many of the early e-tailers spent large sums on advertising in an effort to establish themselves to consumers; and as noted earlier, many ran out of money and did not survive. Deep pockets and an effective marketing campaign are required to succeed in mass markets.

On the other hand, target marketing involves narrowing a mass market into market segments or target markets. This process of segmentation involves isolating a particular product and customer base within the broader industry marketplace. The advantage of market segmentation is that you can better understand your customers and focus your efforts on providing particular products or services to satisfy their needs. In today's competitive marketplace, identifying definable industry segments or spaces can increase both the efficiency and effectiveness of marketing efforts. Consequently, those with more modest resources can attempt to select a segment they can dominate.

ADVANTAGES OF A TARGET MARKET

There is a natural tendency when choosing a market segment to worry about the potential customers that are being left behind. One of the advantages of the online world is that it empowers your venture to capture a vast market. That being said, why would you want to limit yourself? Consider, though, that you are not limiting your business but rather making the most from your core competencies. Businesses that generally try to be all things to all people have a difficult time, even in the online world.

Narrowing your market can be a difficult strategy to accept, particularly in light of the fact that all of the market leaders appear to be embracing broad strategies. Consider the following description of industry leader Yahoo! that was adapted from its 1999 annual report on Form 10-K. In the letter to shareholders, CEO Tim Koogle stated the following about the mission of Yahoo!:

> We set out five years ago to build Yahoo! into the only place anyone in the world would have to go to find and get connected to anything or anybody. Our goal was to attract and retain as large a global audience as possible and give consumers a single, trusted, and comprehensive place to go for all of their daily needs.

This statement appears to describe anything but a target market. But in case you don't already know, Yahoo! was an early Internet pioneer that started by creating a comprehensive navigational guide or search engine for the Internet. It then used the guide as a platform in offering content, facilitating communication, and fostering commerce. Obviously, it would be difficult to challenge it in its broad space of infomediary or portal. Other leaders in this space include Excite@Home, Microsoft Network, and America Online. However, to compete in such a broad market space requires considerable resources.

A better strategy for the start-up is to narrow a particular space and then dominate that space. And the way to dominate the space is to offer superior value. As discussed, in a competitive economy, consumers are only interested in excellent value propositions. In other words, you want to build your company around the things that you do best and target those customers that you can best serve. That is what segmentation is all about: choosing a target market segment that is built around a distinct competency. Often your research can help you determine that part of the market that you can best service. The companies that survive the dot-com gold rush are the ones that follow this advice. Start-ups that try to be all things to all people will have a more difficult time.

There are several advantages to isolating a particular target market:

- Optimal use of marketing resources. Targeting allows you to focus your marketing activities on a particular market space and to therefore focus your efforts on particular products and customers. That enables you to direct your marketing activities to the particular segment you feel is most responsive. Being focused helps to simplify the marketing process by narrowing the message and, as discussed later, simplifies the brand-building process.
- Superior understanding of the customer. As the quotation above from management guru Peter Drucker indicated, marketing is all about understanding the needs and wants of particular customers. Operating in a market segment allows you to become much closer to customers and their particular needs and wants.
- Easy to compete in and dominate. With a narrower focus, the company can more easily identify its competitors. In addition, such a narrower focus makes it easy to spot an unmet need that can be satisfied in a superior fashion, allowing you to dominate that market.

The story below illustrates the pitfalls of trying to be all things to all people, which happened in the case of industry leader Amazon.com.

Not So Fast, Amazon

An Internet pioneer that is trying to be all things to all people is Amazon.com. Its current strategy is to leverage its online market leadership from books to music products and now a broad range of consumer goods. Its ultimate aim is to become the dominant consumer portal. Whether this strategy ultimately proves successful remains to be seen. However, one thing that Amazon can't forget about is maintaining the high level of customer service that has propelled it to market leadership in its original business model.

Many of the other consumer goods that are being marketed by Amazon are distributed through its zShops. The zShop items are not distributed directly by Amazon but rather involve its simply acting as a storefront for other vendors.

I had a recent experience with one of the zShops, and it wasn't particularly good. I attended a recent conference of the Consumer Telephone Industry Association that Amazon Chairman Jeff Bezos was scheduled to attend. He had to be beamed in by teleconferencing for the quite understandable reason that his wife was expecting their first child. After listening to his presentation, I sent him a few cigars to commemorate this special occasion and thought I'd order through his own company. I entered the Amazon site and was directed to the zShop merchants. I selected cigars and began to navigate my way through the order process with another vendor. At the end of the ordering process, I realized there was no way to send the cigars directly to Bezos. Instead they could only be delivered to me, which was not like the fulfillment process at Amazon that allowed you to send items to third parties (even gift wrapped). Worse yet, I didn't realize this until the order went through. When I called the always reliable Amazon customer service, I was told that I had to deal directly with the particular zShop merchant. When I tried to contact the merchant, I found it had no phone number but only an e-mail address. I e-mailed it to cancel the order and received no response. I finally had to surf and find another Web site to deliver the cigars. Although Bezos was courteous enough to e-mail his thanks, the cigar purchase was not my best experience with his company. Even giants can stumble in trying to be all things to all people.

As this book went to press, questions were being raised about Amazon. com's business model, namely its expansion from books and CDs into a broad range of consumer products. The expansion constitutes a significant drain on its resources and also runs the risk of diluting its brand image as a seller of books, CDs, and videos. Whether Amazon can ultimately pull off its ambitious retail strategy remains to be seen.

MARKET SEGMENTATION PROCESS

The process of market segmentation starts with a large, heterogeneous market, consisting of customers with diverse characteristics, needs, wants, and behaviors. The segmenting process divides up this large, heterogeneous market into one or more homogeneous markets, which are made up of individuals with similar wants, needs, and behaviors. The strategy is to provide a product or products for the homogeneous segments, a strategy that allows you to focus your efforts on satisfying customer needs in a superior fashion.

Market Segmentation: An Illustration

The market segmentation process can be illustrated by an example from the retail sporting goods industry, which is defined under the North American Industry Classification System (under NAICS Code 451110) as follows: "This industry comprises establishments primarily engaged in retailing new sporting goods, such as bicycles and bicycle parts; camping equipment; exercise and fitness equipment; athletic uniforms; specialty sports footwear; and sporting goods, equipment, and accessories." Corresponding items that are listed under the same NAICS Code include bowling equipment, diving equipment, golf pro shops, saddlery stores, and tackle shops.

As you can see, the sporting goods industry is quite large and heterogeneous, encompassing a variety of sports for women and men of all ages and preferences. Many online e-tailers, such as mvp.com, fogdog.com, and gear.com, compete in this space. Consider the challenges in becoming known in the sporting goods marketplace and developing a brand identity.

Segmentation would involve breaking down this large marketplace into smaller homogeneous markets, such as bicycle or diving equipment. One company that successfully segmented the sporting goods market is Golfballs.com. As the name suggests, it is an e-tailer of golf balls. Not only did it narrow the sporting goods industry to golf pro shops, but it further segmented the market within that sport to golf balls. Its business model is discussed in more detail later in this chapter.

The actual process of market segmentation is driven by three factors:

1. Product: Which product or service will you offer within a particular industry?
2. Customer: Which customers will you serve?
3. Value-added role: What is your value-added role? What is unique or superior about your participation in the marketplace?

Market segmentation in the sporting goods industry is illustrated in Figure 8.1. Note that each product in the sporting goods industry has a corresponding base of homogeneous customers. But what will distinguish your company in the marketplace is the value-added role that is fulfilled. What advantages can you offer? Typical advantages in the e-tailing sector include price, convenience, and customer service. If you are just another participant in the market, it is hard to distinguish yourself. One reason that many e-tailers are having such a difficult time is the intense competition in many of the larger markets. For example, both the toy space (eToys, Toysmart. com, ToyTime, and Toysrus.com) and the pet space (Petstore.com, Pets. com, Petsmart.com, and Petopia.com) simply became too crowded too fast. In the rush to market themselves, companies found it difficult to distin-

FIGURE 8.1   Choosing Target Segments within Industry Space

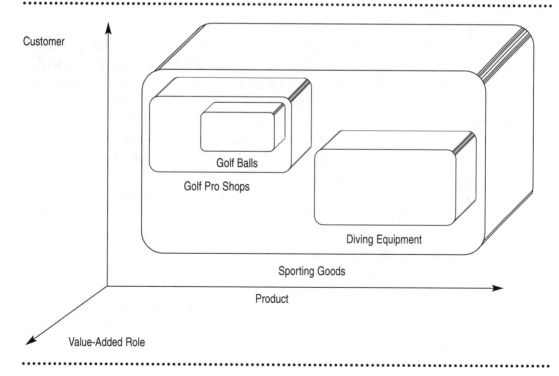

guish themselves and carve out a customer base. Although the survivors may eventually emerge as market leaders, the battle for these large spaces was a very expensive one. Whether it will ever adequately pay off remains to be seen.

SEGMENTATION FACTORS

Although the segmentation process is presented in the order of product, customer, and value-added role, it is actually an integrated process. For example, you might initially decide on a particular product, but a more careful examination of your customer base might push you in a slightly different direction. As mentioned above, the key is to isolate a market space in which you can provide a superior value.

The Product or Service

The first step in the segmentation process is to decide the particular product that you wish to offer. The decision should be made by isolating or determining the particular need in the marketplace discussed in Chapter 2. Within a particular industry, what need is not being met? What products or services are needed in a particular industry? How could you use the Internet to capitalize on a unique opportunity? What type of service would the market be the most receptive to? For an existing business, how could you use the Internet to serve your current customers?

The product or service you choose should be your solution to the pain in the marketplace. However, in selecting your product, you need to consider other products in the marketplace and whether there is sufficient opportunity or gaps in the market.

It's easy to become carried away in the vastness of the Internet. Many Internet entrepreneurs suffer from the "kid in the candy store" syndrome and become infatuated with so many potential opportunities. But it's important to maintain your focus on the product you believe offers a unique opportunity.

The Customers

Closely related to resolving what product or service will alleviate the pain in the marketplace is deciding which customers to serve. A product or service should be developed with a close eye on customer needs. During your market research, what customer needs did you find were not being met? How could the Internet be used to better serve customers? In formulating your business model, consider who the customers actually are. Are they the end users of the product? Would customers be the distributors or wholesalers of the product? Or the retailers? Consider again the market chain examined earlier and presented in Figure 8.2.

In reexamining the market chain, consider again who your potential customer is. Could there be better opportunities in selling to other manufacturers as opposed to consumers? Where do you best fit in the market chain? Where could you provide the best service?

Deciding who your customer is can be a difficult stage in the segmentation process. Sometimes hard choices have to be made. Segmenting on the basis of customers depends on whether your end customer is an individual consumer or a business.

FIGURE 8.2 Market Chain

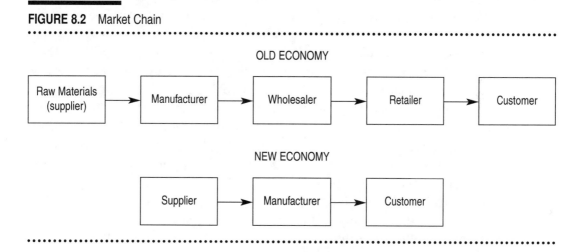

Consumer market. As noted earlier, if your end customer is going to be the ultimate consumer of a product, then your business model would generally be considered B2C, in which case you would want to precisely target the individual user(s) of the product. Traditional factors for segmenting consumers are demographic, geographic, psychographic, and behavioral.

Demographic factors: Demographic factors include age, sex, income, marital status, occupation, education, and nationality. Many online businesses are segmented around one or more of these demographic factors. For example, myprimetime.com (discussed in Chapter 3) is targeting upper-scale baby boomers, establishing a community of interest around this demographic group. Another site directed at a certain demographic group is TheMan.com, which, as its name suggests, is directed at younger men. Its business model is the establishment of a community of interest around younger men. Another example is snowball.com, which is directed to the Internet generation—consumers 13 to 30 years old.

Geographic factors: Prior to the Internet, geography was a traditional way to segment the market. Larger companies opened different stores or outlets in particular markets in trying to capture additional consumers. The Internet, however, is breaking down geographic boundaries and therefore diminishing geography as an important segmentation factor. But if you are combining the Internet with bricks and mortar, then geography would obviously be more relevant than a pure Internet company. For example, gazoontite.com, an e-tailer of products devoted to better breathing, has opened stores in such large cities as New York, Chicago, and San Francisco. As I discuss in Chapter 18, its click-and-mortar approach is to use storefronts in large metropolitan areas to drive its online presence.

Psychographic factors: This basis of segmentation depends on people's lifestyles as well as their personalities. The psychograhic profile is based on consumers' interests as well as their psychological profile. Are the individuals risk takers or conservative? Or are they compulsive or methodical in their decision making?

Behavioral factors: The final basis for segmenting consumers is based on their behavior. How often do they make purchases? What are their purchasing habits? How loyal are they to particular brands? What is their responsiveness to price and promotion? Behavior can be an important basis for determining responsiveness to a particular good or service.

Behavior is obviously a very important factor in segmentation because it is important to understand the responsiveness of selected customers as well as why they respond a certain way to a particular stimulus or promotion. Although promotional methods are the topic of the next chapter, you need to understand the behavior of your loyal customers—those who make repeat purchases. It is important that you know who your repeat customers are and why they respond to particular offers.

Depending on your product or service, one basis of segmentation is more significant than others. However, the more you can understand and segment your customers, the better you can respond to their wants and needs and distinguish yourself in the marketplace. I've said it before: A critical factor in marketing success is to know your customer. The better you understand and fulfill your customer's needs, the more value you provide and the more loyal your customer will be. Remember that success in business is all about knowing and satisfying your customer.

Business market. If your customer is other than an individual user of your product or service, then your business is generally a B2B model. There are many ways to segment the business market. The first is by the NAICS code, which breaks down businesses by their particular industry and also provides the basis to target your market.

Like individual consumers, businesses also have their particular needs and subtleties. Value creation is driven by your understanding of the particularities and needs of an industry and the ability to tailor your product to those needs. There are often smaller segments within a certain business, so keep drilling down until you find the segment where you can provide superior value.

One helpful maxim in deciding on market segmentation is to "go where they ain't." This presupposes that you should avoid competition. If you see a market that you can service better than the existing competition, you are not necessarily avoiding competition but rather directing your resources to a market opportunity that is more promising than another. In this case, you are focusing on the superior market opportunity, which often lies in underserved markets and involves using your specific competence to serve the needs of the industry.

Adding Value

The final factor to consider when targeting your product or service is the value-added function or role that you perform. As noted, market boundaries in the new economy are not always well defined. There is the risk of a larger competitor or even another business in the supply chain swooping down into your market space. Consequently, unless you carve out a value-added role that defines your company in the marketplace, it will be difficult to sustain your business. One question to constantly ask yourself is exactly what you bring to the table in your particular market. What does your business offer that others don't? Another way to consider your value-added role is in terms of your unique selling proposition. What distinguishes your product or service from others in the marketplace?

HOW COMPANIES HAVE SEGMENTED THEIR MARKETS: THREE EXAMPLES

The first example of a company that has segmented its market is Golfballs. com, which segmented a particular market in the golf industry. The second are two public companies—Digitalthink and Saba—that grabbed parts of the online learning market.

Segmentation in the Golf Industry

The first example of a company targeting its market is Golfballs.com, the largest supplier of golf balls on the Web. Its founder, Tom Cox, started the company in 1995 to sell used golf balls over the Internet on a part-time basis. His background included a decade in golf and country club management. The idea to sell golf balls on the Web occurred to him when he was planning the Web site of the club he was managing at the time. Although

Cox considered selling golf clubs as well as other golf accessories, he decided to focus on golf balls. They were the most frequently purchased item and were compact and therefore easy to store.

In 1996, he began selling golf balls on the Web under the domain name myballs.com. The venture was part-time and produced $17,000 in sales in 1996. In 1997, sales had increased by a factor of 5 to $70,000. In 1998, Cox obtained funding from a private placement and purchased the domain name Golfballs.com for the sum of $10,000. He also rebuilt the site and hired someone to run it. That year sales shot up to $200,000. In 1999, sales increased by a factor of 5 again to $1 million. The company is now expecting revenues of $4 million in 2000 and currently has 23 employees.

As opposed to expanding horizontally, Golfballs.com is expanding vertically, working to further penetrate its target market or space of golf balls. It offers new golf balls, custom logo golf balls, and used golf balls. This latter category is particularly promising as the market for used golf balls is estimated at $250 million and is very fragmented. Remember the point made in Chapter 3 that fragmented markets are generally scattered and inefficient, which presents excellent opportunities for Internet businesses to consolidate, become more efficient, and then dominate. Another advantage of used golf balls is that their margins are greater than margins on new golf balls.

Even within its narrow target market, the company has several product offerings for different types of consumers. Within the B2C, or business-to-consumer market, there are sales of both new and used golf balls directly to consumers. The general profile of consumers who buy used golf balls would be different from those who buy new ones. Next is the B2B, or business-to-business market, which consists of sales of used golf balls directly to other businesses for subsequent resale. The other B2B market is the sale of customized golf balls to businesses for their use as promotional products.

The company realizes that each of these different product and customer segments has to be approached differently, and it is currently refining its marketing strategy to do that. Such refinements include customizing its marketing efforts to the individual targeted segments.

Presently, Golfballs.com has no plans to expand its product offering beyond golf balls. Cox feels this product focus is the core of his corporate strategy. The domain name Golfballs.com is intuitive, and the company is rapidly developing a loyal customer base in its space. In fact, one of its more important sources of customers are referrals from other customers. According to Cox, his focus works quite nicely in that the domain name equals the product, which in turn equals its point of sale.

Segmentation in the Online Learning Market

Another example of segmentation occurs within the market for online learning. The Internet presents an obvious opportunity, and many learning providers are rushing to get into this space. However, you must realize the online learning market is vast. Consequently, you have to be careful in the selection of market opportunity. Who are you going to target? Below are excerpts from public offering documents of two companies seeking to carve out different roles in the vast online learning market.

DigitalThink: The Company provides online learning courses and services, which are designed, developed, deployed and delivered on an end-to-end basis. Our outsourced, Web-based courses enable customers to deliver learning to any participant who has access to the Internet using a standard Web browser. Our e-learning offerings are designed to enable our customers to deliver knowledge to a broad set of constituencies and provide customers the ability to monitor, track and measure student participation, performance and knowledge acquisition. Businesses purchase course registrations and offer those courses to participants, including their employees, distributors, suppliers and customers, a group which we refer to as the 'extended enterprise.' We have over 200 customers and over 180 online courses at December 31, 1999.

Our e-learning products and services help customers meet their strategic business objectives by addressing their specific education requirements and delivering targeted, relevant information to increase the productivity of their employees, improve the effectiveness of their sales channels and enhance the knowledge and satisfaction of their customers. We initially focused on delivering information technology courses and have extended this focus to develop courses for customers in the technology, financial services, healthcare and telecommunications industries. Our current catalog of fully developed courses consists primarily of technology-oriented topics. We plan to expand the catalog to include courses on other subject matters.

(Taken from Form S-1 of DigitalThink Corporation filed with the Securities and Exchange Commission)

SABA: We are a provider of software and services that enable businesses and governments to create and deploy global networks over the Internet that connect people to learning. Our Internet-based software platform and related services enable organizations to procure and deliver learning and systematically close knowledge and competency gaps across their base of employees, customers, partners and suppliers, known as the 'extended enterprise.' In addition, we offer learning providers an Internet-based global marketing and distribution channel. We recently launched the Saba Learning Exchange, an Internet-based business-to-business learning marketplace. The Saba Learning Exchange is designed to enable businesses, governments and learning providers to buy and sell learning offerings, such as on-line and off-line courses and related materials, as well as collaborate within learning communities.

As of December 31, 1999, our software was licensed for use by over two million people and more than 20,000 third-party learning offerings were accessible on Saba learning networks. Our learning offerings are available from over 50 third-party learning providers, including DigitalThink, ExecuTrain, IBM Catapult, International Air Transport Association, NETg, PROVANT, SkillSoft and the Sun-Netscape Alliance.

Our integrated software platform consists of the Saba Learning Network and Saba Learning Provider Network software applications, as well as Saba Learning Exchange. Saba Learning Network is an Internet-based software application that allows enterprises to assess the learning needs of individuals and organizations, select and purchase on-line and off-line learning materials and programs, track individual learners' progress, and manage enterprise-wide learning initiatives. Saba Learning Provider Network is an Internet-based software application that enables learning providers to develop, market, sell and distribute on-line and off-line learning materials to organizations worldwide. Saba Learning Exchange is a business-to-business learning marketplace that is designed to serve as a single point of access for the highly fragmented learning market. We also provide a full range of strategic consulting, business process reengineering, and technical implementation and support services for our customers.

(Taken From Form S-1 of Saba Corporation filed with the Securities and Exchange Commission)

POSITIONING YOUR PRODUCT OR SERVICE

After you have targeted your product and customer, the next step is to position your product or service in the minds of your customers—an important step in your marketing strategy that will carry over to your promotional mix (discussed in the next chapter). The definition of the term *positioning* came from the classic book on the subject by Al Ries and Jack Trout entitled *Positioning: The Battle for Your Mind*: "Positioning starts with a product. . . . But positioning is not what you do to a product. Positioning is what you do to the mind of a prospect. That is, you position the product in the mind of the prospect."

Positioning starts with a positioning statement, which is also known as the value proposition. Why should your customer do business with you rather than with your competitor? Positioning is one of the most effective but least understood concepts in marketing. Much like the mission statement, positioning can also be useful in communicating the competencies of a particular organization. In another way, the positioning statement is much like the mission statement; and in some cases the positioning statement can be your mission statement.

In all cases, it is useful to think about how you are going to be positioned in the marketplace. In addition, consider how you're going to build your marketing activities around the statement. The next chapter examines promotional activities—that is, activities that can drive traffic to your site and help you engage in online commerce. At this point, it is helpful to consider the positioning statement as a starting point.

Customers generally limit their thoughts and they hate confusion. Their perceptions are strongly influenced by positioning, so focus on the aspect that gives you a competitive advantage.

Creating a Positioning Statement

A positioning statement is a short description of the essential services your business performs: It should be a simple answer to a simple question, short, conversational and repeatable, and it should be tested.

Examples of Positioning Statements

Although the process of developing a positioning statement can be involved and require an intense focus and evaluation of your business model, the final statement itself is usually quite simple. Let's look at positioning statements of some new economy leaders:

- eBay: Your Personal Trading Community
- Priceline.com: Name Your Own Price . . . and Save
- Cisco Systems: Empowering the Internet Generation
- Andersen Consulting: Helping Our Clients Create Their Future
- Oracle: Software Powers the Internet
- PeopleSoft: People Power the Internet

All of these are very simple, yet effective, positioning statements. They provide the essence of the particular product or service and the benefits received. All of them summarize their business model quite effectively and position their products or services in the minds of the customer.

eBay uses a personal touch in referring to its service as *your personal trading community*. Simply put, the site is where you go to trade goods.

Priceline.com offers a "reverse auction" model that allows customers to submit offers of what they are willing to pay for particular goods and services. The company (see Chapter 12) obtained a patent for this reverse auction process, which is currently being litigated. Note, though, that

Priceline does not describe itself as the home of the reverse auction model. Instead it focuses on the simple slogan of "Name Your Own Price . . . and Save." That is the essence of its business model and the reason that people use its services.

Cisco Systems provides nearly 80 percent of the routers and switchers for the Internet. Suppose its positioning statement reflected this fact—"We Provide 80 Percent of the Routers and Switchers for the Internet." It doesn't have quite the same effect as "Empowering the Internet Generation," which sets them squarely in the middle of the new economy.

Andersen Consulting was formerly part of an international accounting firm. However, its positioning statement seeks to distinguish it from the stodgy impression of accountants as bean counters, who simply report on past results. Instead, accountants help clients create their future, suggesting innovative and out-of-the-box solutions.

Oracle develops most of the Internet software, but a positioning statement touting the company as the Internet's leading software developer doesn't have the same ring as "Software Powers the Internet." Like Cisco, Oracle places itself at the heart of the new economy. Note that both companies use the term *power* in their positioning statements.

Like Oracle, PeopleSoft is a developer of e-business software. However, its positioning statement, possibly a rebuttal to Oracle, claims that *"people power the Internet."*

Some additional thoughts about positioning to keep in the back of your mind include differentiating yourself from the competition on the basis of unique advantages. Clients go with the familiar and do what they perceive is in their best interest. They act in this fashion because of their fears about making a purchasing decision in the marketplace. The main positioning steps include:

- Position yourself in the prospect's mind.
- Position yourself by a singular message.
- Let your positioning set you apart from your competitors.

The goals of positioning are to become defined in the marketplace and to position yourself within your target market(s). Effective use of positioning can lead to creating brand equity. Brand equity can be a tremendous advantage to a business that can be translated into market leadership. The idea behind a brand is its basis on customers' recognition of the brand. Particularly in crowded market spaces, customers don't like to be confused and would rather do business with a company they have positive feelings toward. Consequently, customers go with the brand that is most appealing based on its recognizability.

Many Internet start-ups spent 60 to 70 percent of their initial capital trying to build brand awareness mainly on the basis of advertising. But the branding effort does not start with advertising; rather it starts at the beginning of the marketing process. Branding begins with the selection and targeting of particular products and the careful effort to position these products in the minds of customers. Once the company has developed a positioning statement, the next step is to communicate the essence of the statement to customers via various forms of promotion, discussed in the next chapter. Note that the brand is not solidified in the minds of customers until they have positive experiences using the product.

Brand equity is based on:

- Customers' knowledge of the brand
- Customers' ability to recognize the brand
- Customers' recall of having seen the brand before
- Associating the brand with various messages, attributes, benefits, and experiences
- Using acquired knowledge in decision making

chapter 9

Implementing Your Customer-Centered Marketing Strategy

The previous two chapters dealt with the steps involved in formulating your marketing strategy. These steps include researching your market, targeting a particular market segment, and developing your positioning statement. The next step in your marketing strategy is deciding on your mix of promotional activities. Promotional activities used to attract customers include public relations, advertising, sales promotion, and direct marketing. Other marketing methods include alliances and affiliations as well as additional techniques and considerations specific to online businesses.

After the promotional mix is established, the marketing strategy should be implemented in an integrated effort involving the entire organization. Once the strategy is implemented, it should be constantly monitored to determine both its overall effectiveness as well as the results of the promotional activities. The main question to consider is whether you are receiving an acceptable return on investment (ROI) for your promotional expenditures. The results of such online advertising as banner and text ads can be directly monitored to determine their effectiveness. The impact of other types of advertising and publicity can be traced through questionnaires and consumer responses.

The importance of evaluating the results of your promotional mix is due to the fact that consumer usage patterns, the way that consumers buy over the Internet, are still in a formative stage. In other words, no one is really sure exactly what is most effective in terms of promoting your Internet business and driving traffic to your site. New studies gauging the success of particular types of advertising are frequently released. But for every general conclusion, there are often exceptions. In addition, consumer behavior keeps changing. As a result, it is important to remain flexible and be willing to experiment with your promotional mix. According to venture capitalist Jim Smith, of Mohr, Davidow Ventures, companies that have succeeded were nimble enough to try different strategies to attract customers, leading them to refine their promotional mix and obtain the best return on their investment dollars.

The ultimate goal of your marketing strategy is to develop a strong brand identity in the minds of your customers, as noted in Chapter 8. A common mistake that many dot-coms made was assuming that a positive brand image could be obtained solely via an expensive advertising campaign. Even if successful, high-impact advertising serves only to bring customers to the site. But that's just half the challenge. A bigger challenge is to build your brand by continually providing the best customer service so that your prospect will become a customer for life. According to Robbie Vitrano, the owner of Trumpet Advertising, with offices in New Orleans and New York, branding is developed by the customer experience. You begin to build your brand when your customer has a positive relationship with your company over an extended period of time.

Simply put, if you don't provide an excellent experience, your customers won't return. The experience is everything. You won't be able to build an audience by providing inferior customer service or an inferior experience. A bad customer experience can also result in your losing a previously built audience. This is especially true if a customer's first experience was a bad one. In March 2000, *USA Today* reported that one in four online purchasers had a bad experience during the 1999 Christmas season. A number of e-tailers simply did not produce during the hectic holiday season. Their back office and support operations were unable to handle the demand that resulted from heavy media advertising and the spike in interest in online shopping. Those who were disappointed are highly unlikely to return again.

The customer has been very much empowered in the new economy. Although customer service is the final part of your marketing strategy, it is nonetheless the most important aspect. The successful company has to carefully manage the customer experience to maintain loyalty. Customer expectations are very high, and service and delivery have to be even higher. The good news is that the Internet has vastly expanded the ability for individualized and attentive customer service with the use of customer relationship management tools to be discussed later.

YOUR PROMOTIONAL MIX

Before you can manage your relationship with customers, the first step is to get them to your site. That is the goal of your promotional mix: to create awareness in the marketplace and attract customers. An important aspect of your promotional mix is ensuring that it is coordinated. The activities should converge on a single theme, possibly your positioning statement, to reinforce your message and your product.

In designing your promotional mix, Robbie Vitrano urges you to first determine your constituency and then decide on the particular methods to reach that constituency. Your constituency, of course, begins with your target customers. But your constituency also includes the trade press, the technology community, and the investment community. Different promotional techniques are required to reach each constituency. Public relations can be used to favorably influence the trade press, investment community, and technology community. The company promotes itself to its target customers through a mix of public relations, advertising, sales promotion, direct selling, and other Internet marketing methods.

It is important to coordinate all of these activities to maximize the impact of your marketing dollars. Generally, the more targeted and coordinated your marketing activities are, the more successful they will be. Following is a more detailed discussion of the activities that form your promotional mix

Public Relations

Public relations is the use of nonpaid communication to influence public opinion about a company and its products. Sources of nonpaid communications include the news media, investors, and industry analysts. In addition to being free, public relations also enjoys the added benefit of being more credible than advertising. In other words, people will more readily believe communications from third parties about a company than communications from the company about itself. Companies can either use employees or hire a firm to generate favorable public relations. The objective is to garner free media coverage whose value to the company exceeds the cost of obtaining it.

Many Internet pioneers, such as Yahoo! and Amazon.com, benefited from excellent public relations during their early stages. They received favorable coverage from the press, from industry analysts, and from the investment community. This helped both companies in establishing brand awareness and acceptance in the market. However, with many more Internet start-ups clamoring for attention today, it is much harder to receive favorable publicity. As a result, a well thought-out public relations plan needs to be established as an essential part of the promotional mix.

One aspect of public relations is press relations, the process of communicating with newspapers, magazines, and the broadcast medium about your company and its products. A key to effective press relations is to focus on media outlets that serve your target market. Although national sources will reach your market, such sources are literally bombarded with material, making it very difficult to obtain national coverage. Therefore, in addition to national sources, it is important to target both offline and online sources that cater to your particular industry. Such sources would include the trade press in your industry. Generally, the press is interested in anything that is newsworthy or that could solve a problem for its readers or viewers.

The basic tool for press relations is the press release, or news release. Other tools include the press conference or press briefing. Generally, the press release is a short memo sent to a variety of publications, usually by fax or e-mail, which discusses topics of potential news interest. In addition, video press releases can be sent to television stations. Potential topics for press releases include the announcement of a new product or new technology, the introduction of new company leaders, or any community-related activity the company is involved in. It is also useful to prepare a press kit, which contains publication-ready photos, product samples, background information, and other materials in addition to the press release.

According to John Deveney, the owner of Deveney Communication, there are definite factors that can assist your public relations effort. Deveney is deeply involved in Internet marketing and public relations and is the holder of the designation Accredited Business Communicator from the International Association of Business Communicators. His agency directed a highly successful integrated marketing effort for a new Web site named mardigras.com, which won several awards. He relied extensively on public relations in promoting the site, and his marketing campaign will be examined later in this chapter. According to Deveney, the issues described below are important in your public relations effort. The more your effort matches the criteria, the more likely you will receive media attention.

Topicality. Presenting topical information of particular interest to a news source is by far the most important element in a public relations effort. The media are generally interested in information on a "hot" subject. If your business fulfills a need in what is regarded as a hot category, it is usually easier to obtain press coverage. Note that, unlike the early days of the Internet, dot-com businesses are no longer an automatically hot category. Consequently, the information has to be of topical interest to a particular news source. If the information about your product or company affects a news source's market, affects its readers or viewers, or solves a problem, then you have a much better chance of obtaining media coverage. The question to always ask yourself is whether your topic is of particular interest to that news source.

Timeliness. A public relations effort can be greatly enhanced by timeliness, which determines whether the information is newsworthy. For example, stories that are timed to seasons of the year, government rulings, new laws, new social trends, or even holidays can play a positive role in creating a topical awareness. A timely press release has a better chance of being covered.

Localization. All television and radio newsrooms are dedicated to covering local news, so your release should be relevant to local audiences. Consequently, national trends or statistics have value only if newsrooms can be made to understand what they mean specifically to their community.

Humanization. Your message needs to show how real people are or will be personally affected. Newsrooms want people stories and the trade publications want items that will directly affect their members. Graphics and statistics mean nothing without the appropriate human angle.

Advertising

Public relations may imply free access to various media on the whole, but advertising implies paid media coverage. It can be defined as paid, non-personal communication with a target market. Advertising media include both online as well as offline sources. The most common online sources are banner and text ads and e-mail communications. Offline sources include television, radio, newspapers, magazines, billboards, and direct mail. An effective promotional mix involves the use of both online and offline sources.

Several things need to be considered when planning an advertising campaign. The first is the intended mission of the campaign and the amount of exposure necessary to reach your market. Reach and frequency are important quantitative measurements; reach is the percentage of your target market that sees the ad and frequency is the number of times the target market is exposed to your message. Generally, an audience requires multiple exposures to a particular message before registering awareness. Because your advertising budget is limited, there is often a compromise needed between reach and frequency. You don't want to spend money on sources that few in your target market are exposed to, even if you can obtain higher frequency. On the other hand, it can be risky to spend money on sources with a high level of reach but low frequency.

A good example of high-reach and low-frequency advertising would be Super Bowl ads. Internet start-ups advertised heavily in the 2000 Super Bowl, but shelling out $2 million for 30 seconds of exposure in the 3- to 4-hour broadcast is a considerable gamble. Although the Super Bowl audience is extremely large, it is still difficult for a company to stand out with a single 30-second spot. Many companies hoped to replicate the famous Apple Computer ad in the 1980s, which sought to position Apple as the hip new upstart in the computer industry challenging stodgy IBM. Although the ad played only once, it garnered considerable media attention and the publicity it spun off benefited Apple more than the actual ad. However, nearly half of the companies advertising in the 2000 Super Bowl were Internet companies, which made it considerably harder for any single one to stand out.

Another consideration in advertising is effective ad copy. The main goals of advertising are to (1) capture the attention of the reader or viewer, (2) stimulate interest, (3) build credibility, (4) heighten desire, and (5) motivate action. With these goals in mind, let's examine major advertising locales.

Online ads. As mentioned above, online ads include banner ads as well as text ads. Banner ads consist of a particular graphic, usually your logo, that enables customers to click through to your site. Text ads are links tied to certain key words in the text of another site that are relevant to or describe your product or service, and they are growing in popularity.

Charges for online ads are usually based on click-throughs to the site or actual customer transactions. Placement is very important in the use and flexibility of the ads. Recent research has indicated that click-through rates are dropping, although click-throughs can still be a very effective advertising method. One of the advantages of banner ads is that their effectiveness can be tested relatively quickly.

Print ads. Print advertising pertains to ads that appear in various magazines, journals, and newspapers. Although the effectiveness of print advertising is more difficult to test than that of banner ads, customer questionnaires can determine an ad's effectiveness. Many magazines are extremely targeted and can serve as an efficient way to reach a specialized audience.

Television. Advantages of television include its visual impact as well as its prestige factor. Unlike television, bandwidth is a factor in Internet broadcasts; and even though bandwidth is rapidly increasing, it will still be some time before the average Internet user can receive broadcast-quality transmissions. Consequently, television is still an important advertising medium. Many dot-coms relied almost exclusively on television in promoting themselves—with mixed success.

One drawback of television advertising is its cost. There are production costs in addition to television advertising rates, which are generally high, even for local markets. Cable television has provided a less expensive alternative, and ads on cable can be targeted to specific types of programming (e.g., sports, music, education).

Radio. Radio advertising provides relatively low cost per exposure, and many dot-coms are using radio ads. Radio also allows an advertiser to target messages based on the demographic profiles of the station's listening base.

On the negative side, listeners don't give radio advertising—a completely nonvisual medium—the same degree of attention they give television.

Sales Promotions

Sales promotions are techniques used to stimulate product demand. They include special activities and events, such as live seminars, contests, and celebrity appearances. Chapter 1 discussed the bizarre story of Pixelon and its $12 million iBash, a massive sales promotion to gain attention. However, there were many glitches and David Stanley (alias Michael Fenne), the founder of Pixelon, turned out to be a fugitive from the law. Although Pixelon has received tremendous publicity from its sales promotion and fugitive founder, all of it has been negative.

The Internet has opened up a whole new approach to sales promotions. Such promotional events as live seminars have been used in the marketing world for many years. During seminars, information is provided to prospects that prompts them, it is hoped, to take a second look at the products and services being offered. But, seminars can be very expensive, and to be worthwhile, seminars must generate quality leads from participants. In other words, some of the participants need to be able to be turned into customers.

As opposed to live seminars, promotional events can be marketed successfully over the Internet at a fraction of the cost. There are logistical advantages too, as people don't have to leave their office to attend. The Internet seminar can be live, prerecorded, or a combination of both.

Like any event, however, the Net seminar has to be promoted. You can generate interest or attendance through either e-mail or other direct marketing techniques. In addition, a program has to be developed that creates interest in attending. Many issues must be considered. To start, you need enough lead time to generate an advertising campaign. In addition, you want to focus on your target market. Finally, you want to offer a good program, which depends on the importance of the information, the prominence of the guest speaker, and the ability of the audience to become involved.

In structuring a sales presentation, the delivery mechanism of the Internet must be taken into account. Such items as streaming video will cause bandwidth concerns, but you do want an Internet presence that people can react to and use. There also has to be a server significant enough to host the event and facilitate audience attendance and interaction.

A unique mix of offline and online sales promotion through the use of contests at cybercafés and discussed below has been offered by mardigras.com.

Direct Marketing

Direct marketing is an interactive system of marketing in which your company communicates directly and individually with target customers, and, according to the Direct Marketing Association, employs one or more types of advertising with the goal of creating a measurable response and/or transaction. The advantages therefore of direct marketing are that it is both interactive and measurable. Direct marketing is interactive by including response mechanisms for target customers—toll-free numbers and e-mail, Web site, and/or postcard addresses. In addition, you are able to measure with a high degree of precision the effectiveness of your direct marketing efforts.

The Internet has greatly enhanced the use of direct marketing. The direct marketing model is based on a formula known as AIDA, which stands for awareness, interest, desire, and action.

The first concern of any direct marketing campaign is to generate *awareness*. Awareness is generally the first step in a purchase decision because your prospect or target audience has to know that you exist. The goal of marketing activities is to create a certain level of awareness. These activities include advertising through traditional channels such as the mass media, public relations, telemarketing, and direct mail.

In order to achieve a certain amount of success initially, a direct marketing campaign has to create *interest* on the part of prospects. The goal is to prompt prospects to take some type of action that will move them closer to your product or service.

The next stage of the process is *desire*—when prospects begin to be serious about the product or service. At this point, prospects may request additional information. In the case of an impulse buy, a prospect may even purchase the product immediately. Those who don't buy can still be considered qualified prospects.

The final stage occurs when a prospect takes some *action*. This could be anything from asking for more information to actually ordering a product. The prospect may ask for a demo copy in moving toward making a purchase.

The advantage of the Internet as a direct marketing tool is that it can execute steps to a sale quickly, efficiently, and at very low cost. Compare all the advantages of the online world over brick and mortar:

- The customer's ability to respond by e-mail
- The ability to direct the customer's attention to various online models
- Permitting customers to construct their own products
- Detailed instructions available to customers through e-mail
- The ability to preview a course or demo product already set up online

In the brick-and-mortar world, consider the time it takes a direct sales force to personally interact with the prospect (this still might have to take place in larger orders). You can select and set-up your site to facilitate direct marketing, and the site can lead customers through the steps of the direct marketing model very cost effectively.

Specific types of direct marketing activities are discussed next.

Direct mail ("snail mail"). Generally, direct mail is one of the least expensive and most measurable ways to help sell products or services. Direct mail may use database marketing , in which the company collects and stores information about customers. Some of the drawbacks of direct mail are its poor image (it's often tossed out as junk mail) and its competition with so many other companies relying on direct mailings.

Direct e-mail. Direct marketing e-mail has many of the same advantages and disadvantages of direct snail mail. The main advantages of e-mail over snail mail is that it is virtually costless. Once the database is assembled, there is virtually no cost in sending e-mail. Many companies use e-mail to solicit business or to stay in touch with their target customers. A good example is American Airlines, which e-mails bargain fares to its extensive database at virtually no cost.

Other uses of direct e-mail are generating leads and communicating with existing customers, although there is also the risk of its being considered SPAM and ignored.

Newsletters. Another way to solicit business and stay in contact with customers is through the use of printed or online newsletters. Online newsletters have a cost advantage over their printed counterpart. You could request those interested to complete a preferred customer card or newsletter list online. The list could be used to send out newsletters or to announce specials, promotions, existing services, or changes in services.

Rather than directly promoting your business, newsletters are more of a soft sell by highlighting some of the activities of your business and providing useful information to readers.

Examples of Effective Promotional Efforts

mardigras.com. The integrated marketing campaign for mardigras.com was the brainchild of John Deveney and his associates at Deveney Communication. They launched an online guide designed to bring the best of Mardi Gras to individuals around the world through their computer screens. Mardi Gras, which is French for Fat Tuesday, is an annual celebration in New Orleans to provide one last opportunity to celebrate, before Ash

Wednesday, the beginning of the Roman Catholic observance of Lent. This one-day celebration has evolved into several weeks of elaborate parades and festivities in what is described as the "Greatest Free Show on Earth." The celebration culminates in Mardi Gras Day.

The site mardigras.com featured Mardi Gras event schedules and parade routes, Mardi Gras history and trivia, live cameras with streaming video, and 20-second updated photos of the celebration from hot spots around New Orleans. The site also included an online souvenir shop, restaurant guide, interactive games, downloadable e-cards, screen savers, and audio clips to send to family and friends, as well as online forums for sharing Mardi Gras stories and survival tips.

The goal of the promotional effort was to create interest and awareness in the site and differentiate it from other Mardi Gras sites in order to generate revenue through advertising in the years to come. The agency had 60 days to reach its target objective of 5 million page views during the campaign; page views identify each time an individual page is accessed. Hits, on the other hand, can be inflated by the number of icons and links on a particular page.

The agency selected media outlets nationally, regionally, and within the target markets based on the research of reporters, timely news angles, and lead time. Efforts were made to make media reports topical, timely, and local. The final media list consisted of 26 airline magazines, 98 hospitality publications, 76 national broadcast outlets, 50 national print outlets, 50 travel publications, 12 adult magazines, and 88 local print and broadcast outlets.

A series of news releases was created targeting specific industries, geographic areas, events, audiences, promotions, and items of national interest. For example, press releases were drafted for Mardi Gras seasonal milestones, such as the Krewe de Vieux kickoff of the season and the weekend prior to Mardi Gras. Press releases were also prepared for national dissemination; for example, the site's petition for Mardi Gras to be declared a national holiday; and releases were prepared for specific audiences such as African Americans, gays, and lesbians.

Research revealed that *Playboy* magazine's Web site was among the most heavily accessed and had one of the highest rates of loyalty among applicable Web sites. When Playboy.com announced it would showcase Mardi Gras, the agency worked with Playboy to be featured as a direct link, which gave mardigras.com access to Playboy's heavy traffic and loyal user base. The agency also worked with an Associated Press travel reporter, who included the site in a story on virtual vacations, which was put on the Associated Press newswire. The story was picked up in more than a dozen daily papers across the country and in Puerto Rico. The agency also developed and sent pitches to national talk shows, including E! News, Entertainment Tonight, and USA Today, resulting in coordinating Entertainment Tonight's use of Web cams on the show.

In addition to promotions made through the media, Deveney initiated various other types of promotions—a promotional mix. The site offered free e-cards, which users could personalize and send to friends. Recipients received notification via e-mail and were given a link to the site to retrieve the greeting. This feature was also used as a successful media promotion. Press contacts were sent an e-card with a news release, providing reporters an incentive to visit the site, where they received a personalized news release providing information about the site.

King Cakes, a tasty Mardi Gras staple, were sent to selected members of the national media with other promotional pieces and gifts. The agency created a contest promotion with cybercafés in certain target markets after their research revealed that cybercafés were "hot spots" in many target markets. Cybercafés were identified in the target cities and pitched with a simple online contest. Users from a particular cybercafé could log on and "vote" by entering their contact information and café. The café with the most votes won a full Mardi Gras party with New Orleans food, drink, music, and favors. The contest provided the cafés an incentive to set up and display promotional materials and encourage their patrons to visit the site. Each patron was automatically qualified to win a trip to Mardi Gras 2000, giving each a personal incentive to visit.

Another promotion, which was aimed at college students in the target markets, offered a trip to Mardi Gras to the individual or group that sent the best photo. The plan was for students to send photos of themselves in costumes that would then be posted on the Web site. Students logged on the site to vote for the best photo and thus drove traffic to the site.

All the employees at Deveney Communication sent information to their personal e-mail lists, asking recipients to check out the site and, if possible, make mardigras.com their default Internet home page. The recipients then forwarded the messages to their own personal lists with the same request. The agency tracked messages that were passed to thousands of people in the targeted cities and various organizations.

The agency also coordinated events, and a Web Cam placement at some 40 parades, balls, and locations was cybercast live with a banner displaying a prominent logo from the site and the message "You're on camera. Do something!" An invitation designed to promote the Web site was blank on one side so it could be quickly and inexpensively personalized and sent to everyone on each event's mail list to promote the event and the site.

Certain events were selected to respond to target audiences and provide an insider's panorama of Mardi Gras. The site broadcast the raucous by showing Krewe du Vieux; the intimate with a family's private party for the Krewe of Saturn Parade in their stately antebellum home on St. Charles Avenue; the traditional with the established parades Endymion and Bacchus; and the nontraditional with the Lords of Leather Bal masque. Most of the events used the mardigras.com postcards as their invitations.

The award-winning Mardi Gras campaign was generally considered a big success. The site exceeded its goal of 5 million page views by receiving nearly 28 million page views! The broadcast coverage reportedly reached 7 million viewers, and the print coverage reached another 2.2 million readers. Media relations resulted in some 30 million impressions via broadcast print, radio, and online outlets, with a value conservatively estimated at more than $7 million. The budget for this effort in terms of agency fees and expenses was $28,000, which amounts to one-tenth of one cent per page view—quite a return on the marketing expenditure.

Although not every business will have the unique characteristics of Mardi Gras, many lessons on marketing strategy can be learned from Deveney Communication and mardigras.com. The following have general application:

- *Planning:* Even though their time frame was short, their marketing strategy was carefully planned from the outset. The client and agency planned their objective of 5 million page views and then worked to attain their objective.
- *Targeting:* A key element in their marketing strategy was targeting both potential customers and media outlets. Potential customers were

targeted on the basis of geographic (large cities) and demographic (young adults) characteristics. The media were targeted based on their interest in all the events surrounding the Mardi Gras festival. Media sources included travel, hospitality, and adult magazines in addition to national outlets.

- *Promotional mix:* The results of the campaign were maximized with the effective use of the promotional mix. In particular, the agency was very adept at obtaining free public relations efforts. It displayed imagination with the e-cards and King cakes in garnering favorable media attention. The contests were also relatively inexpensive uses of sales promotion; and partnering with Playboy.com and Entertainment Tonight was very effective.

- *Implementation:* With a short period of time to achieve results, the strategy had to be carefully implemented and coordinated. This was done and culminated in 8 million page views on Mardi Gras day alone.

- *Cost effectiveness:* Compared with many dot-coms dumping money on television, this integrated campaign achieved enormous exposure at the very modest price mentioned earlier of roughly one-tenth of one cent per page view.

Golfballs.com. Golfballs.com is the site discussed in the previous chapter that specializes in the sale of new and used golf balls. The company is careful in the way it spends its advertising dollars and carefully analyzes its return on investment for advertising expenditures. The company's IT architecture enables it to determine the source of its visitors and carefully monitors the unique visitors, registered users, and customers generated by particular forms of online advertising.

Unique visitors are the different individuals who visit the site. Registered users are those who register their name at the site for promotional notices and other e-mail communications. Finally, customers are those who buy something. The company estimates that it converts one in ten of its registered users into customers. For each form of advertising that it uses, the company calculates the cost per registered user and cost per customer acquired.

The company engages in a considerable amount of online advertising on golf-related Web sites such as Golf.com, PGAtour.com, and Golfclubs.com. However, the results from offline print advertising, such as *Sports Illus-*

trated and *Golf Digest* have not proven to generate an adequate return. Other marketing activities include placing advertising and promotions in some of the larger golf-related e-mail newsletters. The company also sends out promotions to its existing database of subscribers. As mentioned above, another important source of new customers is referrals from existing customers. The company also sponsors certain golf-related promotional events and charities that include promotional packets detailing the company's products and Web address. The company is planning an affiliate program later this year and considers this program an important source of new business.

Some advice that Golfballs.com founder Tom Cox provides for Internet entrepreneurs is to spend considerable time (he recommends 100 hours) researching your idea. If you have an idea, someone is probably doing it already. You need to determine how well funded others are and how well established your competition might be in the marketplace. At that point it is important to determine whether there's room for another player in the particular marketplace.

OTHER INTERNET MARKETING STRATEGIES

Search Engine Registration

One of the more effective methods for getting people to your site is to utilize search engines. You do this by registering your site with the various search engines. Effective search engine placement is critical because it can drive sales and increase a company's geographic and demographic reach. Search engines are collections of sites that can be searched on several criteria: keyword, company name, or maybe industry. Some are directories with hierarchal categories of listings like <www.snap.com> or <www.yahoo.com>. These companies have people who check out a site and decide if it will be included in their listings. Others are automated, with software that explores the Web for new sites and adds them to their database; these include engines such as <www.infoseek.com>, <hotbot.com>, and <lycos.com>. For these engines, scatter each page with metatags (see the next section) that you expect prospects to use for their search.

The most important search engine with which you can register your site is Yahoo! It is the most commonly used search engine on the Internet. Be sure to register under the appropriate category so that prospects can find you. Yahoo! also allows registrations in a total of three categories, which allows you to promote multiple products or sell to multiple audiences.

Metatagging. Metatags are commands embedded in the HTML code of a Web site. They cannot be seen by the user, but search engines can see them. Search engines use the keywords or descriptions inside metatags to find and rank sites that match the search criteria inputted by a prospect. Metatags are typically the popular words that marketers think people will use in their search to locate products or services. The existence and frequency of metatags are also used to improve a site's ranking. They are an effective tool and so need to be carefully thought through, and care must be taken when using them.

One type of metatag use to avoid, however, is cyberstuffing. Cyberstuffing occurs when one company uses the name or trademark of another company in its metatags. In such a case, when a potential customer inputs company A's trademark term, he or she will also pull up company B's (the competition) Web site as well, which can cause confusion and be considered infringement. The purpose, of course, is to divert customers' attention from company A so they will buy from company B's site as they were there anyway. Although the results of lawsuits have been mixed, a federal court of appeals saw the practice as infringement. Because both companies competed in the same industry, the court's view was that one competitor benefited inappropriately by using the other company's name in its metatags by diverting customers from the site for which they were really searching.

Viral Marketing

No discussion of Internet marketing would be complete without addressing *viral marketing*. The creation of the concept is credited to the venture capital firm Draper Fisher Jurvetson. The original idea was inspired by Hotmail, an Internet-based e-mail service that included a promotional pitch with a clickable URL in every message sent out by a Hotmail user. In other words, every customer became a salesperson, pitching the e-mail service to his or her circle of acquaintances. One of the advantages of such an approach is its implication of an endorsement from the user. This is generally considered more effective than an advertisement by the company itself. The subscriber base of Hotmail quickly grew to 12 million in 18 months, and the company was eventually purchased by Microsoft.

Another site that has benefited from the use of viral marketing is slambook. com. In the offline world, a slambook is a notebook that teenagers circulate among their friends, usually in school, for input and comments on various issues. The site is structured to allow users to forward their slambook to 25 of their friends, who, slambook.com hoped, would want their own slambook. This technique has increased circulation to 650,000 users per month.

In order for viral marketing to be effective, some motivation or value must be provided to customers to act as uncompensated salespeople and "pass the word." For example, BlueMountainArts allows you to send animated greetings. The site, which is clever and easy to navigate, prompts recipients to return or send others a personalized animated greeting. It also provides value to those who spread the word, specifically the ability to send an animated e-mail greeting to others at no cost and requiring very little time.

Strategic Alliances

The use of strategic alliances or affiliates can be very beneficial to the marketing effort of your company. Many companies in the new economy, in fact, are judged on the strength of their alliance partners. These strategic alliances range from placing links on related sites to a formal partnership. As already discussed, speed is of paramount importance in the new economy, and so using a strategic partner can allow you to offer your product or service more quickly to your customers. My earlier recommendation that your company perform what it does best and then outsource the rest applies equally to competing in the marketplace.

Several approaches are available in forming strategic alliances. The first is a purely marketing approach in which alliances are used for their reach into a particular market—banner ads, for example. Another approach is to give your customers access to products that compliment your products and thus enabling you to become the one-stop source for your customers. For example, Auto-By-Tel is an online auto retailer; in addition, through strategic partners it provides financing and insurance. These additional services generally accompany the purchase of an automobile. As a result, Auto-By-Tel provides a complete solution for its customers.

A key driver in forming strategic alliances for complimentary products is assessing how necessary an alliance is as part of a customer solution. However, don't forget your core market and be distracted by offering too many ancillary products. You have to question whether a particular alliance serves a useful purpose in serving your customers or assisting you with market penetration.

Another example of an alliance is the use of market affiliates, which can be an important way to generate leads for your Web site. You could have free links to others to get them to your Web site, also known as using marketing affiliates and creating an affiliate network. We're all familiar with the Amazon.com banners.

Although you may be tempted to think of quantity instead of quality in developing your affiliate marketing program, remember that you want to build a brand recognition or name outside of your marketing affiliate network. You want to achieve high awareness among your market base outside the network and establish a good relationship with your affiliate partners. Finally, remember that quality is better than quantity with affiliates; it's better to selectively enlist a few successful affiliates than to use a scattered approach in attracting a multitude of marginal ones. Next, it is important to work with your partners in adding value to their sites that will assist you in generating revenues from your site. The referral network has to be enticing or no one will bother. The key is to seek out strategic affiliate partners with whom you have complementary services and with whom you can bundle services.

CUSTOMER-CENTERED MARKETING

●●●

"You pounce in here expecting to be waited on hand and foot. Have you any idea of how much there is to do? Do you ever think of that? Of course not, you're all too busy sticking your noses into every corner, poking around for things to complain about, aren't you?**"**

Basil Fawlty, a.k.a. John Cleese (born 1939), actor and comedian

An overriding theme of promotional activities is their need to be customer focused. The traditional view of marketing mix was revised in a study by Richard Barry, a professor at the University of Wisconsin-Madison, which arranged the marketing mix from the most important to the least important:

1. Customer sensitivity: customer treatment and response to customers
2. Product: product reliability, quality, and features
3. Customer convenience: customer convenience in selling, availability to the customer
4. Service: customer convenience, resale service, sales service
5. Price: pricing terms and offers as well as the price
6. Place: provider facilities, availability to the customer, and provider accessibility
7. Promotion: publicity, advertising, selling, resale services, and pricing offers

Although this model was designed for traditional businesses, it does have a lot of merit in the online world. As is evident in the model, it is customer responsiveness and customer service that are paramount. The Web is allowing customer interface and sensitivity to customers in a way that has never been done before. The irony of the high-tech world is that even with the seeming impersonal nature of technology, customers still want their desires to be taken into consideration, particularly in one-to-one marketing to individual consumers.

Customer Relationship Management

Renewed focus on the customer has led to increased emphasis on customer relationship management, or CRM. The CRM model is built around some telling statistics. The first is that it generally costs six times more to sell to a new customer than to sell to an existing one. In a typical setting, dissatisfied customers will tell eight to ten people about their experience, as noted in an earlier chapter. On the Internet, this dissatisfaction can be multiplied by a factor of 100. In addition, the odds of selling a product to new customers are 1 to 5 percent, whereas the odds of selling a product to existing customers are 40 to 50 percent. In addition, more than 90 percent of existing Internet companies don't have the service integration to support their e-commerce.

A new company can gain an instant competitive advantage by already having in place a good CRM system. Companies that treat their customers well are able to grow revenue through the use of existing relationships. This is done in a traditional manner by either cross-selling additional products or up-selling customers more expensive products. The key is to identify and retain the best customers. What helps is having the entire relationship with customers digitized so that customers don't have to continue entering your site over and over again.

The first step in using the integrated CRM technology is to acquire new customers. As noted earlier, CRM technology fits well within the traditional AIDA model (awareness, interest, desire, and action) for integrating customer awareness and interest with a direct response from you. You are empowered to respond to a nibble from customers, with a direct response technology that allows you to maximize and leverage your relationship. This permits you to field inquiries quickly and efficiently and even return with a quick response when a customer gets in touch with you.

Another advantage of CRM technology concerns retaining the customer relationship, which in turn allows you to make the buying cycle permanent and easy. Once you already have a customer's business, it is much easier to retain that business.

Selling-Chain Management

Another type of software that enhances the customer experience is selling-chain management, which integrates order acquisition strategy and thus makes it easier for the customer to buy. Obviously, the great example is Dell computers, which allows customers to order and configure their computers online. Dell makes it easier to custom order the products with its integrated form of selling-chain management.

The goal of integrated systems of supply chain management and CRM is to provide the total solution for customers. Those sites that provide the total solution are the sites that customers visit again and again. The point is that you have to make it easy for customers to do business with you—

either in core competencies that you offer or in competencies or advantages that you obtain on your own.

Instant customer fulfillment. An important part in setting up customer service architecture is being able to fill an order online; instant fulfillment is very important. Your company has to be able to give customers instant information concerning order fulfillment, which includes acknowledgment of the order as well. Of course, a leader in order fulfillment is Amazon.com, which uses instant response for your order and also lets you know when the order will be shipped.

This gets back to CRM technology that allows instant execution. In the Christmas season of 1999, many companies overpromised their deliveries—in particular, a toy company was not able to fill its orders in time for Christmas. To miss Christmas had to be the ultimate nightmare of any marketer.

One of the best ideas in generating orders over the Internet uses the speed and efficiency that the Internet supplies, greatly reducing transaction costs. Internet efficiencies can be used either to generate more profits or to reduce selling costs. An example of how the Web can greatly reduce selling costs is Cisco, which allows customers to configure orders; this also reduces human errors and saves administrative time, all of which translates into savings.

Personalization

Another part of the customer-oriented focus is marketing and the use of the Web to create stronger bonds with customers. In the book *Enterprise One-to-One*, the authors recommended the model of one-to-one marketing. Instead of selling one product at a time to as many customers as possible, the one-to-one marketer uses customer databases and interactive communications to sell to one customer at a time and to sell that one person as many products and services as possible—the precise model used by Amazon.com. To fully exploit one-to-one marketing, you have to track the customer and know the customer's wants and needs. You can facilitate interactive communications and then have mass customization, which allows your company to know particular customer preferences and allow them to access your services. Obviously, such software is expensive, so be cognizant of the cost of one-to-one marketing.

10

Financial Accounting in the New Economy

"Business is many things, the least of which is the balance sheet. It is a fluid, ever-changing, living thing, sometimes building to great peaks, sometimes falling to crumpled lumps. The soul of a business is a curious alchemy of needs, desires, greed and gratifications mixed together with selflessness, sacrifices and personal contributions far beyond material rewards.**"**

Harold Geneen (born 1910), CEO of ITT, famous for his dedication to the balance sheet

"An accountant is a man who puts his head in the past and backs his ass into the future.**"**

Ross Johnson (born 1932), American executive and former Nabisco CEO

Nearly every book about accounting describes it as "the language of business." This continues to be true. Although accounting has some drawbacks in the new economy, most of its principles of measurement and value are still relevant. The promise or market potential of a business will carry it only so far; at some point, the business will have to prove itself. Financial accounting provides the proof by measuring how well the business has performed. The investment community has discovered a new Internet buzzword: profit. The honeymoon is over for Internet business models that cannot at least demonstrate prospects of profitability in the short term.

I have taught accounting to college students as well as to entrepreneurs as noncredit and credit courses and know that its principles can both scare and bore students at the same time. Accounting textbooks tend to be large and intimidating, and some intricacies of accounting can be mind numbing in complexity. However, your goal in preparing the e-plan is not to master every convoluted detail of accounting. Rather, it is to gain a broad understanding of the most important accounting principles so that you can quickly evaluate the performance and condition of your business or determine its bottom line. Such a broad understanding can be considered financial literacy.

By understanding the financial aspects of your business, you can better manage the direction of the business and employ resources more productively. Successful companies need to carefully manage their finances. In fact, the number one cause of mortality for start-ups is poor financial management. Lately, the press has been chronicling the obituaries of promising Internet start-ups that burned through their initial financing with little to show for it. Such businesses perished outright, were sold at a discounted value, or lingered on as the "walking dead" in trying to somehow revive themselves. Proper financial management will not save every business, but improper financial management will doom almost every business, particularly start-ups.

The technology companies that have sustained themselves in the marketplace, such as Cisco, Microsoft, and Intel, show continuing profit expansions as well as market savvy. When Wall Street is in a sober mood, it is very sensitive to earnings. Companies that miss their earnings and report lower-than-expected profits are often punished severely. Therefore, it is not just accountants—the so-called bean counters—who need to worry about the bottom line; every business owner needs to focus on it as well. Basic financial accounting principles can equip you with such a focus so that you are able to stretch your budget, not only during flush times, but during lean times as well.

ACCOUNTING AS A VALUE MEASUREMENT

One of the harshest criticisms of accounting today is that it is behind the times as a value measurement. The assets of a business are valued on a historical cost basis. In other words, assets go on the books at the amount that you pay for them. Such treatment ignores many of the important resources of new economy businesses, such as the knowledge, talent, and ability of the workforce. Consequently, present financial reporting standards are biased in favor of companies with hard assets, such as natural resources and manufacturing, and against businesses based on intellectual and intangible resources.

Some have suggested that the financial accounting model should be expanded to incorporate the value of a company's intangible and intellectual assets, such as high-quality products and services; motivated and skilled employees; responsiveness of internal processes; and satisfied and loyal customers. Such an evaluation of intangible assets and company capabilities would be especially helpful because, for information age companies, these assets are more critical for success than traditional physical assets. In cases where intangible assets and company capabilities could be properly valued within the financial accounting model, organizations that are able to improve those assets could rapidly communicate this improvement to the market and their shareholders. On the other hand, the market could also quickly recognize companies that have depleted their share of intangible assets long before the negative effect would appear on their income statements.

The issue, of course, is how to formulate a reliable financial value on intangible assets. Yet, despite this difficulty, such assets are very important to the success of a business. The American Institute of Certified Public Accountants (AICPA) currently recognizes the issue and is suggesting ways to update accounting practice to make it more relevant in today's economy. Some of the suggestions currently under consideration include:

- Provide more information about plans, opportunities, risks, and uncertainties.
- Focus more on the factors that create longer-term value, including nonfinancial measures indicating how key business processes are performing.
- Better align information reported externally with the information reported internally to senior management.

Until such standards are modified by the AICPA, we will have to put up with outdated valuations on balance sheets, discussed below. This is not to say that the balance sheet is not useful. It still serves as a practical method of categorizing the resources and obligations of a business as well as determining its financial strength. Just realize that the balance sheet is not always a good indicator of the valuation of the company.

Valuation analysis is the topic of Chapter 17 and is particularly significant in raising money as well as attracting quality employees. The greater the valuation, the less of your company you will have to give up to raise money, and potential employees will be more interested in equity participation or stock options.

USES OF ACCOUNTING IN PREPARING YOUR BUSINESS MODEL

Despite its limitations, accounting is indispensable in preparing your business model. The key to any business is making money. In other words, a business has to attract sufficient revenues to sustain a profit through one or more of the following activities:

- The sale of goods and services
- Advertising
- Subscriptions
- Commissions from other sources
- Joint venture agreements

These potential sources of revenue should be combined with your market research (based on Chapter 7) to determine whether your business has a viable business model. Although Internet commerce is predicted to increase, so will the competition from aggressive start-ups as well as from established businesses that begin to pursue viable Internet strategies.

Financial Components of the Business Model

The construction of a viable business model requires an understanding of basic accounting concepts as well as primary accounting statements. Some of the basic terms of accounting are as follows:

- *Assets:* resources that have future benefits and are owned or controlled by a company.

- *Capitalization ratio:* total liabilities plus the owners' equity divided by the owners' equity that provides a quick overview of how leveraged a business is.
- *Cash flow statement:* the presentation of cash inflows and outflows for a particular period of time and grouped into major categories (such as cash flows from operations, cash from investing activities, and cash from financing activities).
- *Expenses:* outflows of resources used to generate assets.
- *Financial flexibility:* the ability of a company to raise cash to expand operations, reduce debt, or pay off shareholders's equity.
- *Income statement:* the matching of a company's sales (accomplishments) with its expenses (effort) or expenses of operation during a particular period.
- *Liabilities:* commitments to pay out assets, generally cash to creditors.
- *Liquidity:* ability of a company to meet its short-term cash needs
- *Owners' equity:* representation of the owners' investment in a business from direct investment, the investment of others, or profitable operations.
- *Pro forma statement:* a financial statement that details the predictions of management.
- *Revenues:* inflows of resources or assets into a business that are generated through operations.
- *Working capital:* a common term that refers to resources of a business— those assets and liabilities used or worked with on a daily basis. Working capital can be a very quick measure of liquidity and is determined by subtracting current liabilities from current assets (Working capital = Current assets – Current liabilities).

The primary financial statements of accounting are the balance sheet, income statement, and statement of cash flow.

Let's examine each of these financial statements.

Balance Sheet

Although the earlier part of this discussion detailed some of the problems with the balance sheet as a measure of valuation, it still provides a quick overview of the financial condition of a company. Simply put, the balance sheet is a snapshot of a business that lists its assets, liabilities, and owners' equity at a particular time. In viewing the balance sheet of a business, you can rapidly assess its financial health and determine the amount of its obligations to creditors.

The balance sheet is built around a basic equation that reflects the fundamental order of the accounting universe:

Assets equal Liabilities plus Owners' equity, or $A = L + OE$

The basic equation $A = L + OE$ is derived from $A - L = OE$, or assets minus liabilities equals owners' equity. This equation should be intuitively obvious: If you subtract the obligations or debts from the assets or resources of a business, you have the net equity of the business. This is similar to a financial statement, where your net worth is equal to your assets minus your debts.

Another way to view the fundamental equation is to consider that assets can be divided between the claims of the creditors and the claims of the owners.

$$\text{Assets} \begin{cases} \text{Liabilities: Claims of creditors} \\ \text{Owners' equity: Claims of owners} \end{cases}$$

Assets. Assets are resources that promise future benefits and are owned or controlled by a company. To qualify as assets, benefits have to be quantifiable. In other words, the amount of the benefits has to be able to be determined with some certainty, which is the reason that financial accounting is so stingy with intangible assets. Assets include the following:

- Cash
- Marketable securities (a.k.a. cash equivalents)
- Prepaid assets: expenditures already made for benefits to be received in one year that would include such items as insurance or professional fees paid in advance
- Inventory: items held for sale
- Accounts or customer receivables: all payments your customers owe

- Intangible assets: assets that lack physical substance but have a high degree of certainty regarding their future benefits. They include patents, franchises, goodwill, trademarks, trade names, secret processes, and organization costs.
- Equipment: all the equipment of the business that you do, or that you might own, including computers, certain personal property, and so on
- Buildings: real estate and other types of property interests
- Other assets: a wide variety of items that may include deferred charges and special assets

Assets are generally valued at their historical cost; in other words, the amount paid for the asset would be the amount listed on the balance sheet. This applies also to intangible assets such as patents, so even though a patent has a huge market value, it would be valued on the balance sheet at the cost involved to obtain it.

The two general categories of assets are current and noncurrent. *Current assets* are cash and other assets expected to be converted into cash in one year and generally include accounts receivable, prepaid assets, and inventory. *Noncurrent assets* are assets that would be held for longer than one year and include buildings, equipment, and intangible assets.

Liabilities. As mentioned earlier, liabilities are claims on assets. They represent probable future sacrifices of economic benefits arising from present obligations to transfer assets or provide services in the future. These obligations include:

- Payables resulting from the purchase of goods and services, such as accounts payable, wages payable, and the like
- Accounts payable: amounts that you owe your trade creditors
- Wages payable: any wages payable to your employees
- Taxes payable: taxes that are due but unpaid
- Long-term debt

Like assets, liabilities may be current or noncurrent. Liabilities such as accounts payable and other short-term payables due in less than one year are considered current. Long-term debt is considered a noncurrent liability, but the portion of the long-term debt due within one year is considered a current liability.

The purpose of classifying assets and liabilities as current or noncurrent is to assist in measuring the performance and condition of a business. For example, working capital is a measure of short-term liquidity that is determined by subtracting current liabilities from current assets. The classification is also important in the preparation of accounting ratios, presented in Chapter 11.

Owners' equity. The final component of the balance sheet is known as owners' equity, which represents the portion of a business belonging to the owners. Another way to consider owners' equity is the owners' equity or net worth in the business after all liabilities have been satisfied. Owners' equity consists of the following components:

- Capital stock: stock valued at the par or stated value of the shares issued. Most securities either have no par value or a nominal par value.
- Additional paid-in capital: amounts paid in over the par or stated value
- Retained earnings: the cumulative earnings of the business

For example, a start-up business funded with the sale of 1,000 shares of common stock with a $.10 par value for $20 per share would have the following owners' equity:

Capital stock ($.10 par value)	$ 100
Additional paid-in capital	19,900

Any earnings of the business would flow into retained earnings. In the event of losses, the retained earnings would appear as a cumulated deficit.

Figure 10.1 is an example of the balance sheets of Loislaw.com, an online provider of legal research to attorneys and other legal professionals.

In reviewing Loislaw's balance sheet, note that most of the assets of the company are divided between its initial cash infusion and the legal databases, which are listed on the balance sheet at their costs; other assets include prepaid licenses and fees. Liabilities are generally split between deferred revenues, accounts payable, and long-term debt. In addition, owners'

FIGURE 10.1   Loislaw.com Balance Sheets
•••

LOISLAW.COM, INC.
BALANCE SHEETS

	December 31, 1997	December 31, 1998	June 30, 1999	June 30, 1999 Pro forma (note 7)
			(unaudited)	(unaudited)
ASSETS				
Current assets:				
Cash and cash equivalents	$ 3,233,172	$ 99,042	$ 3,274,946	$ 3,274,946
Accounts receivable	896,001	1,540,052	1,889,283	1,889,283
Prepaid commissions	114,936	311,394	748,193	748,193
Prepaid software license	—	96,958	271,125	271,125
Other current assets	19,654	138,811	631,302	631,302
Total current assets	4,263,763	2,186,257	6,814,849	6,814,849
Databases, net (notes 3 and 5)	6,460,547	10,766,967	15,672,406	15,672,406
Property and equipment, net (notes 4 and 5)	501,218	1,446,459	2,931,468	2,931,468
Deferred loan costs	4,528,723	3,992,278	4,017,634	4,017,634
Other assets	544,081	820,721	652,779	652,779
Total assets	$16,298,332	$19,212,682	$30,089,136	$30,089,136
LIABILITIES AND STOCKHOLDERS' EQUITY (DEFICIT)				
Current liabilities:				
Current installments of long-term debt (note 5)	$ 26,443	$ 954,893	$14,557,184	$14,557,184
Accounts payable	1,906,319	2,559,631	3,676,373	3,676,373
Deferred revenues	2,540,459	2,961,067	3,566,185	3,566,185
Accrued expenses	304,708	461,549	557,861	557,861
Total current liabilities	4,777,929	6,937,140	22,357,603	22,357,603
Deferred revenues	981,722	967,046	440,037	440,037
Long-term debt, excluding current installments (note 5)	4,080,941	11,317,631	28,614	28,614
Other noncurrent liabilities	—	170,373	245,938	245,938
Total liabilities	9,840,592	19,392,190	23,072,192	23,072,192
Redeemable equity securities (notes 5 and 7):	11,216,279	11,720,353	25,324,065	4,940,157
Stockholders' equity (deficit) (notes 5 and 7):				
Common stock, $.001 par value	7,180	7,180	8,083	17,049
Additional paid-in capital	415,352	—	1,168,777	21,543,719
Accumulated deficit	(5,181,071)	(11,890,941)	(19,467,881)	(19,467,881)
Treasury stock	—	(16,100)	(16,100)	(16,100)
Total stockholders' equity (deficit)	(4,758,539)	(11,899,861)	(18,307,121)	2,076,787
Total liabilities and stockholders' equity (deficit)	$16,298,332	$19,212,682	$30,089,136	$30,089,136

Source: Registration Statement on Form S-1 filed by Loislaw.com with the Securities and Exchange Commission.

•••

equity includes various redeemable securities. Note also that Loislaw.com had an accumulated deficit, which is not uncommon for start-ups.

Income Statement

The income statement is historical as its main use is to evaluate the past performance of a business. It can also help predict future profitability by analyzing the viability of the enterprise. (As noted earlier, Wall Street is particularly sensitive to the income or earnings of companies.)

The primary difference between the income statement and the statement of cash flow (operating portion) is the use of accrual accounting in the income statement. Accrual accounting measures income and expenses prior to the actual exchange of cash. For example, income is measured when services are rendered or goods are shipped. At that point, a bill is dispatched and the income is booked, creating an account receivable. Expenses are incurred when the liability or obligation occurs, as opposed to when the money is actually paid. The main components of the income statement are as follows:

- Revenues: inflows during a period from delivering or producing goods, rendering services, or performing any other activities said to constitute the ongoing major or central operation of the business
- Expenses: outflows or other using-up of assets or incurrence of liabilities during a period as a result of delivering or producing goods, rendering services, or performing any other activities said to constitute the ongoing major or central operation of the business

Figure 10.2 is an example of an income statement, or a statement of operations.

In reviewing the statement of operations, note that the primary source of the company's revenue is from its sale of CD-ROM products; in fact, its sales of Web-based products are growing rapidly. Its primary operating expenses include the costs of maintaining the legal database, selling and marketing expenses, and general and administrative expenses.

FIGURE 10.2   Loislaw.com Statements of Operations

LOISLAW.COM, INC.
STATEMENTS OF OPERATIONS

	Year Ended December 31,			Six Months Ended June 30,	
	1996	1997	1998	1998	1999
				(unaudited)	
Revenues:					
Web-based products	$ 28,333	$ 208,357	$ 842,112	$ 272,054	$1,171,184
CD-ROM products	1,854,605	3,157,056	3,182,067	1,515,506	1,621,188
Other	—	—	1,000,000	353,090	—
Total revenues	1,882,938	3,365,413	5,024,179	2,140,650	2,792,372
Operating expenses:					
Database costs	1,459,845	1,563,152	2,623,717	1,015,866	2,704,417
Costs of other revenues	—	—	393,357	147,248	—
Selling and marketing	2,152,638	2,363,028	4,606,638	1,902,504	4,320,448
General and administrative	1,524,997	1,535,179	1,977,424	1,023,306	1,708,179
Product development	101,057	86,465	540,866	368,228	333,075
Total operating expenses	5,238,537	5,547,824	10,142,002	4,457,152	9,066,119
Loss from operations	(3,355,599)	(2,182,411)	(5,117,823)	(2,316,502)	(6,273,747)
Other income (expense):					
Interest expense, net	(250,964)	(454,667)	(1,548,931)	(643,290)	(1,308,678)
Other, net	2,644	(6,353)	41,953	1,002	5,485
	(248,320)	(461,020)	(1,506,978)	(642,288)	(1,303,193)
Loss before income taxes	(3,603,919)	(2,643,431)	(6,624,801)	(2,958,790)	(7,576,940)
Income tax benefit	(52,184)	—	—	—	—
Net loss	$(3,551,735)	$(2,643,431)	$(6,624,801)	$(2,958,790)	$(7,576,940)

Source: Information taken from Registration Statement on Form S-1 filed by Loislaw.com.

Statement of Cash Flow

The last accounting statement examined here is actually the most important. As noted, the main difference between cash flow and the income statement is that the income statement uses accrual accounting. Under accrual accounting principles, revenues are recognized when sales are made as opposed to when cash is received, and the same principle applies to the recognition of expenses.

Although the accrual statement is thought to be superior from a reporting standpoint, cash is more important to a start-up. In fact, cash is king. A business can survive many adversities, such as an abrupt change in the market, a new competitor, or some other bump in the road, but no business can survive a lack of cash. The purpose of the cash flow statement is to detail information about the cash receipts and cash payments of the enterprise during a particular period.

One of the grim facts of an emerging business is that it can crash and burn even while turning a profit. Success and growth often strain the cash resources of a business, and it is not uncommon for a new business to outgrow its cash resources. Consequently, all businesses, particularly new businesses, need to focus obsessively on cash.

The statement of cash flow has three basic components:

1. *Operating activities:* transactions in which cash enters into the determination of net income. Cash in and cash out as a result of operations are reported. A net inflow of cash from operating activities exists when cash revenues exceed cash expenditures.
2. *Investing activities:* changes in cash from (1) making and collecting loans to third parties, (2) selling and buying investments, and (3) purchasing and selling property, plant, and equipment
3. *Financing activities:* cash inflow and outflow resulting from changes in a company's debt and equity that would include raising funds from lenders and equity investors as well as repaying those funds

Statement of cash flows from operations. Cash flow from operating activities can be reported in two ways. The first is to simply track the cash in and the cash out. The second way, which is shown in Figure 10.3, is to take net income calculated on the accrual level and then back out the noncash expenses as depreciation and amortization. Next, calculate the impact of changes in working capital on cash. An increase in accounts receivable represents a use of cash and decreases available cash. Reductions in accounts receivable increase available cash. Conversely, an increase in accounts

FIGURE 10.3   Loislaw.com Statements of Cash Flows from Operating Activities

LOISLAW.COM, INC.
STATEMENTS OF CASH FLOWS

	Year Ended December 31,			Six Months Ended June 30,	
	1996	1997	1998	1998	1999
				(unaudited)	
Cash flows from operating activities:					
Net loss	$(3,551,735)	$(2,643,431)	$(6,624,801)	$(2,958,790)	$(7,576,940)
Adjustments to reconcile net loss to net cash provided (used) by operating activities:					
Depreciation and amortization	638,210	645,416	1,361,238	642,836	1,411,375
Deferred tax benefit	(52,184)	—	—	—	—
Loss on disposal of property and equipment	—	—	3,979	—	—
Change in operating assets and liabilities:					
Accounts receivable	(154,920)	(1,025,210)	(758,773)	(368,645)	40,852
Prepaid expenses and other current assets	174,168	(132,655)	(412,573)	(295,774)	(1,103,457)
Accounts payable	1,371,768	(175,172)	823,685	261,211	1,192,307
Accrued expenses	326,070	(132,129)	156,841	(200,669)	96,312
Deferred revenue	1,597,149	1,768,429	405,932	332,176	78,109
Net cash provided (used) by operating activities	$ 348,526	$(1,694,752)	$(5,044,472)	$(2,587,655)	$(5,861,442)

payable also represents an increase in available cash; and decreases in accounts receivable represent uses of cash.

The implications of these calculations for cash flow purposes is that you want to receive your cash as quickly as possible and pay it out as slowly as possible. The idea is to carefully monitor and conserve cash.

Cash flows from investing activities. Cash flows from investing activities, illustrated in Figure 10.4, concerns the long-term investments by the company. It generally involves the effect of transactions on noncurrent assets in the balance sheet and usually includes the purchase or sale of a building or piece of equipment or investments in other businesses.

FIGURE 10.4 Loislaw.com Statements of Cash Flows from Investing Activities

	Year Ended December 31,			Six Months Ended June 30,	
	1996	1997	1998	1998	1999
				(unaudited)	
Cash flows from investing activities:					
Database costs	$(2,741,984)	$(1,972,244)	$(4,769,562)	$(1,793,658)	$(5,737,218)
Purchase of property and equipment	(218,045)	(92,528)	(1,224,665)	(870,359)	(1,668,324)
Decrease (increase) in other assets	8,892	(8,827)	(161,918)	(138,788)	(222,141)
Net cash used by investing activities	$(2,951,137)	$(2,073,599)	$(6,156,145)	$(2,802,805)	$(7,627,683)

Major investments in the case of Loislaw.com included database costs as well as property, plant, and equipment. Because database costs were non-current assets, they were broken out separately from operating activities.

Cash flows from financing activities. The final part of the statement of cash flows is the cash flow from financing activities illustrated in Figure 10.5. Companies can raise money from either equity or debt (see Chapter 15). Overall, the change in cash position is as follows:

Net increase (decrease) in cash and cash equivalents	$(215,867)	$3,131,126	$(3,134,130)	$(2,400,427)	$3,175,904
Cash and cash equivalents at beginning of year	317,913	102,046	3,233,172	3,233,172	99,042
Cash and cash equivalents at end of year	$102,046	$3,233,172	$ 99,042	$ 832,745	$3,274,946

FIGURE 10.5   Loislaw.com Statements of Cash Flows from Financing Activities

	Year Ended December 31,			Six Months Ended June 30,	
	1996	1997	1998	1998	1999
				(unaudited)	
Cash flows from financing activities:					
Repayment of capital lease obligation	$2,406,000 —	(25,183)	(15,385)	(9,967)	(5,910)
Deferred loan costs (note 5)	—	(553,614)	(143,681)	—	(13,273)
Proceeds from sale of Series A convertible preferred stock, net of $237,263 costs of issuance (note 5)	—	2,762,737	—	—	—
Proceeds from sale of Series C convertible preferred stock, net of issuance costs of $624,023 (note 5)	—	—	—	—	8,893,850
Proceeds from notes payable	253,705	6,117,446	8,661,077	3,423,077	9,362,500
Repayment of notes payable	(573,905)	(2,240,855)	(423,077)	(423,077)	(2,050,623)
Proceeds from related party borrowing (note 7)	2,406,944	688,946	—	—	—
Proceeds from exercise of warrants (note 5)	—	—	3,653	—	—
Proceeds from sale of common stock	300,000	150,000	—	—	478,485
Repurchase of treasury stock	—	—	(16,100)	—	—
Net cash provided by financing activities	$2,386,744	$6,899,477	$8,066,487	$2,990,033	$16,665,029

The advantages of analyzing the cash flow statement is to determine whether a company is really profitable or whether it has to borrow to stay alive. Another issue concerns the company's ability to generate cash. A company might throw off a lot of cash even though its income statements indicate it is only marginally profitable. Generally, the true measure of a company's financial health is whether it generates cash from operations. Companies that generate cash are sustainable, whereas those that burn through their cash too quickly could face problems. A company can only finance unprofitable operations for so long.

11

Accounting Analysis: Developing the Financial Portion of Your Business Model

··

"Annual income twenty pounds, annual expenditure nineteen six, result happiness. Annual income twenty pounds, annual expenditure twenty pounds nought and six, result misery.**"**

  Charles Dickens (1812–1870), Victorian novelist

··

"The debt is like a crazy aunt we keep down in the basement. All the neighbors know she's there, but nobody wants to talk about her.**"**

  H. Ross Perot (born 1930), American executive and would-be politician

This chapter examines two important accounting statements in developing the financial portion of your business model: the *initial capital requirement* and the *pro forma cash flow statement*. These statements make up Slide 9 of your e-plan and are designed to demonstrate how much cash is required to launch and sustain your business until you reach a break-even point. This chapter also reviews accounting ratios, which are important indicators of financial health and performance, as well as certain nonfinancial indicators of performance.

DETERMINING YOUR INITIAL CAPITAL REQUIREMENT

The first financial calculation of importance for the start-up is the accurate determination of its initial capital requirement. The goal of calculating your initial start-up capital is to estimate the amount of funds necessary to start, operate, and sustain your business until you reach a break-even point. Initially, funds will be spent on items necessary to "open your doors" and would include set-up costs for site design and e-business architecture. Further uses of funds include the costs of running the business and attracting customers. Finally, the business needs sufficient capital to fund operating losses until it reaches a break-even point and is able to sustain itself. These start-up and operating costs are also known as the "burn rate," which is the amount of cash the business uses each month to pay for everything.

In an ideal world, the initial capital needs of a business would be completely funded at the outset, leaving the owners free to concentrate all of their attention on operating the business and attracting customers. However, this would require an accurate estimation of the initial funding requirements as well as the future financial performance of the business. Such an estimation of future financial performance is determined in pro forma cash flow statements (discussed later in this chapter).

But we don't live in an ideal world, and it is rare for a start-up to accurately estimate and then fully fund its initial capital requirement. For a while, the Internet frenzy did create a fantasy world where incomplete business models received substantial funding. Investors literally threw money at many "business out of a box" dot-com ideas, but such practices have come to an abrupt halt and venture capital is much more difficult to raise.

As a result, start-ups cannot count on the easy availability of capital. They cannot assume they will be able to obtain additional resources if their initial funding runs out. Although venture capital is commonly raised in stages, the business needs to reach its objectives at each stage of funding. Some fledgling companies that failed to reach their target objectives found their funding cut off. (Financing is discussed in more detail in Chapter 15.) The point is to develop a realistic estimate of your initial capital requirement before you seek financing. That way you know how much to ask for.

Failing to properly estimate the start-up funds needed can shut your business down before it even gets off the ground. Many budding entrepreneurs, in their zeal to get started, often overlook or underestimate items in determining their initial capital requirements, which can lead to a shortfall of cash at a critical time. Not only must the *amount* of the various expenses be properly estimated, but it is also important not to overlook any expense *category*. It is often the missing cell in a spreadsheet that can lead to later problems.

Twelve Components of Your Initial Capital Requirement

1. *Information technology costs:* the costs associated with the construction and maintenance of your site as well as your e-business architecture.
   a. Web site design: funds necessary to create and design your company's site.
   b. Web site maintenance: fees necessary for the ongoing hosting and maintenance of the site, including whatever services are not done in-house.
   c. E-business architecture (see Chapter 6): includes all costs needed to transform your business from e-commerce (simply selling goods off of the Web) to e-business, which integrates all aspects of the Internet into your operations. The more the Internet is integrated into the business, the better the benefits for the business. The e-business architecture should support the integration of business processes and the interaction between customers and suppliers. From a customer standpoint, the following are goals of your e-business architecture:
      i. Convenience: The experience needs to be convenient for end users. Customers want your site to be the entire solution for their problems. In addition, full integration in the supply chain is important; order entry, fulfillment, and delivery must be smooth and seamless.
      ii. Speed: In the online world, there is no such thing as too fast. Customers expect a response that is not only instantaneous but also accurate.
      iii. Personalization: Customers want to be treated as individuals. It bears repeating that your business needs to be responsive

and customer centered, which requires your business to have the necessary attributes for outstanding customer service. Another important quality is the empowerment of customers to transact business themselves.

d. One of the advantages of a start-up over an existing business is that the start-up doesn't have to reconstruct its business architecture; it's much easier to begin from the ground up. The types of software applications to be considered are those that have outstanding supply chain management, selling-chain management, operating resource management, and customer relationship management. Many of these applications are offered by large software vendors such as Oracle, IBM, and SAP.

    i. Customer relationship management (CRM): Integrated customer relationship applications combine sales, service, and marketing into one application. These applications assist in the acquisition of new customers and increase the profitability of existing customers.

    ii. Selling-chain management: These applications manage the order and acquisition process throughout the entire sales procedure and range from identifying potential customers to preparing orders. Issues to be addressed in the order acquisition process include fully understanding customers' needs, configuring cost and price, allowing changes in the order, and bidding the product to potential customers.

    iii. Enterprise resource applications: These include some of the processes listed above and integrate the management of the enterprise from the front to the back.

2. *Prepaid items:* prepaid deposits on real estate leases and equipment rentals. Some real estate leases require a deposit to cover several months. In hot Internet locales, such as the San Francisco Bay Area and East Coast, lease expenses have skyrocketed to as much as $45 per square foot. In addition, it is not uncommon for lessors to require as much as 12 months' rent in advance in addition to stock warrants. Some prepaid items can be quite significant, so you have to accurately determine them in advance.

3. *Leasehold improvements:* remodeling or improvement expenses.

4. *Office supplies and equipment:* items for the brick-and-mortar component of your business, such as stationery, business cards, and basic office supplies. Although many of your office expenses are included under IT costs, don't forget to budget for office supplies and equipment.

5. *Marketing costs:* expenses for direct marketing, print advertising, and other items in the promotional mix. With competition lining up at virtually every space on the Internet, the importance of marketing can't be overestimated. Start-ups have to plan and budget for both online and offline marketing activities. As mentioned earlier, many Internet start-ups are budgeting as much as 70 percent of their initial budget for marketing.

6. *Personnel:* the cost of high-quality employees and the ability to attract and maintain competent individuals that adds value to the company and on which your business will be judged.

7. *Licenses/fees:* the cost of certain occupational licenses, some of which can be significant.

8. *Taxes:* sales taxes, payroll taxes, occupational taxes, and other taxes that affect your business.

9. *Hidden costs:* costs that all businesses have and that you'll have to figure out and budget for.

10. *Inventory:* expenses of a start-up inventory if you sell products directly.

11. *Professional fees:* fees for legal, accounting, consulting, marketing, and other professional services.

12. *Working capital:* the proverbial lifeline for the start-up business. Working capital is defined as the excess of total current assets over total current liabilities. A good rule of thumb is to determine how much working capital you believe you will need and then double it. Every business needs adequate working capital until cash flow is sufficient to sustain operations.

Issues in Calculating Initial Capital

Despite major categories of start-up expenses applicable to all businesses, be aware that every business is unique. Thus, careful research of the costs is required, particularly if a technology process in involved. The technology start-up frequently faces the issue of expense overruns. It is also important to plan for contingencies and obtain reliable estimates for all of the expenses listed above. In preparing your start-up budget, it may be useful to prepare budgets based on different levels of funding.

In addition, you should not hesitate to seek outside assistance in determining your initial capital requirement as well as in preparing your pro forma financials discussed below. A good CPA or business consultant can be of tremendous assistance in the financial area. As mentioned earlier, when estimating start-up capital, every cell of a financial spreadsheet matters, particularly when you forget about it.

The estimation of your working capital—funds used to sustain operations before your business becomes profitable—requires particular attention. After you have estimated your initial working capital needs, compare them with your pro forma cash flow statement. When preparing your pro forma cash flow statement, you should use a range of scenarios based on the likelihood of your business's success. But also be sure that you have the money to sustain your worst-case scenario.

Although your initial capital requirement may appear daunting, it is much better to know your true capital needs up front. That is far superior to underestimating your capital and running out of money. Therefore, be accurate, even conservative, in determining your initial capital requirement.

PREPARING YOUR PRO FORMA CASH FLOW PROJECTION

After you have determined your initial capital share, the next step is to prepare your pro forma cash flow projection. The traditional way to do this is to

- determine your market share on a per customer basis;
- estimate your revenues per customer;
- identify and estimate your expenses per customer;
- determine whether your expenses are fixed or variable costs; and
- estimate pro forma cash flow and your break-even point.

Note that accurately estimating pro forma cash flow can be difficult, even in the most predictable of businesses. Consider, for example, a well-established franchise in a defined market area. In such a case, the franchiser would have plenty of historical information about the business model on which demographic data of the target area could be overlaid. Such an analysis would generally yield fairly reliable results. An entirely new product or service, however, does not have these data to draw on. With no geographical limits, the estimation of market share and resulting financial performance becomes considerably more difficult. In fact, one venture capitalist told me that he and others put very little faith in the estimations of revenue because they are so difficult and unpredictable.

Nonetheless, estimating revenues is not simply a shot in the dark. If you have developed good research methods and understanding about your target market and your competition, you can begin to make educated assumptions to guide the preparation of your business model. Anyone can plug numbers into a spreadsheet. But it is determining the assumptions behind those numbers that requires the effort. The more you know about your business, the better the assumptions you can make. In addition, it is always better to be conservative in your estimation of future performance.

Estimating Your Market Share on a Per Customer Basis

The first step in determining revenue is to estimate your market share. Careful research will assist you in accurately estimating the size of the potential market. Then, estimating your market share involves determining the realistic percentage of the market that you can attract as your customers.

In determining your market share, it is more useful to calculate your share from the ground up as opposed to simply picking an arbitrary percentage of the market. In other words, break down your target market into individual customers and then use the individual customer as a basis or metric for your financial projections.

For example, estimate your projected revenue per customer. Then calculate your projected cost per customer. That will enable you to determine the number of customers you need to break even. (An example of this calculation is provided later in the chapter.) Note how closely related your financials are to your marketing plan. Once you determine the number of customers or transactions required for breakeven or a particular performance level, you need to attract those customers. Is this realistic based on your market research? Have you prepared a plan that can attract the necessary customers?

If your business serves as a conduit or exchange between buyers and sellers, you could use each transaction as a basis or metric. For example, how many transactions would your business process in the first year? What would be the revenue per transaction? Cost per transaction? How many transactions would need to be processed for breakeven?

If, after reviewing your marketing plan, you don't feel you can attract the particular target, then adjust your financials. Also consider the impact of customers who leave. What are your assumptions for attracting new customers? What is your strategy for retaining customers?

As discussed, the e-plan is interrelated and involves constant revision. Changes in your assumptions in one part of the plan makes an impact on others. The main advantage in preparing the e-plan is that it forces you to think through the important aspects of your business model—particularly valuable once you begin operations. Actual data can then be input into your plan and serve as a basis for evaluating your strategy.

A good example of a business that chose a financial metric and then focused relentlessly on it is America Online. Many snickered at the avalanche of AOL disks that seemed to show up practically everywhere. The financial press blasted the marketing efforts as too expensive—more than $100 per customer. However, AOL Chairman Steve Case maintained his focus on attracting new customers because AOL had estimated lifetime revenues per customer to be much greater. This one financial metric (lifetime revenue per customer) propelled AOL's aggressive marketing effort and also its success.

Determining Pro Forma Revenue

Pro forma revenue can be derived, as noted above, by multiplying the number of customers with the average revenue per customer. Following are recommendations for preparing your assumptions when calculating pro forma revenue.

Use a relative range. As stated earlier, estimating revenues is an imprecise process even in a stable environment, such as a well-established franchise in a defined market area. When done in an unstable environment like the Internet, it is particularly difficult to anticipate all the changes. Thus, it is advisable to assemble ranges for a best-case and a worst-case scenario—that is, ranges for the number of customers and the revenue per customer.

Gather as much information as possible. This, of course, was the objective of your market research. If your target market is a particular industry, that industry's trade association often has considerable information on the size of the market and even the size of various market segments. Perhaps there are studies of buyer behavior that could guide you in your estimates. If you're not the first company in your particular space, perhaps you can gather information from direct or indirect competitors, but this information may be difficult to gather if your competitor is not a public company.

Brainstorm potential revenue sources. One of the advantages of preparing projections is that it gives you the opportunity to brainstorm potential revenue sources. Consider every possible way to extract revenue from your product or service. What spinoff products or services could you offer? What alliances or partnerships could lead to additional revenue? Are there additional advertising opportunities? Are there any other ways to create value?

Be conservative in your estimates. It is advisable to be conservative in your estimates of market penetration and resulting revenue. Remember that it takes time for a new product or service to gain acceptance and usage.

Consider external factors that affect revenue patterns. Consider the various external factors that could impact the revenue stream. One factor is seasonality, which has a profound impact on the retail industry. Unless your revenue stream is based on subscriptions, it is rare for businesses to receive their revenues in a completely uniform fashion. Consequently, consider the particularities of your market in calculating your revenue. Avoid straight-lining your accounts—that is, taking one monthly revenue figure and using it for every month.

Update your projections. Because the new economy is a dynamic environment, your projections have to be constantly reviewed and updated to take into account changes in the marketplace. In addition, as your business begins to gather its own historical data, your projections will probably need to be revised.

Use projections as a benchmark. One of the advantages of preparing projections is the creation of a benchmark with which to evaluate your operations. Benchmarking is a process used by management to develop goals, standards, and expectations for the business's financial and operational data. Comparing actual data with your projections is a way to test your assumptions as well as your marketing plan, allowing you to quickly adjust your strategy or tactics.

Determining Pro Forma Expenses

Your pro forma expenses are generally easier to calculate than your revenues. The calculation involves an exercise similar to the calculation of your initial capital requirement and projecting the expenses of your business. It is easier to start on a monthly or per customer basis and then expand your calculations. Many of the recommendations for preparing revenues are applicable to expenses, namely, information gathering, preparing a range of expenses, and considering the impact of change. The following are some additional recommendations to help you prepare your pro forma expenses.

Be inclusive. The flip side of being conservative with your revenues is to be inclusive with your expenses. Because it is the overlooked cell on your spreadsheet that will cause you problems, consider all possible sources of expenses.

Consider external factors. Just as revenues don't occur uniformly, neither do expenses. Consider the various patterns of expenses and how your business responds. Just as you shouldn't straight-line revenues, you shouldn't straight-line expenses. You must be able to fully understand business cycles and anticipate times of additional demands on cash.

Separating Fixed and Variable Costs

Fixed costs are costs that remain constant regardless of your sales volume. They are required to "keep your doors open" and include your rent, IT maintenance costs, debt service, professional fees, salaries, and utilities. They are incurred before a single customer is served. Another term for fixed costs is *overhead.*

Unlike fixed costs, *variable costs* vary directly with sales; they occur only if sales are made. Variable costs are the individual components involved in producing goods and include direct materials and direct labor. Variable costs are more significant in manufacturing and retail than in personal services business and scalable businesses. Scalable businesses are those that can handle considerably larger volumes at only incrementally higher costs—a factor considered one of the main advantages of the Internet. However, even the most refined business models are going to experience some degree of variable costs. Consequently, variable costs may generally be lower for businesses in the new economy, but they are still relevant for calculating breakeven.

Break-Even Analysis

Break-even analysis involves the following four steps:

1. Separate your revenue, variable costs, and fixed costs into separate categories:

$$Profit = Revenue - Variable\ costs - Fixed\ costs$$

To illustrate this analysis, I'll use as an example Loislaw.com, whose financial statements were excerpted in Chapter 10. For the last full year presented, its revenue was approximately $5 million, but because expenses were approximately $10 million, Loislaw.com had a loss of approximately $5 million.

2. Calculate the variable cost percentage as follows:

$$Variable\ cost\ percentage = Variable\ cost \div Revenues$$

Although Loislaw.com's fixed and variable expenses are not broken out in the financial statements, let us assume that its variable cost percentage is 20 percent.

3. Calculate the contribution margin—that is, the amount left after subtracting variable costs:

$$\text{Contribution margin} = 100\% - \text{Variable cost percentage}$$

Because we have assumed that the variable cost percentage is 20 percent, the contribution margin would be 100 percent − 20 percent, or 80 percent.

4. Calculate break-even revenues:

$$\text{Break-even revenue} = \text{Total fixed costs} \div \text{Contribution margin}$$

Because fixed costs would be $8 million and the contribution margin is 80 percent, break-even revenue would be calculated by dividing $8 million by 80 percent for an amount of $10 million. This is approximately the amount of revenue that would have produced breakeven.

In addition to calculating breakeven for revenue, it can also be calculated for volume. When this calculation is combined with your financial metric, it produces breakeven for unit volume.

The steps for calculating breakeven on a unit basis are as follows:

(a) Classify costs as fixed or variable; we assumed variable costs were 20 percent in our example.

(b) Calculate price per unit:

$$\text{Price per unit} = \text{Total sales} \div \text{Number of units sold}$$

From its financial statements, we determined that total sales for Loislaw.com were approximately $5 million for the last full year reported, and it had approximately 7,844 customers. An average price per unit can be calculated by dividing $5 million by 7,844 for a price per unit of $637.

(c) Calculate variable cost per unit:

$$\text{Variable cost per unit} = \text{Total variable cost} \div \text{Total units sold}$$

The variable cost per unit is $1 million divided by 7,844, or $127 per unit.

(d) Calculate contribution dollars per unit:

Contribution dollars per unit = Price per unit − Variable cost per unit
($637 − $127 = $510)

(e) Calculate breakeven for units:

Breakeven = Fixed costs ÷ Selling price per unit − Variable cost per unit

Breakeven for units is derived by dividing $8 million by $510, or approximately 15,686. In this case, units represent customers.

FINANCIAL ANALYSIS

Ratios

Accounting ratios can serve as key indicators of financial performance and quickly highlight selected problems or issues with your business. Ratios compare the relationship of one number to another to provide quick information about the fiscal health of your business. Because the numbers are relevant, ratios are accurate no matter what the size of the numbers involved. They can quickly diagnose problems and point out issues with the business. In addition, ratios can be compared with previous operating results as well as with similar businesses. Ratios are based on the balance sheet and the income statement. There are four major types of ratios:

1. Liquidity ratios: measure the short-run ability of the business to pay its maturing obligations.
2. Activity ratios: measure how effectively the business is using its assets.
3. Profitability ratios: measure the financial performance of the business.
4. Coverage ratios: measure the degree of protection for long-term creditors and investors.

Liquidity ratios determine the ability of a business to pay its current debts.

Current ratio: The current ratio is determined by dividing current assets by current liabilities.

Current ratio = Current assets ÷ Current liabilities

The current ratio is one of the most commonly used indexes of the short-term solvency and financial strength of a business. It predicts the short-term ability of a business to meet its current obligations, or short-term solvency. The lower the ratio, the greater the risk that the business could default on current liabilities.

Quick ratio: The quick ratio is a measure of short-term liquidity.

Quick ratio = Cash or Cash equivalents ÷ Current liabilities

Activity ratios are also performance based. They are efficiency ratios designed to measure some of the specific operating data for the business. Note that some of these ratios, specifically the inventory turnover ratio, are not applicable for businesses that have no inventory.

Accounts receivable turnover: This ratio measures the rate that your accounts receivable are being collected by the business. This ratio is important if you have significant accounts receivable because it determines the number of times that you can collect your accounts receivable. The accounts receivable turnover is determined as follows:

Receivables turnover = Revenues ÷ Receivables

Usually, this is calculated on an annual basis, and, usually, a higher number shows that your receivables are not out of line with your sales.

Inventory turnover: This ratio measures how quickly inventory is sold. It is computed by dividing the average inventory into the cost of goods sold. Then, dividing 365 days by the inventory turnover indicates the average number of days it takes to sell inventory (or average number of days' sales for which inventory is on hand).

Inventory turnover = Cost of goods sold ÷ Average inventory

Inventory turnover is particularly important for e-tailers as the measurement is a staple of the retail industry. Generally, the higher the inventory turnover, the better, because it means the company is selling its products. As this book was going to press, Amazon.com received a negative report from a research analyst at Lehman Brothers, one of the criticisms at the time being that its inventory turnover ratio had declined significantly from the previous year.

Profitability ratios indicate how well the business has operated during the previous period.

Net margin: The purpose of the net margin ratio is to measure profitability at the net profit level. It calculates the amount of net profit produced for every dollar of sales. The net margin of a business is calculated as follows:

$$\text{Net margin = Net profit} \div \text{Revenue}$$

Asset utilization: This ratio measures the efficiency of assets in generating sales. The asset utilization ratio is calculated as follows:

$$\text{Asset utilization = Revenues} \div \text{Total assets}$$

Return on assets: This ratio is similar to the asset utilization ratio but focuses on net income instead of revenue. The return-on-asset ratio is calculated as follows:

$$\text{Return on assets = Net income} \div \text{Total assets}$$

Return on investment: This ratio determines the type of return that owners are receiving for their investment in the business. The return on investment is calculated as follows:

$$\text{Return on investment = Net profit} \div \text{Owners' equity}$$

Coverage ratios are computed to help predict the long-run solvency of the firm.

Debt-to-total assets ratio: This ratio provides creditors with an idea of the ability of the business to withstand losses without impairing creditors.

Debt to total assets = Total liabilities ÷ Total assets

Debt-to-worth ratio: This ratio measures financial risk—the percentage of debt load for every net worth dollar of the business. The debt-to-worth ratio is determined as follows:

Debt to net worth = Total liabilities ÷ Owners' equity

Performance Measures

Considerable discussion has taken place in the business and accounting community over instituting a new type of measure for business. Although the financial measures discussed above can be helpful, they are lagging indicators as opposed to leading indicators; and it is preferable for a business to focus on measures that are leading indicators. Many of these measures, such as customer acquisition rate, pace of innovation, and customer satisfaction, fall outside traditional areas of financial measurement.

One of the ideas behind performance measurement is that generally what gets measured is what gets done. Therefore, instead of relying solely on financial indicators, perhaps a business would want to implement measures of nonfinancial areas such as business operations, marketing, and sales and management. The reason is that these areas can also have a significant impact on the performance of the organization. Ideally, a business will isolate five to ten key performance measures and then track them to gauge performance.

Performance indicators should be structured in the context of a company's overall goals, business strategies, and specific objectives. While developing new performance indicators, companies should consider a number of objectives:

- Make strategic objectives clear.
- Look for core processes.

- Focus on critical success variables.
- Signal where the performance is headed.
- Identify which critical factors warrant attention.
- Use the indicators as a basis for rewards.

What many firms need is a performance indicator system that focuses *externally* on the business environment and its changing demands and on market/customers and competitors, and focuses *internally* on key non-financial indicators (such as market penetration, customer satisfaction, quality, delivery, flexibility, and value) as well as more typical financial measures (such as sales growth, profits, return on investment, and cash flows).

Another way of looking at performance measurement is to consider that a business is a function of its activities. The traditional paradigm of measuring profit for a business is as follows:

$$Revenue - Expenses = Net\ profit$$

However, this measurement does not consider what could have been made had the business operated more efficiently. As stated above, every business is made up of activities, and the profit of a business depends on how well the employees consistently perform specific activities. In addition, they generally perform their best when the measurement of activities is clear. So the key is to develop performance measures for key activities. Although a full discussion of performance measurement is beyond the scope of this book, next are some examples to consider in the operation of your business.

One key measure of marketing effectiveness is revenue per customer. Because it is much more expensive to attract new customers, focusing on increasing revenues from sales to existing customers can have a significant effect on the bottom line and could be a key indicator that is integrated with CRM technology. But revenue per customer is just one type of performance measure.

Other types of marketing standards measure the increase in number of customers served as well as the frequency of customer contact. The business would then measure such activities as the cost of goods sold, overhead, lifetime value of a customer, cost of customer acquisition, leads generated, and the conversion ratio. In measuring such activities, the business could determine how market or customer focused it is. For manufacturing concerns, business rework and returns could be key operating measures. For management, employee turnover ratios and employee satisfaction levels are key measures.

The main question is whether your business is keeping score. Generally, businesses that keep score for critical functions perform much better than companies that don't. That, in a nutshell, is what performance measurement is all about—an effective way of keeping score for your business. So when you sit down to plan the goals of your business for the 21st century, don't rely on 20th-century techniques. Use your version of performance measurement to ensure that your business is operating effectively, because what gets measured is usually what gets done.

chapter 12

The Fundamentals of Internet Law

With its rapid development and adoption, the Internet has proven to be as much a challenge to the legal establishment as it has been to the business establishment. As technology expands and evolves, the legal system must run to keep up. Common law and statutory doctrines that have developed over time must now contend with a whole new type of busi-ness that was not remotely envisioned even five years ago, much less a century ago.

The best way to describe the state of the legal system regarding the Internet is its uncertainty. Every day it seems the Internet is raising new issues involving some previously ingrained part of the law, ranging from personal jurisdiction to electronic signatures, the applicability of the Uniform Commercial Code, and online transactions. Individual states are trying to plug the holes where they can, and most have adopted legislation authorizing electronic signatures. As this book went to press, Congress authorized electronic signatures on a national level. Congress has also begun to take action on various fronts, such as protecting children online and prohibiting cybersquatters. Courts have become jammed with lawsuits raising a host of new issues about electronic commerce and intellectual property. Many judges and legislators will probably learn more about technology than they had planned.

A federal judge in San Francisco recently announced her plan to log on to the Internet to check out Napster, a popular Web site for trading MP3 digital music files, which can be downloaded by users to create their own CDs. The reason for the judge's plan was not because the judge was a music buff, but rather because she had been assigned to hear the lawsuit by the Recording Industry Association seeking to shut the site down. Both the Recording Industry Association and the heavy metal group Metallica have sued Napster for copyright infringement. As this book went to print, the Ninth Circuit Court of Appeals had issued a stay on the judge's order to close down Napster.

Another judge had to make a determination of whether nude postings on the Internet with the Playboy bunny symbol violated Playboy's signature trademark. The learned jurist concluded that the Internet postings happened to be similar to Playboy's business of featuring nude women in conjunction with the Playboy trademark. Consequently, the judge sided with Playboy and ordered the site to cease its postings with the Playboy trademark.

In this climate of uncertainty, start-ups are advised to err on the side of caution and seek proper legal advice. The legal issues in this chapter are the major ones to keep in mind. Some are Internet legal issues such as privacy and intellectual property. For purposes of the e-plan, any significant intellectual property issues could be outlined on a miscellaneous slide.

PRIVACY

Privacy has emerged as a highly controversial issue on the Internet from a marketing and public relations standpoint as well as from a legal angle. Much of the concern from consumers and the Federal Trade Commission center on innocuous-sounding computer files called "cookies," which are placed within the individual computers of visitors to particular sites. Ostensibly, cookies are designed to track user behavior within a particular site, thus allowing the site to customize its offerings based on users' needs and preferences. This doesn't seem so bad—somewhat like a salesperson that already knows you and your tastes.

However, enter the Net, and particularly Internet ad specialists like DoubleClick, Inc., Real Media Inc., and MatchLogic. The ad specialists assist companies that want to advertise on other sites, especially larger companies that advertise on thousands of sites. Instead of having to insert all the ads themselves, the companies rely on the networks to store and place the ads. The cookies assign unique tracking numbers to site visitors and allow the ad network to track individual meanderings throughout cyberspace.

The issue of cookies became particularly controversial when Double-Click Inc. purchased Abacus Direct, the repository of names, addresses, and buying habits of millions of consumers. DoubleClick planned to combine this information with the data that it already had on Web sites that people visit. This information would have provided it with users' names and addresses along with details of all the sites they visited and purchases they made online.

This intended use of cookies proved so controversial that it prompted a probe by the Federal Trade Commission as well as a lawsuit by the state of Michigan. The resulting firestorm led DoubleClick to back off from its previous plans to combine the information despite having paid $1.7 billion in stock for Abacus.

The basis of the legal right to privacy begins with the United States Constitution. Although the Constitution does not contain the word *privacy*, the Supreme Court has found privacy to be protected by various penumbrae within the Constitution and the Bill of Rights. The Supreme Court has upheld that this right to privacy applies to individuals in such cases as abortion as well as to their homes in case of unreasonable search and seizure. However, it is less clear how such privacy rights would apply to an ISP server located outside of your home.

This constitutional vagueness, however, has not deterred lawyers from piling on lawsuits against DoubleClick and offering creative theories of recovery in addition to an expansive range of companies that might be liable. For example, some lawsuits claim that DoubleClick violated the Electronic Communications Privacy Act, which makes it unlawful to intercept any wire, oral, or electronic communication. Lawyers allege that this wiretap provision applies to DoubleClick because the company is accumulating data about Web users without their consent while the users are "communicating" on a Web site. In addition, everyone in the chain of information who passed it on to others would be liable also, which would include the various companies that use DoubleClick for their advertisements.

For example, Intuit, the financial software developer and manufacturer of Quicken, is being sued by users of its Quicken.com Web site for the unauthorized release of certain personal information. Apparently, individual financial information that was input into the site's loan calculation tools was gathered up in cookies and sent off to DoubleClick. To top it off, the Federal Trade Commission is investigating the use of cookies, and Congress is considering legislation in the area.

Consequently, it is advisable for start-ups to avoid this legal quagmire by adopting and following a comprehensive privacy policy. Lawyers are much like investors in that both are attracted to lucrative businesses. But instead of investing money in the business, some lawyers seek to separate the business from its money.

Some large companies such as IBM and General Motors are preventing the ad networks from collecting information from cookies. The companies are doing this by contracts or, in the case of GM, by the use of its own cookie, which keeps its data segregated and private. Above and beyond the legal obligations, you want to be sure that your customers are comfortable in using your Web site.

Below is a sample privacy statement for reference. Note that the statement addresses cookies and pertains to a site that still uses cookies. The statement also contains certain language that distances itself from the cookies of ad agencies but will not necessarily guarantee insulation from any privacy-related lawsuit. You should consult with your counsel regarding the state of the law concerning cookies. Instead of cookies, you may want to consider having customers register voluntarily.

Sample Privacy Statement

Netco.com Privacy Statement

Introduction

Netco.com, Inc. (Netco.com), has created this privacy statement in order to demonstrate our firm commitment to privacy issues. The following discloses the information-gathering and dissemination practices for Netco.com.

At Netco.com, we are very committed to your privacy, so here is our PRIVACY PROMISE TO YOU: Netco.com will never sell, exchange, or release any of your individual personal information to a third party without your express permission.

Information We May Collect

From time to time, we may conduct online surveys or run a contest for promotional purposes, during which we may ask users for contact information (like e-mail addresses) and demographic information (like zip codes, age, or income level). We use contact data to send consumers information about our company and, of course, to notify people if they win the contest.

We understand, though, that you may want to participate in these surveys or contests but may not want us to send you e-mail. Accordingly, as part of these surveys or contests, we will always give you the option of declining to receive information from Netco.com. Hey, if you don't want to receive e-mail, just let us know, and we won't send it. Simple as that.

Like other Web sites, your IP number is visible to us when you visit our Web site. What is an IP address, you may ask? It is a number automatically assigned to your computer whenever you're connected to the Internet. Your IP number is visible to most of the Web sites that you visit. Don't worry, though; at Netco.com we only use IP numbers to help diagnose problems with our servers and to administer our Web site. Other sites may use your IP number for marketing purposes. We don't.

From time to time, we may share with third parties aggregate information—such as how many of our users are men, or how many Netco.com consumers search on flyfishing-related topics, or how many are Yankees fans. Such information will not contain any personal identifying information.

Cookies

Like many sites, Netco.com uses cookies. Cookies are data files that are stored on your computer. They contain identification information that enables us to see how our users are interacting with our site and how frequently they are returning. Cookies do not contain any personally identifiable information.

We use cookies for the benefit of our users. Cookies let us know if we have repeat visitors (a strong indication of happy consumers) and if we are delivering a quality product to our consumers. We also use cookies to identify which sites our repeat visitors are coming from so that we can place more of our online advertising on these sites. Essentially, it is an anonymous way to survey how we are doing and to look for other consumers who we think will like our site.

Also, speaking of cookies you should know that Netco.com employs an outside ad company to display banner ads on our site. These ads may contain cookies. Cookies from banner ads are collected by our ad partner and are used for tracking the performance of banner ads. Netco.com may not have access to this information.

If you do not want to accept cookies from Netco.com or other sites, your browser software should allow you to not accept cookies. Look in the Preferences (Netscape) or Internet Options (Microsoft Internet Explorer) feature to do this.

Links to Other Web Sites

Netco.com contains many links to other sites. Netco.com is not responsible for the privacy practices or the content of such Web sites. Netco.com does not share any of the individual personal information you provide Netco.com with the sites to which Netco.com links, although Netco.com may share aggregate data with such sites (such as how many people use our site). This includes other third-party sites on the Internet for which Netco.com provides search services.

Please check with those sites to determine their privacy policy.

Opting Out

If you do not wish to receive future communications from us, you can send an e-mail to privacy@Netco.com.

Contacting Netco.com

If you have any questions about this privacy statement, the practices of this site, or your dealings with Netco.com, please contact webmaster@Netco.com.

INTELLECTUAL PROPERTY

Another hot legal area related to Internet commerce is intellectual property. This onetime sleepy area of the law has been jolted awake by the Internet. Financial columnists and e-business leaders are sounding alarms at the way business process patents are issued, and the Patent and Trademark Office has vowed a review. Another development concerns the unauthorized replication of music among users; although once largely ignored by the recording industry, it has now become a major issue. The digital age has vastly expanded the scope of copyright violations from simply borrowing a friend's CD and making a usually inferior copy. Now, a wide range of music is posted on such sites as napster.com and is available for anyone to download in a high-quality format. As discussed above, the recording industry and individual artists have come out swinging with lawsuits, but the practice of posting music on Web sites is now so vast that the industry has a lot of holes in the dike to plug.

The intellectual property concerns of start-ups, however, are not always related to headline-grabbing lawsuits. The first major concern of start-ups is to protect their own intellectual property, which includes patents, copyrights, and trademarks. Intellectual property is behind much of the wealth creation in the new economy, and intangible assets can be an important part of a start-up's worth. A company that is not careful in protecting its own intellectual property could very well lose an important competitive advantage.

The second concern for start-ups is they may unlawfully—and often unwittingly—be infringing on the intellectual property of others. Your company needs to maintain its focus on attracting and retaining customers and does not have time to be distracted by lawsuits.

The three basic forms of intellectual property—patents, trademarks, and copyrights—are particularly relevant to the Internet.

Patents

A patent is the grant of a property right to an inventor by the Patent and Trademark Office. Patents are generally issued for

- new and useful industrial and technical processes;
- machines, devices, and apparatus;
- articles of manufacture;
- compositions of matter; and
- any new and useful improvements to the above.

A patent lasts for 20 years from the date that the application was filed in the United States; patent grants are effective only within the United States and U.S. possessions. Generally, a patent is a right that excludes others from making, using, or selling the invention covering the claims of the patent.

A patent is generally the highest level of protection given to intellectual property in the United States and involves a fairly extensive process. Patents are not just simply filed but rather "prosecuted" by the inventor or their counsel. Each application is assigned to a patent examiner, who determines whether the patent is a new and unique process. The application has to set forth the invention with particularity so that the Patent Office can determine what the patented process is. Often, counsel has to modify the application to fit within the stringent patent requirements.

Controversy has recently arisen over patenting certain business processes. In July 1998, the Court of Appeals for the Federal Circuit confirmed that computerized business processes can be patented. In August 1998, Priceline.com was granted a patent on its reverse auction method, which allows shoppers to offer to buy goods from merchants at a particular price; the merchants then decide whether to accept the bids. In September 1999, Amazon.com was granted a patent for its "one-click" process for Internet purchases. As its name suggests, the process allows consumers to purchase goods from the site with a single click. Shortly after obtaining its patent, Amazon.com sued Barnesandnoble.com for allegedly infringing the one-click patent. Most recently, Intouch sued Amazon.com for violating its patent governing the way that consumers sample music online. Intouch patented the preview of music products over the Internet, which was an extension of its earlier patent pertaining to kiosks in music stores.

Now Amazon.com CEO Jeff Bezos and others are calling for an end to patenting business processes. The Patent and Trademark Office is apparently listening and announced an overhaul of the way that it awards patents for online processes. The office pledged to add additional steps in the review process, but it is not certain at this time what impact a change will have on business process patents.

The good news is that the apparent change could make the Net more democratic. The bad news is that it will be harder to patent business processes that could lead to a competitive advantage. This, however, does not mean that start-ups shouldn't consider patents for any new and useful processes. Any process thought to qualify should be reviewed by an intellectual property attorney. The company should also consult with their counsel in the event its practices might potentially violate another patent.

Trademarks

A trademark is generally a distinctive symbol, picture, or phrase that sellers use to distinguish and identify the origin of their products. One of the best-known examples of a trademark is the Coca-Cola logo. The service mark is the same as the trademark except that it identifies and distinguishes the source of a service as opposed to a product. The terms *trademark* and *mark* are commonly used to refer to both trademarks and service marks. In addition to distinctive symbols, trademarks may also be granted to distinctive and unique packaging, color combinations, building designs, product styles, and overall presentations.

The source of trademark law is the Lanham Act in addition to the statutory law and common law of particular states. Like patents, trademarks are registered with the Patent and Trademark Office. The approval process for trademarks is much like that for patents, and the person filing has to convince the office of the mark's uniqueness.

One way to view a trademark is as a shortcut by which purchasers can select a particular product based on their recognition of its symbol as well as its goodwill. In this case, the trademark is generally used to distinguish your goods, guarantee consistent quality, and advertise and sell your products.

Trademarks have a direct impact on domain names. Currently, to acquire a domain name, you have to represent that the name, as used, will not infringe any third-party rights, which include such intellectual property rights as trademarks and service marks. Just because you acquire a particular domain name is no guarantee that you won't be sued because of the underlying trademark. Unlike trademarks, domain names don't indicate the type of goods and services. Consequently, it is advisable to obtain both a trademark and a domain name.

Early case law in the area established that trademarks do protect domain names. One of these cases was *Princeton Review* v. *Kaplan.* When Princeton registered its own domain name, it also registered the name *kaplan.com,* possibly to annoy its major rival in the standardized test review market. However, under the kaplan.com address, the *Princeton Review* created a site with phony comparison charts and recommended that people enroll in the Princeton course. The arbitration panel found that Princeton had obtained the name in bad faith and ordered Princeton to relinquish the site.

Another case involved music station MTV. An employee of MTV registered MTV.com and developed the site with the network's permission. When the employee left MTV, he refused to relinquish the domain name to MTV. The court analogized domain names to mnemonic alphanumeric telephone numbers (e.g., 800-CALLATT), which allows consumers to locate businesses with easy-to-remember names. Remember that the IP address for most sites is a series of numbers, such as 56.789.321, but to make Internet addresses more user friendly and easier to remember, domain names were used. Consequently, the court held that the MTV trademark was protected in cyberspace.

An inherent conflict between trademark law and domain registration nonetheless still exists. Generally, trademark law allows different parties to register a particular mark if they're determined to be in noncompeting and different areas of the marketplace. Under domain name registration, however, only one entity is able to have the domain name address. Consequently, this area is still evolving and the recommendation is to protect your domain name like a valuable piece of property. Obtain the assistance of competent counsel and seek trademark protection in addition to registering your domain name.

In the fall of 1999, Congress addressed the issue of cybersquatters—those who register the trademarks of well-known companies as their own domain names. Sometimes these individuals have attempted to sell the names back to their original owner for a profit. The new law prohibits the bad-faith registration or use of Internet domain names that infringe an original owner's trademark and provides for statutory damages as high as $300,000. The law also offers protection to individuals with famous names.

The new provisions assist in bringing claims against cybersquatters because actual harm need not be demonstrated. The law further allows an action directly against a site, even if the owner cannot be found, and it provides for a streamlined dispute resolution procedure for domain name challenges. Such actions are enforced through the Internet Corporation for Assigned Names and Numbers (ICANN), which is located in Marina Delray, California. Under these procedures, you can engage an arbitrator for a fee of approximately $1,000.

Some have claimed that the law went too far. Take the case of the Los Angeles resident who registered veronica.org after his infant daughter. Archie Comics threatened to sue, claiming that it had the right to Veronica as well as Archie, Jughead, and Betty. Although the comic book company did back down, it could have sued the owner of Veronica.org for damages under the new law.

Copyrights

Copyright is a form of protection that is provided to authors of original works, which include literary, dramatic, musical, artistic, and certain other intellectual works both published and unpublished. A copyright protects the form of expression rather than the subject matter of the writing; and copyright protection attaches from the time the work is created into a fixed form.

One exception for copyright protection is the fair use doctrine, which allows limited copying of copyrighted works for the purpose of teaching and research, including criticism and news reporting. Some of the issues to consider in deciding whether copying in fair use depends on the purpose and character of the use, the nature of the copyrighted works, and the amount of the portion used. Note that fair use is a limited exception and does not allow indiscriminate copies.

The term of a copyright is 70 years after the death of the author. The nature of the Web has made copyright violation relatively easy; for example, cutting and pasting information from a site into another document or Web page generally violates the copyright. In addition, the simple act of viewing pages on the Web actually creates a copy within your hard drive, but there is an implied license to make those copies. A copyright is not violated until you actually misappropriate Web content. Generally, the content of databases is not subject to copyright protection unless there are original features about a particular database.

Common misconceptions about copyrights abound. To begin with, the material does not have to bear a copyright notice to be protected. Most nations, including the United States, follow the Berne Convention, which is an international agreement that provides that anything published after April 1, 1989, can be copyright protected, even without notice. People can also violate copyright law even if they don't charge for, or profit from, the copyrighted material. In addition, just because something is posted to Usenet or is in the public domain doesn't necessarily mean that it is not subject to copyright protection. Like other areas of intellectual property, copyright law can be complex and requires the advice of counsel.

CONTRACTS

Another traditional area of law with broad application to the Internet is contracts, which are created regularly in commercial transactions. Contracts are the body of law that regulates the rights and responsibilities between parties and are generally enforced according to their meaning and intention. First, you want to be able to enforce contracts you've made with others, so you must be aware when you have entered into an enforceable contract. Second, you want to be sure that a contract says what you think it says, which is why it is advisable to have your attorney review the terms of your major contracts.

Generally speaking, contracts are promises that the law will enforce by providing remedies if a promise is breached. There are generally two primary elements in a contract for it to be enforceable:

1. *Agreement between the parties.* A contract is not in place until the parties have reached a mutual agreement, and for there to be a mutual agreement, a valid offer has to have been made and accepted. The person making the offer must objectively intend to be bound by its terms, the terms of which must be reasonably certain and communicated to the offeree. A communication that is uncertain or merely an expression of opinion is generally not an offer. The offer also has to be definite

and must identify the parties, the subject matter, the quantity, the consideration to be paid, and, finally, the time of performance. The traditional common law of contracts has become more flexible with the use of the Uniform Commercial Code, under which only the price and quantity have to be agreed to in order to have a binding contract.

2. *Consideration.* Consideration is the bargained-for elements of a contract, which are usually the goods or the funds exchanged. Consideration does not always mean money; a promise to perform services is valid consideration.

Some contracts are required to be in writing. They include the following:

- Contracts involving interest in land
- Contracts that cannot be performed within one year
- Collateral contracts in which a person promises to insert the debt of another, or a guarantee
- Sale of a good for more than $500
- Contracts hiring agents

The writing need not necessarily be long and detailed. The law only requires a written document to contain the essential terms of the parties' agreement. Any writing will suffice, and that includes letters, telegrams, invoices, sales receipts, checks, handwritten agreements, and e-mail messages.

The law does require that a written contract be signed by the party against whom enforcement is sought. Many states have adopted laws permitting electronic signatures and Congress recently passed a bill giving online signatures the same validity as a signature in pen and ink.

BUSINESS ORGANIZATION

One of the first issues that must be addressed by a start-up is the particular form of organization in which business will be conducted. This is another area for which it is advisable to consult with professional advisors, such as your attorney and CPA. The major forms of organization are sole proprietorships, partnerships, corporations, and limited liability companies.

Generally, the following factors are important in deciding the form of organization you choose:

- Tax implications
- Owners' liability and assurance that personal assets are insulated from business liability
- Convenience and ease of use
- Opportunity for growth
- Cost to maintain

Other factors to be considered in choosing an ownership structure include (1) whether owners are other business entities; (2) projected profits and losses; (3) whether the owners are active or passive participants; (4) whether prospective owners will make different types of contributions; (5) family status of owners; (6) form of compensation; and (7) distribution of capital. These many factors illustrate that the choice is not necessarily an easy one but requires careful deliberation and professional assistance.

Sole Proprietorships

The main advantages of a sole proprietorship are that it is simple, flexible, inexpensive, and provides centralized management. The disadvantages are the unlimited liability and lack of continuity of existence. The sole proprietorship simply treats the business as an extension of the owner for tax and legal purposes; its income is the same as the owner's, and the owner is liable for all of its debts and obligations. Although most businesses are still conducted through sole proprietorships, the form cannot support a growing enterprise.

Partnerships

The advantages of partnerships are that they are flexible and simple. Unlike sole proprietorships, however, a partnership is a separate entity. The main disadvantages of partnerships are the unlimited liability and lack of continuity of existence.

Under the law of most states, partnerships are separate legal entities that can hold title to personal real property and transact business in the name of the partnership. From a taxation standpoint, partnerships don't pay federal income taxes. Rather, the income and losses of partnerships flow through to the individual partners' federal income tax returns. The partners have a right to participate in management, share in profits, collect compensation, and be indemnified. After termination of a partnership, the partners are entitled to have their contributed capital returned to them. The partners also have a right to information and the right to an accounting.

Besides regular partnerships, there are also limited partnerships. A limited partnership is a special form of partnership that has both limited and general partners. General partners invest capital but also manage the business and are personally liable for partnership debts. Limited partners invest capital but don't participate in management and are not personally liable for partnership debts beyond their capital contribution.

Corporations

A corporation is a separate legal entity created according to the laws of the state of incorporation. As such, it is considered an artificial person who is able to own property, enter into contracts, sue, and be sued. Advantages of the corporation include limited liability, centralized management, and certainty in the law.

The main disadvantages of the corporation are a degree of complexity and double taxation of profits; profits are taxed at the corporate level, and shareholders also pay taxes on their salary (if employees) and dividends. The S corporation is a form of corporation with a flow-through formula similar to a partnership, but S corporations are limited to 75 shareholders and face other restrictions.

Limited Liability Companies

A limited liability company (LLC) is a new form of business entity that combines the tax benefits of partnerships with the limited personal liability of corporations. Started in a handful of states, the LLC has swept across the country with amazing speed. Its tax structure is very similar to that of the general partnership. Although there was initial uncertainty as to how limited liability companies would be taxed, the Internal Revenue Service ended the uncertainty in 1997 with "check-the-box" regulations. Now, LLC owners can indicate if they want to be taxed as a regular corporation, a sole proprietorship, or a partnership.

Currently, the LLC is very popular for start-ups because of its flexible structure, simplicity, and tax advantages. However, an LLC is generally not a good vehicle for a public entity because its flow-through tax structure can create considerable tax complexities for its public owners. Consider that owners of shares of corporations are taxed on dividend distributions, which are relatively simple to report on tax returns. However, LLC distributions pass on all of its tax attributes to its owners (e.g., depreciation and capital gains and losses) and can require more extensive reporting on individual tax returns.

chapter 13

Finalizing Your E-plan

"It is a bad plan that admits of no modification."

Publilius Syrus (43 B.C.), Latin writer

Now, it's time to prepare your e-plan. Following is a checklist of the e-plan slides.

I. **Slide 1—Company Name**
   A. List the domain name of your company.
   B. Elaborate on the following points in the written part of the e-plan:
      1. Legal form of the business
      2. Brief company history
      3. Development stage of the company (e.g., start-up, short operating history)

II. **Slide 2—Mission Statement**
   A. Set forth the mission and vision of the company.

III. **Slide 3—Management Team**
   A. Present an organizational chart of your key management team and a brief explanation of their experience.

B. Elaborate on the following points in the written part of the e-plan:
   1. Discuss the management team members in greater depth, including their experience, background, responsibilities, and any unique skills, and can also include copies of their résumés.
   2. List members of the board of directors and advisory board.
   3. List your attorney, CPA, and other consultants you plan on using.
   4. Discuss any planned hiring additions.

IV. **Slide 4—Market Analysis**
   A. Describe your target market, which includes its size, growth rate, and any particular segments of interest.
   B. Discuss the general condition of your target market, such as whether it is highly fragmented, inefficient, and so on.

V. **Slide 5—Industry Analysis**
   A. Present a more detailed discussion of your particular industry, including its market chain or value chain, major suppliers and customer groups, and competition.
   B. Identify your target market.
   C. Elaborate on the following points in the written part of the e-plan:
      1. Prepare a competitive matrix profile identifying existing and potential competitors.

VI. **Slide 6—Market Opportunity**
   A. Describe the current pain of the market and how your product or service helps to alleviate that pain.
   B. Discuss the particular benefits offered to customers.

VII. **Slide 7—Solution**
   A. Describe how your product provides the solution to the marketplace.
   B. Elaborate on the following points in the written part of the e-plan:
      1. Distinguish your service/product from others in the marketplace.
      2. Detail the need that your product fulfills.

VIII. **Slide 8—Marketing Plan**
   A. Present the overall strategy for marketing your product or service to your target market.
   B. Discuss any unique marketing advantage that you have.
   C. Elaborate on the following points in the written part of the e-plan:
      1. Analyze particular market segments and present a profile of the target customers.
      2. Discuss how you will capitalize on the uniqueness of your product or service.
      3. Describe your promotional mix, mentioning both offline and online promotional activities, including
         a. public relations,
         b. advertising,
         c. sales promotion, and
         d. direct marketing.
      4. Elaborate on any assumptions that you will make with your marketing plan.

IX. **Slide 9—Financial Portion of the Business Model**
   A. Present your pro forma cash flow statement.
   B. Discuss your breakeven in terms of the most suitable financial metric (e.g., customers, transactions).
   C. Elaborate on the following points in the written part of the e-plan:
      1. Detail your assumptions and provide any supporting schedules behind your pro forma cash flow statements and breakeven analysis.

X. **Slide 10—Valuation Analysis**
   A. Present the valuation of your company based on the most appropriate financial analysis.
   B. Elaborate on the following points in the written part of the e-plan:
      1. Detail your assumptions and provide any supporting schedules behind your valuations.

XI. **Slide 11—Miscellaneous**
   A. Present any relevant issues to the business such as the following:

1. Discuss issues related to product development.
2. Present any legal issues regarding the product or service as well as copyrights, patents, trademarks, and licenses.
3. Describe any research and development activities that are in progress.

EXAMPLE OF MEDSUPPLY.COM (SEE SLIDES)

A sample e-plan for you to review as an example is for a company entitled MedSupply.com. The company is developing and implementing an online business-to-business e-commerce marketplace for the purchase and sale of medical and nonmedical products, supplies, and equipment used by alternate site, hospital, and other health care providers. The company will aggregate both purchasers and suppliers to create an efficient, secure, and real-time exchange for the large and highly fragmented health care industry. Such services and information will more efficiently and effectively manage the business.

The services offered:

- Procurement: automates the purchasing and requisition process.
- Management: inventory management, contract compliance, physician and procedural cost data, and product marketing data.
- Selection: access to superstore where purchasers can evaluate a broad range of products from manufacturers and distributors.
- Resource center: provides current information on innovative surgical products.

SLIDE 1   Company Name

MedSupply.com

SLIDE 2   Mission Statement

- **Become the leading online marketplace for medical products, supplies, and equipment.**

- **Provide comprehensive services to address entire health care procurement process.**

SLIDE 3 Management Team

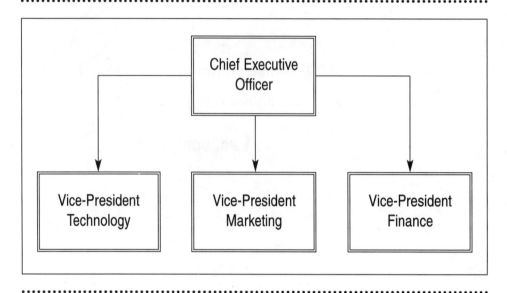

SLIDE 4 Market Analysis

- **$150 Billion World Market for Medical Products**
- **Annual Growth Rate 6% to 7%**
- **United States segment of that marketplace is $60 billion to $80 billion**
- **Market highly fragmented**
- **Competition from e-commerce providers with online marketplace**

SLIDE 5   Industry Analysis

- **Highly fragmented industry**
- **0,000 manufacturers**
- **100 distributors, various integrated delivery networks, and numerous group purchasers**
- **Supply chain serves**
  - 60,000 alternate site facilities
  - 6,000 hospitals
  - 600,000 physicians
  - 185,000 physician groups

SLIDE 6   Market Opportunity

- **Independent study determined that supply chain costs of distributing medical products totaled approximately $ 3 billion annually.**
- **$11 billion of such costs could be eliminated by more efficient sharing of information, management of orders, and movement of products.**

SLIDE 7 Solution

- **Business-to-business e-commerce marketplace for the purchase and sale of medical and nonmedical products, supplies, and equipment.**

- **Aggregate purchasers and suppliers for efficient, secure, and real-time exchange for highly fragmented health care industry.**

SLIDE 8 Marketing Plan

- **Provide solutions for industry**
- **Strategic alliances within industry**
- **Aggressively promote brand**
  - advertising
  - participating in industry events/trade shows
  - targeted promotions
  - public relations

SLIDE 9   Financial Portion of the Business Model

- **First-year pro forma**

- **Financial metric**
  - 1% per transaction
  - 3,200 customers (first year)
  - heavy spending on marketing to establish brand name

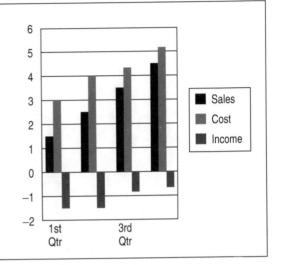

SLIDE 10   Valuation Analysis

- **Revenue Multiplier**   **($250M)**

- **Net Present Value**   **($75M)**

- **Size of Market**   **($60B to $80B)**

- **Market Value**   **($1B)**
  - based on number of transactions
  - compare with other publicly traded companies

chapter 14

Confident Execution: Performance Strategies for the Entrepreneur

"Nothing in this world can take the place of persistence. Talent will not; nothing is more common than unsuccessful people with talent. Genius will not; unrewarded genius is almost a proverb. Education will not; the world is full of educated derelicts. Persistence and determination alone are omnipotent. The slogan "press on" has solved and always will solve the problems of the human race."

Calvin Coolidge (1872–1933), 30th American president

Given the very competitive online world and new economy, product life cycles have shrunk considerably and competitive advantages have practically evaporated with the intense rate of change and competition. Much of your success will depend on how well your company can perform in the marketplace. In previous chapters, we discussed planning your venture, but effective planning is just one part of the equation. Another part is confident execution, the ability to act decisively and effectively to implement your e-plan so that you can stay ahead of your competitors.

Although the ideal e-business is digitized from front to back, people are still its most important resource and often the critical distinctive factor in the venture. Their performance, both individually and collectively, will determine the ultimate success of the company. Therefore, it is important that the entire team perform as effectively and confidently as possible in moving the company forward. As noted, there's no monopoly on good ideas in the new economy, so it's not uncommon for many different companies to emerge and attack the same market space at the same time. Generally, the company that executes better will win.

PERFORMANCE STRATEGIES

The performance strategies discussed below have evolved from the peak performance and self-help strategies made popular in the latter part of the 20th century. One of the forerunners of this self-help movement was Dale Carnegie, who pioneered self-development programs that enhanced personal interaction skills. His classic book *How to Win Friends and Influence People* was a precursor to many of the relationship skills and personal effectiveness programs today. Since Carnegie, there have been numerous other self-help gurus. Dr. Wayne Dyer informs us how to be a "no-limit" person. Tony Robbins advocates the use of neurolinguistic programming, or NLP, as a way to more effectively communicate with others. Dr. Stephen Covey instructs us about the seven habits of highly effective people. Deepak Chopra equips us with strategies to combat aging and tap into the collective wisdom of the universe.

Much of the material espoused by these self-help gurus as well as other motivational speakers is based on timeless wisdom, management development strategies, and common sense. The authors put their own spin on the material, some more unique and successful than others. One problem that struck me with some of the self-help strategies was that they were often too simplistic as well as overhyped. Problems don't just disappear because you have a good attitude. You will not become wealthy and successful simply by repeating a certain mantra to yourself every day. Success will not happen by simply visualizing it. Although all of these are important attributes of outstanding performance, there are other necessary qualities and steps.

There is no easy formula for success. Behind every great success is discipline, focus, and, of course, work. That being said, certain qualities, many of which are espoused by the self-help gurus, *can* contribute considerably to your performance and success. I discuss them individually below.

Perseverance

The reason I opened this chapter with the quotation by Calvin Coolidge on persistence is because of its extreme importance to overall success. Few notable accomplishments have ever been achieved without some setbacks, failures, and bumps in the road. Few quality businesses have ever been built without a dogged and dedicated effort. Although vision and focus are important for entrepreneurial success, perseverance is the glue that holds them all together.

One of the fables of the new economy is that success is easy. Although some of the early Internet successes seemed to experience phenomenal success overnight, the effort and the challenge involved should not be minimized. Some early high fliers were veterans of other businesses. Others had been associated with various business failures. For example, entrepreneur Jay S. Walker experienced several business failures before he founded Priceline.com, which pioneered the use of the reverse auction model for selling goods on the Web. As discussed in Chapter 8, the reverse auction model allows consumers to bid on items, such as airline seats, that various venders can review and decide whether to accept. Although Priceline.com has experienced its ups and downs, it is a major Internet company.

Another way to view perseverance is the ability to persist despite massive rejection. One of the better self-help books, *The Road Less Traveled*, begins with the phrase "Life is difficult." Likewise, competing in the new economy is difficult. Entrepreneurs should anticipate considerable rejection from various sources, ranging from investors to potential customers and employees. It is rare that start-up operations proceed exactly as planned. The successful entrepreneur has to be able to withstand all of the rejection and press on in the face of inevitable setbacks. Just because you don't win every battle doesn't mean you can't ultimately win the war. Realize there will be failures along the way.

Actually, failure is relative; you never fail until you throw in the towel and quit. Persistent people simply keep at it until they succeed. There are some notables, such as famed inventor Thomas Edison, who made a career of failure. Edison made several thousand attempts before developing the lightbulb. When asked how he felt about his numerous false starts, Edison claimed that he didn't fail but simply discovered thousands of ways of how not to invent the lightbulb. The key is to learn from your mistakes and not to quit too soon. During difficult and frustrating times, focus on solving the problems instead of lamenting the situation. Success could often be just around the corner.

A poignant example of someone who did stop short of eventual success was John Kennedy Toole, the author of the Pulitzer Prize–winning novel *A Confederacy of Dunces*. Kennedy wrote the novel in the 1960s while a young man. He was not successful in having the novel published and became deeply despondent; and tragically, he later committed suicide. His mother, Thelma Toole, however, persisted on her son's behalf to have the novel published and eventually persuaded famed author Walker Percy to review the manuscript. Although skeptical at first, Percy became quickly captivated by the novel's bizarre humor and helped to get it published. It later was awarded the Pulitzer Prize for fiction. The book was a success all along; unfortunately, the author stopped trying before its phenomenal success was realized.

Vision

Vision is fueling the new economy. It started with the development of the personal computer and other information technology. Later, it evolved into a digital framework that is transforming commerce and communications at a rapid speed.

In turn, the new economy is fueling vision. The immense scalability of digital ventures has fueled visions and dreams that are massive in scope. Few entrepreneurs today fail to dream about becoming the market leader, but the vision should not be couched in terms of present markets and applications. Rather, the goal of visioning is to provide newer and improved structures and value.

One of the misnomers about visioning in the new economy is that a technical background is necessary for success. Although a technical background is helpful, many of the leaders of the new economy are decidedly nontechnical. Instead, they are focused on the applications and practical uses of a particular technology.

One example is Steve Case, the chairman of America Online. Case readily admits that his focus was not technology. Instead, his vision was viewing technology through a "consumer prism" and was based on the fact that real people lead real lives. Many technically savvy people scoffed at AOL and its remedial treatment of the Internet. Case realized that the average person knew nothing about high-speed Internet connections but simply wanted an easy path to the online world. Case provided that path, and over 20 million customers are using the AOL thoroughfare.

The consumer prism applies to business as well as consumer markets. What subtle or unmet needs could you address? Keep visioning your target market though a consumer prism.

Expertise

Expertise or knowledge is obviously the main currency in the information economy. First and foremost, you need to be an authority in your chosen segment of the market. Note that I did not say well read or extremely knowledgeable, but an *authority*. According to venture capitalist Jim Smith of Mohr, Davidow Ventures, entrepreneurs need to be experts in their economic space. Your first priority in acquiring knowledge or expertise is to completely master your space.

Knowledge demands on the entrepreneur are particularly fierce, and it is often difficult to handle the pertinent flow of information relevant to your business. Undoubtedly, you are besieged by a constant barrage of information. It seems that trade journals, magazines, newspapers, newsletters, and similar sources of information come cascading over people's desks on a daily basis. And that's not even counting the online world—with its infinite amounts of electronic information. For entrepreneurs, the challenge is to keep current in their field of business without being overwhelmed or distracted.

I know about being overwhelmed by information firsthand, as I must confess that I am a recovering information addict; my addiction started quite innocently and then got quickly out of hand. In response to solicitations, I ordered a few books here and a few magazines there, resulting in even more solicitations I couldn't resist. Before long, I'd filled up all my bookcases, my closets, my attic, and then my parent's attic. Eventually and fortunately, I was able to gain control of the situation with the following advice I share with you.

Be selective. Remember that you can't possibly read everything, so be selective in your choices. Focus on the sources of information that are most important to your business—and even be selective within those sources. No one ever said you had to read a magazine cover to cover. Look at the table of contents and decide ahead of time which articles are most important. Read those carefully and then skim the rest. Usually, your trade periodicals are more important than general business news. Rank in order of importance the information that you can get to and ignore the rest.

An advantage of being selective about material you read is that you force yourself to focus on the items that truly matter. You may come across an important article that you want to save for future reference. Technology has made such information storage a lot easier and leads to my second suggestion for conquering information overload.

Leverage technology. An important development for business owners is digital technology, which permits the conversion of photographs or articles into a digitized format for easy storage and retrieval. Digital cameras can now store photographs in your computer. Scanners, which were prohibitively expensive not that long ago, can be used to scan and save articles and photos in your computer.

For those who like to save articles or other information, the scanner is indispensable. Improved optical recognition processes allow material to be converted to your word processor. For the information that you obtain directly from the Internet, use the cut-and-paste functions to store it in your word processor rather than printing the articles out. Take advantage of the digitized format and avoid paper wherever possible. (Don't let this ease of use lure you to violate copyright law, however.)

Leverage your time. My final suggestion is to take advantage of downtime by leveraging your time. One way to do this is by listening to books on audiocassettes; in fact, most of the books I get through, I listen to on tape. Listening to audiotapes is an outstanding way to leverage time because you can listen while you are driving, exercising, on an airplane, or even relaxing. You'd be surprised how the time accumulates and how much you can learn during these listening periods. Another way to leverage your time is to use your downtime productively. Waiting at the doctor's office or getting your oil changed are chances to keep up with information, so take it with you and take advantage of downtime.

Courage

Courage is closely related to perseverance and involves continuing on under adverse circumstances—it's also known as facing down and surviving the "Dark Night of the Soul." There are countless stories of start-ups that had to survive many brushes with extinction and were propelled on by the valor of their owners. Competing in the new economy is not for the faint of heart.

Steve Case is a prime example of courage too. At a recent convention, I heard AOL Chairman Case describe his "Dark Night of the Soul" with America Online. At a time of considerable criticism of AOL's operations and expensive marketing tactics, Case received a phone call from Redmond, Washington, that often struck fear in the heart of technology companies. On the other end of the phone was Bill Gates. Case recounted that Gates expressed an interest in acquiring America Online, adding that Microsoft would either "buy AOL or bury it." As it turned out, Microsoft did neither. But it required considerable pluck on the part of Case and AOL to stare down what at the time was an ominous threat.

Another display of courage that has never been chronicled in the media involved Internet start-up NetEx and its founder Greg Meffert. NetEx is a leading provider of document encryption software for e-mail delivery that originally started as Imaging Technology Solutions (ITS) and was engaged in document imaging and management. Chapter 6 mentions Meffert's first crisis when his investors tried to buy him out and how his programming staff rallied around Meffert with his ending up buying out the investors.

Meffert's next challenge was to expand the company beyond consulting projects and retail shrink-wrapped versions of his document management software called Zydeco. The software provided the bridge between document scanners and financial software for managing and storing financial records. Meffert was able to raise part of the money he needed from Advantage Capital and found the remaining $3 million from an unlikely source, actress Sandra Bullock. Bullock happened to be in New Orleans and was looking for a technology-related venture to invest in. She met with Meffert and reviewed his product; the next day her financial advisors called him and scheduled dinner. Meffert showed up thinking that her financial advisors wanted to meet him, but the event turned out to be a closing dinner where he was presented with a check for $3 million.

ITS quickly sold 50,000 copies of Zydeco and appeared in *Inc.* magazine's list of fastest-growing companies. However, production and marketing expenses were eating deeply into cash reserves. To make matters worse, Visioneer, one of the leading scanner manufacturers at the time, rebuffed Meffert's offers for any type of strategic alliance. Instead, it sought to develop its own product to interface directly with financial software. Although Visioneer's product was not as sophisticated as Zydeco, it confused consumers and crimped Zydeco's marketing efforts. Then, a leading financial software developer filed suit against ITS. Already reeling from high distribution costs, dwindling cash, and a confused market, when Meffert realized he didn't have the resources to fight the suit and continue selling Zydeco, he decided to pull the plug on the software operation and sought to refocus his company on the Internet. Corporate clients that used his document-managing software particularly liked one feature that enabled them to e-mail documents easily. With the growing popularity of the Internet, Meffert saw an opportunity in the encryption of e-mail documents.

Meffert had run through his initial capital with Zydeco, and his investors were not happy. He pared his expenses to the bone and was sustained only by month-to-month advances from Advantage Capital and Bullock. Working practically alone, Meffert struggled to perfect his document encryption software while trying to raise additional funding. Several promising financing arrangements fell through. One venture capital firm backed out when it realized he was headquartered in New Orleans, which was apparently too far from Austin, Texas, the closest location of its other funded start-ups. With Bullock and Advantage Capital growing increasingly antsy, Meffert was introduced to Silicon Valley veteran Jim Clark, the founder of Silicon Graphics, Netscape, Healtheon, and MyCFO. Clark had received his master's degree in engineering at the University of New Orleans and maintained ties to the city. He became interested in NetEx and wanted to invest, but the conditions of the term sheet he faxed were quite stringent.

Although Meffert's equity position would be drastically reduced, he felt he had no choice but to accept the offer. Then, Clark abruptly changed his mind when he found out that Sandra Bullock was one of the initial investors. Apparently, the successful and hardened Silicon Valley operator became skittish at the prospect of offending a popular Hollywood actress.

NetEx was finally able to hook up with Deutsche Banc Alex. Brown for its financing and transportation giant TNT as a business partner. The company is expanding rapidly and its prospects are promising.

Effectiveness

In today's hectic world, entrepreneurs are constantly challenged by time demands. Entrepreneurs seem to be at war with time, and each day brings another battle with the crushing demands of the business. People scurry to get things done as quickly and efficiently as possible, but efficiency is not always the answer. Instead, it is preferable to be *effective* in handling business matters. Efficiency can be thought of as doing things right, whereas effectiveness is doing the right things. It does little good to do efficiently things that don't need to be done at all.

No one explains the principal of effectiveness better than noted author and economist Peter Drucker, who is regarded as the father of modern management, whose book on the subject is aptly titled *The Effective Executive*. Although nearly 40 years old, the book is timeless in its wisdom and practical advice.

The bad news, according to Drucker and others who have researched this area, is that people are generally not nearly so effective as they can be, but the good news is that effectiveness can be learned. The major key to effectiveness is proper time management. Time is the one true scarce resource. All of us get the same amount of time. We cannot produce any more of it, and once it is spent, we can't get it back. Proper time management can be broken down into three steps.

1. *Prioritize:* Determine those tasks that are most important to your business and then rank them in order of priority so you can focus on what is most important. According to the Pareto principle, we derive 80 percent of our results from 20 percent of our activities. Wilfredo Pareto, a 19th-century

Italian economist, stumbled across the principle while measuring patterns of wealth and income in England. He found that the majority of wealth went to a very small percentage of people. Even more significant was a predictable mathematical relationship, which was that 20 percent of the population enjoyed 80 percent of the wealth. Pareto began studying it and found the 80/20 pattern to be practically everywhere he looked: 20 percent of customers produced 80 percent of sales, and 20 percent of sales produced 80 percent of profit and so on.

The Pareto principle is one of the most important guides in the field of management today. Because time demands are so overwhelming, it is important to concentrate on activities with the highest payoff. You seldom will complete all the items you want to; the practically infinite demands on business owners can crush the most zealous workaholic. Therefore, prioritize your business activities and focus on that magic 20 percent, which produces 80 percent of the results.

2. *Log your time:* Management consultants have recommended logging your time for at least a week to determine how you spend your time. People are often shocked to find they spend the most time on the least-productive activities. For example, corporate executives are often surprised to discover how little of their time is actually spent in strategic planning activities. The time log can be used to redirect your activities or even eliminate or delegate them.

Logging your time is a good way to determine whether you're spending your time on what you have determined to be higher-payoff activities. Are you focusing on that important 20 percent or are you allowing yourself to be distracted by less valuable uses of your time?

3. *Schedule blocks of time:* Notice I said "blocks" of time, because the effective individual needs to have disposable time available in fairly large chunks. This is also known as consolidating your time. Despite all the technological advances, important tasks require adequate time. How often do we rush through something and make a mistake that causes us embarrassment and, yes, even more time to resolve? Allow adequate time to *complete* your priorities. We know how much time can be wasted by constantly stopping and starting an activity. Block the time and finish it. And remember that sometimes you have to take the time to make a point with

coworkers; a casual conversation in the hall doesn't have nearly the impact of a focused meeting where a topic is properly considered.

Scheduling blocks of time is not always easy. It often requires determination and even cooperation in holding your calls and visitors. Sometimes it's easier to schedule uninterrupted periods at home. Ideally, you want to use the 80/20 principle to determine those critical activities for which uninterrupted planning time is necessary. Not all management decisions and business problems are created equal. The key is to devote the necessary time to the important decisions.

Planning

Implicit in the term *effective* is the practice of planning your activities ahead of time. Planning is one of the corollaries of effective management and involves setting forth different goals and objectives. Planning can be thought of as establishing the direction for your business and your life and then following through. Your e-plan should be used as a guide to follow through the implementation of your strategy. If your business strategy is going to be executed in a consistent matter, break the strategy down into activities and then schedule the activities. To make your e-plan into an action plan, I suggest the following four steps:

1. Go through your e-plan, note your strategy, and break out your strategy items into separate activities.
2. Once you have made a list of all activities, schedule a time to do them, and then proceed to do them.
3. As you develop other strategies with your e-plan, go though the same process: break out the strategies into activities, and then schedule the activities and do them.
4. Use your e-plan to keep track of any new strategies and the activities necessary to implement them.

Although this system of setting and following through on your business plan goals and activities can be tedious, it is not particularly complicated.

Your main challenge is to establish a system to keep track of your plans, strategies, and activities.

An important corollary to effective planning is to not delay on important items. Learn to do the important things *now!* We all have a tendency to delay projects that strike us as either difficult or intimidating. If there is someone important that you need to contact, don't delay—do it now. If you blink, a competitor could get there ahead of you.

Balance

In addition to working hard, you also need to establish balance in your life. Balance replenishes your energy and restores a sense of perspective. Activities that assist in maintaining a balance include such things as recreation, your important relationships, a regular spiritual practice, proper health and nutrition, and a good attitude. Balance can help you withstand the slings and arrows of outrageous fortune and continue on during times of turbulence.

Recreation can provide a sorely needed break from the daily grind. Although hard work is essential, so is scheduled relaxation. Ideally, your recreational activities should be things that you most enjoy.

Another aspect of balance is tending to your significant relationships. Don't let work completely overshadow the important people in your life. Success doesn't mean that much if you don't have special people in your life to share it with.

Advocating a regular spiritual practice might seem out of place in a business book. Although the Internet is vast, the universe is even vaster. Therefore, it is important to have a regular practice that puts you in touch with your spiritual side and provides renewal. Deeprak Chopra recommends the use of a regular spiritual practice to tap into the collective wisdom of the universe.

Many use organized religion as a means of engaging in a regular spiritual practice. The organizational structure and fellowship help to guide their spiritual renewal. Others approach it from a more individual perspective. What is important is taking the time to contemplate or meditate and put yourself in contact with a Higher Power and those portions of yourself and the world that are most significant. A regular spiritual practice can help rid your mind of clutter and negative thoughts. It can sustain you, particularly during times of high stress. Not only can a regular spiritual practice quiet the mind and produce inner peace, but it can also produce the strength to draw from during times of adversity.

Personal health and fitness are also aspects of balance that should not be overlooked. Everybody, even the young, needs to properly address diet, exercise, and nutritional needs. A healthy diet leans to protein and complex carbohydrates and away from fats and refined sugars; in other words, more fruits, vegetables, lean meats, fish, poultry, and less fatty foods and candy. In addition, it is also wise to avoid excess caffeine or alcohol and refrain from tobacco use. Regular exercise includes both aerobic and strength-conditioning activities. Engaging in one or both forms of exercise for 45 minutes three times a week can produce significant health benefits. Note that unlike the promising e-business, exercise benefits are not scalable, tending to level off after moderate use. So unless you are planning to be a professional athlete, you can get most of the benefits of exercise in less than three hours a week. In addition, all of us need a certain amount of rest to function as well as we could. Determine the amount of rest that you need and resolve to get it.

The final type of balance is emotional balance, remaining cool during times of pressure. In the competitive new economy, entrepreneurs need to carefully manage their emotional state. Many balancing activities discussed above will help you remain emotionally grounded during turbulent times. One critical aspect of your emotional base that cannot be overstated is your *attitude*. People with positive self-expectancy or an optimistic attitude tend to respond better to adversity. People with a negative or pessimistic outlook simply don't respond as well.

Maintaining a positive attitude depends on the way you cope with adversity. Coping behaviors can be divided into two types: control oriented and escape oriented. Escape-oriented coping is generally negative and involves lamenting any setback; it includes worrying or obsessing on a problem and can even lead to substance abuse. On the other hand, control-oriented coping behaviors are more positive and are centered on finding solutions to problems. In other words, focus on the good of a situation and the steps needed to address it. Control-oriented coping and perseverance often go hand in hand. Those who can bounce back from short-term defeats with a new approach are those who can press on. Resolve to turn challenges into opportunities. Don't dwell on your failures. Learn from them and try again.

••

"Advance confidently in the direction of your dreams. Live the life that you have imagined.**"**

Henry David Thoreau (1817–1862), American writer

Confidence

Confidence may be thought of as a composite of the other performance strategies described in this chapter. In essence, confidence is based on the *belief* that you will ultimately succeed. This belief may be based on your planning, expertise, vision, and effectiveness, although it is natural to harbor doubt. First-time entrepreneurs wonder whether they can make it. Even those who have succeeded in the past wonder whether they can pull it off again.

Like effectiveness, confidence can be a learned behavior. If you don't *feel* particularly confident, start *acting* confident. Part of your confidence can be based on your mastery of a particular market. Another part can be based on your faith and belief that you will be able to achieve your goals. Everyone is naturally afraid of failure. But remember the earlier discussion on perseverance. Failure occurs only when you say it does; so simply refuse to fail. Most of the historical research by the Small Business Administration and other sources indicates that approximately one in five business start-ups fails. Ninety percent of business failures can be traced to poor management and undoubtedly apply to companies in the new economy, so no one should be especially surprised when Internet businesses fail. However, my experience indicates that if you plan carefully, execute confidently, and learn from your mistakes, you have at least an even chance of succeeding. It might not be as soon as you'd like, but that is the price of success. All in all, those are not bad odds. Believe that you are doing everything in your power to achieve success. In many cases, the people that succeed are not that much different or better than the ones who fail. It is often the little things, the marginal things, that make the critical difference between success and failure. Focus on doing that little bit extra, push a little harder for new opportunities, and, most of all, stay that much more attuned to your customers.

15

The Financing Hurdle: Overview of Business Finance

"Money doesn't talk, it swears."

Bob Dylan (b. 1941), singer, songwriter

"Yes! Ready money is Aladdin's lamp."

Lord Byron

"For the love of money is the root of all evil."

Holy Bible (I Timothy 6:9)

That available opportunities for financing a start-up today are promising does not necessarily mean that it is easy to get financed. Raising money for the new and unproven business can generally be quite difficult, the odds quite daunting. Much of the popular press perpetuates the myth that businesses are like hamburgers—they can be started and flipped at a moment's notice. But the path from start-up to going public can be winding and treacherous. There are several stages of financing before a company can issue its shares to the public, although today's new economy has compressed the time for a start-up to become a public company into a matter of months.

In some cases this compression has created enormous short-term wealth and propelled some Internet pioneers into instant market leaders. In other cases, some not-ready-for-prime-time companies have been put in the public arena far too soon. Being publicly traded can provide a company a heady experience, but the scrutiny of public markets can be brutal, particularly for those companies still refining their business model. It's a good idea to know what you are doing before stock analysts start nosing around your operations.

One of the downsides of the financing market is that it is notoriously fickle. Business models considered hot one day can run cold the next. Perceptions about a particular industry or space in the market can change on a moment's notice. As noted, the B2C sector of the Internet economy was very hot in the early part of 1999; one venture capitalist even referred to it as "business out of a box." Consumer plays in virtually every sector of the retail market were being generously financed. However, just as quickly as a window of opportunity opens, it can also close, as many of those planning Internet ventures discovered.

Take the case of Pupule Sports Inc., an online women's sports news and shopping site. Its heartbreaking experience with the changing winds of Silicon Valley venture capital was chronicled in *The Wall Street Journal*. Apparently, Pupule did just about everything right in staking out its claim to women's sports products. Its founder, Laura Jarrell, ran a successful outdoor-gear store in downtown Palo Alto. She attracted such impressive investors as the former head of 3Com and struck alliances with former tennis great Billie Jean King. Prominent women's sports commentators contributed to the site as did Briana Scurry, the goalie of the World Cup–winning U.S. women's soccer team. But Pupule's one mistake was not raising sufficient funds in the beginning. They stopped at $750,000 of seed money and decided to grow the company more before seeking venture capital when the market suddenly turned, leaving the company unable to raise additional funds.

Souring on a particular space is closely related to downturns in the stock market, particularly the Nasdaq. Much of the venture capitalist funding of business start-ups is related to the success of related businesses in the public market (see Chapter 1). Venture capitalists that are bullish one day can quickly become bearish and vice versa. Consequently, timing plays a critical role in funding a start-up. This, however, does not mean that timing should totally guide your business model. In other words, don't simply base your entire model on what is currently hot in the world of finance. It might not be tomorrow. Although financing trends are important considerations, they should not be the sole determinant of your business model. Instead, you want to scour the market for the best business opportunity in terms of market need, potential return, and your understanding of the particular space.

It is not unusual for entrepreneurs to build successful businesses around their own interests. Their interest in a particular subject leads them deeper and deeper and creates a higher level of understanding and insight. Although you can outsource much of the expertise you need, as a founder you need to be an expert in your economic space. Your interests and expertise should play a bigger role in selecting your business model than what's attracting the buzz at the time. The perception of the financing community toward a particular business model can change by the time you've printed out your plan.

Although venture capital can assist a business tremendously, it is not indispensable; Microsoft, for example, did not use venture capital. There are many ways to finance your business; the key is to be creative and persistent. A viable business that has been carefully researched and is based on a sound business model has a reasonable shot at being funded. Just because some of the purportedly smart money passes on your idea doesn't mean it's an invalid business concept. Bessemer Venture Partners at one time had a listing on its Web site of all the successful businesses that it had passed on. Among them were Compaq, eBay, and Federal Express. So don't be deterred by rejection from financing sources. In fact, expect some.

FACTORS IN OBTAINING FINANCING

Business plan. The first step in obtaining financing is a carefully prepared business plan, which, of course, is the major focus of this book. Not all financing sources want your entire plan initially. I hope your e-plan format provides a basis and framework to respond to requests by financing sources.

Your format, however, is secondary to your business model. Financing sources want a compelling model backed by the team that can execute it. The more convincing you are about your model and your team, the easier it will be to obtain financing. Promising business models attract the necessary attention, but these models need to be well researched and achievable.

Persistence. Nowhere is persistence more important than in obtaining financing. With competition for financing so fierce, you must be persistent in attracting the attention of investors, who are bombarded with business plans and ideas. You need to somehow be insistent without being annoying in obtaining their attention and interest.

You need to also be dogged in approaching funding sources in addition to venture capitalists. Not everyone you contact is going to think that your business is as promising as you do. In fact, I've said you must expect some rejections. Consider carefully the feedback you receive; some of it could be extremely useful constructive criticism. Certain criticisms of your idea may save you from going down the wrong path. Your initial idea, properly revised, could easily be refashioned into a viable business. Viafone, a wireless Internet service, was initially rejected by prominent venture capitalists Draper Fisher Jurvetson. After Viafone revised its business model, it was accepted for funding. On the other hand, some suggestions might not be valid. Don't let a few negative opinions discourage you. Investors are not infallible. Everyone has his or her own opinions and biases. The key is to find the right investor or funding source that is committed to your business and will best help it.

Obtaining financing can be a frustrating process but also an enlightening one. You must develop a plan for obtaining financing and then follow it. Both this chapter and Chapter 16 should help you develop a financing plan.

Creativity. Another requirement for obtaining financing is to be creative. Creativity goes hand in hand with persistence. Start-ups are seldom financed from one source; their bootstrap financing frequently comes from a multitude of sources that include both debt and equity. Be original in searching out different financing sources as well as choosing the proper mix of debt and equity. Sources of financing may be as traditional as conventional bank loans or as nontraditional as money advanced by suppliers and affiliates.

Knowledge. The final requirement for raising funds is to be knowledgeable. The primary goal of this chapter and Chapter 16 is to educate you about the various forms of financing so that you can fund your venture.

Risk/Reward Ratio

An important concept during the financing process is the risk/reward ratio, according to which, both risk and reward increase proportionately. In other words, as the risk to an investor increases, so should the available rewards, a principle supported by many individual as well as professional investors. On one end of the risk/reward ratio is the venture capitalist and other equity investors. The venture capitalist is betting money on perhaps the riskiest stage of the business. Such investments involve a brand-new company with a new product and a new market. Consequently, venture capitalists demand a higher reward or return on their investment (at least 33 percent per year) because the risk is higher. On the other side of a risk/reward ratio is the commercial bank. As a general rule, commercial banks don't invest in start-up companies; they are much more conservative and have little tolerance for risk. They seek out established companies with an existing cash flow or collateral, and their reward is generally less (under 10 percent per year) than it is for venture capitalists.

A venture capitalist is much like the home run hitter who is seeking home runs only and doesn't mind striking out once in a while as long as he has enough home runs. A commercial bank doesn't accept striking out in stride, so it lends money only when there is a fairly well established cash flow or collateral.

STAGES OF THE FINANCING PROCESS

In the following discussion of the usual stages for financing a fast track start-up, the amounts listed are fairly general. Different ventures have different needs.

Seed capital. This is the initial capital needed to get your business off the ground. The money is used to organize your venture, prepare your prototype site, and further flesh out your business model. The seed capital enables the founders to quit their day jobs and let the venture assume the look and feel of an independent business. Funding could also be used for further refinement of the business plan through marketing surveys and for research and development. It would also fund filing patents for businesses that have a unique prototype or process.

The amount of seed money can range from $250,000 to $1.5 million. Some bootstrap operations could be started for even less. Although these funds aren't usually very large, they are the most difficult to get because they represent the earliest and highest-risk investment that can be made. Most venture capital firms don't fund at this stage, and owners must either raise funds through angel investors or self-funding.

First-stage funding. This is typically the stage at which venture capitalists enter the picture. The first stage of funding is the amount necessary to put the company in business. It represents the money that basically opens the door of your venture and begins to attract customers. It includes funds to hire necessary personnel and launch a marketing campaign. First-stage funding can range from $15 million to $30 million.

Second-stage funding. These are the funds used to expand the working capital of a business that is successful and expanding at a greater rate than it is generating its own working capital. The second stage is generally designed to maintain the momentum of the company. Much of the money for second-stage financing is also derived from venture capitalists or similar investors. However, risk is reduced at this level as the business is already operating and presumably is adhering to a viable business model. Second-stage fundings can raise an additional $15 million to $30 million.

Third-stage funding. The third stage refers to the funds used to finance further expansion of a break-even or profitable company. These funds can finance acquisitions or the development of new markets and products. At this stage, the company could be eligible for commercial financing from lending institutions or use more venture capital. Third-stage fundings are dependent on the size and prospects of the business.

Bridge financing. Bridge financing, which can be obtained from various debt or equity sources, is used as interim financing for a company preparing to go public. The public registration process is quite extensive and involves considerable effort and expense.

Initial public offering (IPO). This process requires registration of the securities of a company with the Securities and Exchange Commission as well as with various state authorities. The public-offering process is intricate and involves hiring an underwriter or investor and compliance with the securities laws that govern the company before, during, and after the registration process. This process includes full disclosure on a continuing basis of all material facts regarding the operations of the business. The company must also list itself on an exchange and comply with the requirements of that exchange.

In many cases, the new economy has compressed the normal time between the funding stages as well as the stages themselves. The several years that would have usually elapsed between the start-up of a company and public funding has been compressed to a matter of months. In some cases, companies used the public markets as a lever to finance more growth and acquisitions; in other cases, they went public much too soon. But many companies found it hard to resist the overheated markets of 1999 and early 2000. The ripe markets also allowed companies to leap-frog over several stages of financing. Some literally went from seed or first stage to a public company, although many have come crashing down, and the shakeout will likely continue.

The fast-track model is appealing to entrepreneurs and one that many Internet market leaders have used. However, it's very difficult to obtain venture funding. Venture capitalists are looking for a certain business profile, which is generally based on a large market and their ability to exit the investment quickly. Many viable business models don't fit that profile and won't receive venture capital funds.

Money Makes You Stupid

A contrarian approach to the fast-track financing model is one entitled "money makes you stupid." It can also be entitled the "get rich slowly" approach, which advocates a more measured growth. Comparing the two approaches reminds one of the fable of the tortoise and the hare. As opposed to spending heavily to quickly increase operations and become known in the marketplace, the measured approach follows a flatter development curve. It allows the company more time to iron out its business model and work out the bugs. The growth follows a more natural projection instead of a turbocharged one. Management has the benefit of a learning curve at each stage of development instead of making major marketing and operational decisions in a vacuum. Some start-ups, in their rush to capture market leadership, neglect to spend their money wisely and burn out before reaching the finish line, but the tortoise approach is not without its risks. Its main disadvantage: a tortoise company can be easily passed up by a better-funded rival that copies its business model. On the other-hand, it could position itself for a sale if it builds up a sufficient presence and customer base.

One Internet entrepreneur who advocates the get rich slowly approach is Mark Lewis, who has bootstrapped all of his ventures. A former IBMer, Lewis started an Internet service provider (ISP) in 1994, funding the venture with credit card debt and a $50,000 SBA loan. His target market in the young days of the Internet was businesses wanting to become connected. Lewis focused relentlessly on customer service, and his business prospered. Three years later he sold his company to Verio, a large ISP.

Lewis is presently involved in several Internet ventures, among them slambook.com, described in Chapter 9. Lewis bought the site for $125,000, which he financed through conventional bank borrowing, and to date has not spent any money on marketing. He has used viral marketing (the technique in which customers drive the marketing process) and has driven traffic up to levels that make venture capitalists drool.

Lewis is currently developing strategies to continue to enhance user experience. Through various equity arrangements with marketing and Internet personnel, he is keeping his operating costs to a minimum and actually answers the site's e-mail himself. The site currently turns a profit, and although he has received several inquiries from venture capitalists, Lewis isn't interested at this point. One of the reasons he cited was that "money makes you stupid."

Debt or Equity

Debt. Debt consists of funds borrowed from lenders that must be repaid. There are many forms of debt as well as many repayment terms. Debt can be is simple as a demand note and as complicated as convertible callable subordinated debt. Although the terms of debt, such as interest rate and repayment terms, may vary, the common factor of debt is that it constitutes borrowed funds that have to be repaid. Failure to pay back these funds in a timely fashion can subject the business to legal action as well as bankruptcy.

In terms of financial analysis, debt appears on the right side of the balance sheet and creates a liability for the business. This causes a decrease in the balance sheet equity and can affect the borrowing power of the business. As a result, debt must be taken on carefully as it represents a claim on your assets. From an operating standpoint, debt imposes a certain drain on short-term liquidity. Consequently, excessive debt not only erodes the balance sheet of the business but its operating capacity as well.

Debt also has a negative impact on the borrowing capacity of the company. Obviously, the more money that you borrow, the greater the leverage of the company. Companies that are highly leveraged create a greater credit risk than those with more modest leverage. Prospective lenders consider many of the same financial ratios that we examined in Chapter 11, such as current ratios and debt-to-equity ratios, in determining the creditworthiness of a business.

Debt does have some advantages. One of the main ones is that it doesn't dilute equity. Most debt issues are simply repaid according to their terms. Equity investors receive an amount of ownership in the company in exchange for the funding.

There are generally two types of debt: unsecured and secured. Typical debt transactions, such as the use of credit cards, constitute unsecured debt. The most familiar type of secured debt is a home mortgage. Secured debt imposes a direct claim either against particular assets or a class of assets and receives a higher priority for repayment in the event of bankruptcy than does unsecured debt. Unsecured debt is simply claimed against the company as a whole and is only paid after all of the secured debt has been paid.

In addition, there are many forms of debts. For smaller companies, debt can take the form of a line of credit or a revolving note. Many businesses use a line of credit to finance their day-to-day operations. Generally, the main variables in a line of credit are the interest rate and the repayment terms.

Larger companies can issue debt securities or fixed income securities to the public or private investors. There are generally three types of debt securities: debentures, bonds, and notes. A *debenture* is a long-term security (usually 30 years or more) and is often an unsecured debt instrument based primarily on the ability of the company to pay. However, should the company encounter financial difficulties, the unsecured holders of the debentures would be treated as general creditors of the corporation, which means they would be paid only after the secured parties are paid.

A *bond* is a long-term debt security that generally is secured by some form of collateral. Bonds are very similar to debentures except that they are secured. This allows the bondholders to foreclose on collateral in the event of default. Bonds sometimes contain a conversion feature that allows them to be converted into equity securities, such as common or preferred stock.

The final classification of debt security is a *note.* Also known as a promissory note, it is a debt security with a maturity of five years or less. Notes can be either secured or unsecured and can sometimes be redeemed or called back by the company.

Equity. As opposed to creating a liability, equity allows investors to share in the profits of the business. Note that equity is still a claim on the assets of the venture, appearing on the right side of the balance sheet. However, instead of creating debt, issuing equity security simply dilutes the ownership of the company. The main advantage of equity is that the funds need not be repaid.

In a legal sense, equity entitles owners to receive a ratable share of assets and dividends of a company. Depending on the size of the equity, the owners may have certain rights under state law.

In some cases, the various professionals connected with start-ups receive an equity interest in exchange for their services or perhaps in conjunction with payment for the services. For a cash-strapped business, this could represent an opportunity to raise money at a relatively inexpensive price. But always remember to be stingy with your equity: the more equity you give up at the earlier stages of the business, the less you will have later on. Be aware that granting equity does come with a cost—the claim on the future profits and assets of the business, or, basically, a claim on the value of the business. Another thing to keep in mind is that raising equity from a number of private sources can trigger federal securities laws (see Chapter 16).

Equity participation comes in various forms and sometimes in even a hybrid of the forms explained below.

Common stock. Common stock is the most common form of equity in a company, representing ownership in businesses organized as corporations. Most of the equity securities traded on the public markets are common stock, an equity security that represents the residual value of a company. Certain rights are granted to common shareholders, such as the right to elect directors and vote on mergers.

Common shareholders receive dividends from the corporation but generally have no influence on the payment of dividends nor a direct claim on the earnings of the company. (As noted previously, however, earnings flow through directly to the shareholders of an S corporation.) Earnings are important for valuing shares, which explains why earnings per share is an important investment indicator. Common shareholders have a right to share in the growth of the corporation, and as the corporation grows in value, the value of the shares grows. If the corporation is sold, common shareholders receive a ratable share of the corporation's ownership. But common shareholders receive no preference if the company is liquidated. They are outranked by creditors and preferred shareholders. If the corporation were to be liquidated, creditors and then preferred shareholders would be paid first by operation of law.

This discussion is not to imply that venture capitalists who become minority shareholders don't have substantial influence on your company. However, their influence is not based on corporate law but rather on their control over the purse strings. They usually don't give you the money all at once but in accordance with a fixed schedule. In addition, they are usually provided at least one seat on the board of directors and can also assist in obtaining additional funds.

Preferred stock. Preferred shares of stock are also an equity security; and some preferred shares trade on the national markets. The difference between preferred shares and common shares are that holders of preferred shares enjoy certain priorities and rights over holders of common stock. Generally, preferred shares are issued in a particular class or series; and one class of the preferred shares can be given priority over another class. Preferred shareholders usually don't have the right to vote for the election of directors and generally don't share in the growth of the value of the corporation. Preferred shares generally have a stated value and a fixed dividend. The attributes of preferred shares are established in the articles of incorporation and typically include the following:

- *Cumulative dividend right:* Corporations that have earnings must pay the fixed preferred dividend out of earnings; and any missed dividend payments must be paid in the future. Common shareholders have no such protection.
- *Participating versus nonparticipating preferred stock:* This can be a critical distinction in the start-up world. Participating preferred stock allows the shareholder to participate in the profits of the corporation along with the common shareholders. Consequently, the value of the stock will be gauged by the amount of the dividend. Nonparticipating preferred stock would not generally share in the increase in value in a stock.
- *Conversion right:* This right allows preferred shareholders to convert their shares to common stock. Generally, the terms of the exchange rate of the conversion are established before the shares are issued. Preferred stock without a conversion feature is called nonconvertible preferred shares.

Other types of equity interest are *stock options* and *stock warrants*. Neither options nor warrants are actual shares. Rather, they permit an investor to purchase shares at a certain price for a set time. Stock options are often issued by corporations to its senior managers. Generally, a stock option is nontransferable and grants the recipient the right to purchase shares from the corporation at a stated price (the strike price) for a certain time (option). The use of stock options as compensation is playing an increasingly important role in the new economy. Generally, if the stock price increases, the difference between the strike price and the market price benefits the holder of options. In many cases, this value can represent a significant portion of the employee's compensation package. Companies whose stocks decline have a more difficult time attracting qualified employees. Certain stock option plans, called incentive stock options (ISOs), don't tax employees until they actually sell the shares.

A stock warrant is an option generally evidenced by a contract and is usually issued with another security. Holders of a stock warrant can exercise the warrant and purchase common stock at a strike price anytime during the life of the warrant. The warrant can either be transferable or nontransferable.

16

Financing Strategies in the New Economy

....

"Money, it turned out, was exactly like sex. You thought of nothing else if you didn't have it and thought of other things if you did."

James Baldwin (1924–1987), American novelist

....

"We all need money, but there are different degrees of desperation."

Anthony Burgess (1917–1993), prolific novelist

SOURCES OF FUNDING

With the many available sources of funding for the start-up venture, the key is to develop a strategy for obtaining funding that is based on the validity of your business model, your persistence in seeking funds, and your knowledge of the funding market. This chapter presents the various funding sources and discusses strategies for approaching those sources.

Self-Financing

Even with the tremendous amount of available funds to finance start-ups, self-financing by owners is still one of the most common forms of financing and in most cases is required. Sometimes a new business can be financed from income or resources accrued in a previous business or career. Self-funding involves putting your own money on the line and is the direct opposite of OPM, other people's money. Some degree of self-funding is usually involved in most businesses as it can be difficult to ask others to risk capital for your business if you are unwilling to risk any of your own.

Depending on their respective financial circumstances, everyone takes a different position on the amount of funds he or she can or will invest in a start-up. Sometimes even successful entrepreneurs are required to fund their ventures themselves. Stuart Skorman, the founder of Hungryminds, was forced to put his own money into his online education portal despite the fact he had a very successful record as an entrepreneur. In 1998, he sold his online video operations Reel.com for $100 million to Hollywood Video (which recently closed down the operations). When Skorman started Hungryminds, however, the market had turned against B2C business models, and he couldn't raise any venture capital despite his track record. Consequently, he funded his venture himself along with some angel investors.

Friends and Family

Many business start-ups rely on resources from friends and family members, who are often considered the first form of angel financing. In general, friends and family have more than a simple financial interest in the business and are motivated by their relationship with the entrepreneur.

Investments by friends and family can be in the form of debt or equity. Although turning to family and friends might involve some humility, family and friends are often an important, and perhaps the only, available source of funds. It is advisable to deal with them at arm's length in a businesslike way. If you are borrowing money from them, execute a promissory note. If you are giving them an equity position in your business in return for the investment, issue them shares of stock or other equity interest in your business.

Sometimes, money raised from family members is described as "blood money." As the name connotes, such funds can have negative aspects, including resentment and bad feelings among family members. You can minimize the fallout from blood money by addressing potential problems in advance. It is generally better to be up front with other family members about the financing situation rather than letting them find out from others.

Bank Financing

Although it is difficult to raise money for start-ups through traditional banks, don't be too quick to scratch them off your list. To begin with, many banks do have venture capital groups. A referral from their lending side could assist you on the venture capital side. In addition, although your initial funding might not come from a bank, you're going to need a bank at some point, maybe even sooner than you think. Although the financial markets are changing rapidly, commercial banks are still the primary source of day-to-day operating capital and lines of credit.

Bankers are generally more favorably disposed to start-up companies in the current economic climate. Like other professionals that cater to businesses, they know that start-up companies may eventually become large clients. In addition, many banks work very closely with the Small Business Administration (SBA) in processing loans that are guaranteed by the government, and Uncle Sam is taking a larger and larger role in funding small businesses. The SBA itself is becoming aggressive and operating more like a private enterprise then a bureaucratic organization. Sometimes the quickest way to an SBA loan is through a commercial bank that does a great deal of SBA lending. In that case, the traditional lending requirements of the bank would be loosened a bit because as much as 80 percent of an SBA loan is guaranteed by the government. This represents a significant decrease in risk for the bank.

Nevertheless, when dealing with banks, keep in mind they are generally not risk takers. Unlike venture capitalists, banks must comply with stringent regulatory requirements that govern their operations. Many of the requirements that banks impose on borrowers are actually mandated by the regulatory authorities. As mentioned earlier, banks are not looking for the home run but rather to be repaid. Their tolerance for risk as well as their return is comparatively low.

Consequently, banks' main focus is the assurance that their loan will be repaid. If the start-up is not generating sufficient funds, it will need another income source, which could be a family member. If no steady income is able to fund repayment, banks consider using collateral and often require collateral even when a steady income source is available. It is not uncommon for people to mortgage their home to start a business.

Banks are also interested in the accounting ratios discussed previously. The main ratio they are concerned with is the debt repayment to cash flow. Banks typically like $1.40 of cash flow for every $1 of debt repayment. They also examine your credit history, consider your debt ratio, and find out the amount of your current assets. Naturally, a good business plan is also a considerable advantage in dealing with banks.

Some bankers also serve a useful advisory role. As the new and old economies continue to converge and bankers become more experienced with digital businesses, bankers may even provide valuable advice. Some bankers have become particularly knowledgeable about certain areas of the economy and can provide useful feedback about your business plan. Often their experience in dealing with similar businesses can be invaluable, particularly in pointing out the various holes and gaps in the analysis of the financial statement.

Credit Cards

Credit cards are the mother's milk of the new economy. Many Internet start-ups have relied on credit cards for at least some of their financing. Among the many advantages of credit cards are a certain amount of security and quick access to cash. One Internet entrepreneur I know but will remain nameless financed his entire start-up with credit cards. First, he obtained several credit cards in his own name. When he ran out of available credit, he applied for several cards in his wife's name. Then he applied for several credit cards in the name of his infant children. Fortunately, his business succeeded and all of his credit card debt was repaid. But it's not always this easy.

You have to keep in mind that the credit card is not manna from heaven. The charges are personal debts that will eventually have to be repaid. Businesses that are too free and easy with credit cards could eventually get into debt over their heads. Therefore, like any type of debt, credit card debt has to be managed.

A disadvantage of credit cards is their typically higher rates of interest because the debt carries a higher risk. However, in many cases, introductory rates are very competitive, so it is not uncommon for businesses to transfer debt to the card with lower interest rates while paying off those with the higher interest rates. But managing credit card debt not only requires you to transfer debt to the lower interest rate card; it also requires you to make the minimum payments to avoid default. More important, business owners have to discipline themselves to pay down the balances when they have free cash.

Managed properly, credit cards can be an excellent financing tool. A caveat is that credit cards can be very tempting and can turn on you if not properly managed.

Government Agencies

Government agencies can be an important source of financing. In particular, the SBA has emerged as an important source of capital for the start-up. With its variety of programs and loan guarantees, the SBA has done much to help small businesses. Depending on where you are located, a national or local government entity may have loan guarantees and programs directed to help the small business. You never know until you ask. You may want to begin with your local or regional department of economic development. Many government agencies offer not only loan assistance but professional and technical assistance as well.

Below is a list of the most common SBA loan programs:

- *SBA Basic 7(a) Loan:* This is the most common general purpose SBA loan program. Loan proceeds may be used for the purchase of inventory, furniture and fixtures, machinery and equipment, land or construction, leasehold improvements, and real property as well as for working capital. Small businesses operating for profit are eligible for a loan, which is made by either the SBA or approved participants. The maximum loan amount is $750,000, with a loan maturity of 25 years for real estate and 10 years for working capital.

- *Basic Guaranty Business Loans:* These are loans made exclusively by commercial lenders and certified nonbank lenders. The SBA cannot guarantee more than $750,000 to any one business, including its affiliates.
- *LOWDOC (Low Documentation) Loan Program:* This general purpose loan guarantee program is designed for quick processing of loans of $100,000 or less. Using a one-page application, the program focuses on the strength of character and credit of the applicant; and personal guarantees of the principals are required.
- *Caplines Loan Program:* This is an umbrella program under which the SBA guarantees short-term working capital lines of credit. The types of working capital available under this program are seasonal, contract, builder, and asset-based lines of credit. There is no limit on a loan, but the SBA cannot guarantee more than $750,000 to any one business, the line of credit cannot exceed five years.
- *Microloan Program:* This is designed for the start-up, existing small businesses, and home-based businesses that need relatively small loans to purchase equipment, machinery, and fixtures and to make leasehold improvements, finance increased receivables, and obtain working capital. Loans made by selected nonprofit lending organizations go up to $25,000, although most are under $10,000. Lending decisions are based primarily on the basis of the credit history and the personal character of applicants.

Other programs available for start-ups are these:

- *Certified Development Loans:* These emphasize generating or retaining jobs in a specific geographic area.
- *Defense Loan and Technical Assistance Program:* This is a joint effort by the SBA and the Defense Department to minimize the effects of defense downsizing.
- *Minority and Women's Resources:* These are various programs and policies to promote full participation in the economy by minority-owned and women-owned businesses.

In addition to the U.S. government, many states have programs specifically geared to technology companies and emerging businesses. Many state programs represent a partnership between state government, private companies, and academia and are generally funded by various economic development funds sponsored on state and local levels. These programs provide various services that include assisting with obtaining venture capital, providing incubator space, providing individual and group counseling, and underwriting educational programs.

It would be wise to check with your state to see what types of programs exist. States are realizing that technology and the new economy is the future of the country and are trying to develop technology within their state.

Venture Capitalists

Venture capitalists are generally at the top of the pyramid in funding start-ups in the new economy. As noted earlier, many of the current leaders in the new economy received their jump start with venture capital financing. It is clearly one of the most sought-after and desired forms of financing for start-ups replete with numerous advantages.

Besides being merely funds, venture capital can also be "smart money" that cuts years off the learning and growth curve of a business in the competitive new economy. Soon Yu, the founder and chairman of Gazoontite. com, which sells allergy products from its Web site as well as through stores, is very keen on venture capital. He stated that the particular quality of a venture capital partner is even more important than the valuation provided your business. The valuation given to your business by the venture capitalist determines the amount of equity that must be relinquished in exchange for the financing. However, the smart money aspects of the venture capitalist can be more important than the financing terms. According to Yu, a venture capitalist can assist start-ups in many ways, including (1) providing important contacts in the business world; (2) helping to find management talent; and (3) assisting in locating additional funding.

The general role of the venture capitalist is to provide the first and second stages of funding for your venture. As discussed, venture capital firms typically do not provide the seed funding but do provide the funds that enable a business to open its doors and begin marketing. Generally, venture capitalists don't want to stay invested in a business for a long time but would rather be out of the business within 18 or 36 months. Their exit strategy is achieved either by an IPO or by the sale of the business. They can offer guidance in addition to funding; so venture capitalists remain actively involved in the funded business, oversee most of the strategic decisions, serve on the board of directors, and closely supervise funding draws during the few months they remain invested.

Venture capitalists inject money into promising projects in return for a significant equity position that varies depending on the valuation rate and the stage of the investment. Generally, venture capitalists receive an equity interest in the particular business in the 25 percent range in exchange for first-round funding, whereas the second-round financing can require as much as an additional 20 to 25 percent. The terms of the funding vary in accordance with the company and are usually set forth in a term sheet that forms the basis for the transaction. For example, some companies require the business to reach certain targets before obtaining funding draws. Consequently, a financed company runs the risk of being cut off if it fails to hit certain targets.

The biggest issue in dealing with venture capitalists is the valuation given your business, which determines how much equity the founders have to give up in exchange for the financing (valuation is included in the e-plan). Another important part of the term sheet is the vesting schedule of shares in the company to the owners. To ensure the owners' commitment, shares vest over a four-year period. In some cases, owners are given "credit" in the vesting schedule for prior work done on the business. For example, if the founder worked on a product for a year before being funded, he would be given credit in the vesting schedule. In addition, other shares in the company are required to be set aside in a pool to attract key employees.

Many venture capitalists are based in Silicon Valley and cluster around the famed Sand Hill Road, which is considered the Wall Street of the venture capital community. The venture capitalists I spoke with were unanimous about several aspects of the process. The first was making contact with venture capital firms; all of them cited referrals as a very important factor in having particular business plans considered. Although none said that unsolicited business plans were never considered, it was apparent that referred prospects received considerably more attention. In addition, the venture capitalists agreed that less is better with respect to business plans. Your plan needs to get to the point quickly and present a compelling case.

Steve Dow: Sevin Rosen Funds. Sevin Rosen is a venture capital firm with offices in Dallas and Palo Alto and focuses on business opportunities driven by new Internet-enabled business models and technology break-throughs in communications. As with many venture capitalists, its decision to invest in a new venture is based on several key criteria, which includes a large growing market opportunity; the experience, vision, and energy of the founding team; a clear and compelling business model; and a strong competitive advantage.

The Web page of Sevin Rosen bears the following quotation by partner Steve Dow: "I love the challenge of working and molding creative new ideas, but success requires more than ideas. Building something that lasts takes incredible effort. In other words, vision without execution is just hallucination."

Dow mentioned that the types of opportunities that would attract his attention would not be duplicates of brick-and-mortar businesses but rather businesses that change an existing market. He is most attracted to products that are completely new and solve problems bigger and better than their counterparts. The parts of the business plan that Dow finds most important are those that (1) describe a compelling market need or pain, (2) detail the team that will execute and deliver on the opportunity, and (3) detail the execution of the plan.

Common mistakes that Dow finds in plans are those that are too clever—too many charts and acronyms and unclear about the problem they are solving. Dow recommended that the business plan be short, something that could be explained in no more than 20 slides. In addition, he preferred receiving an executive summary before seeing the entire plan.

Dow admitted that many viable businesses with smaller target markets won't receive funding because of the financing requirements of the venture capitalists. As mentioned earlier, venture capitalists are seeking a significant return on their investment and desire a quick exit. This is not to say that the businesses that don't receive venture capital won't be successful. Dow quipped that outside Silicon Valley, $1 million to $2 million is still real money.

Brendon Kim: Altos Ventures. The founder of Altos Ventures, Brendon Kim leads its Internet media and media content investment activities. The items Kim is looking for in new ventures in their order of importance are (1) a good management team, (2) the size of the market, and (3) the competitive advantages of the business.

According to Kim, the investment is made in the people and not necessarily in the business process. The question he faces is whether the principals of the business are worthy of the investment. Specifically, Kim is seeking people who are committed to building a company.

He too prefers initially receiving an executive summary, one that addresses the following three criteria: (1) market opportunity, (2) the people, and (3) the competitive advantages. A full-fledged plan is generally no more than 20 pages long. One mistake he sees with most plans is their inclusion of too much hype. If the market opportunity is compelling, the plan should speak for itself; a good plan quickly gets to the point rather than burying it.

Jim Smith: Mohr, Davidow Ventures. Mohr, Davidow Ventures has broad expertise in the types of ventures that it funds, which include semiconductors, enterprise software, networking and communications, electronic commerce, and the Internet. According to Jim Smith, an associate at the firm, the companies that his firm invests in are those that address difficult problems in large markets uniquely. Smith prefers a plan that is concise and hard-hitting and presents team strengths and weaknesses as well as the unfair advantage the company is trying to seize.

The advice that Smith offers to individuals for raising funds is to become an expert in your market or space and learn everything possible about the particular market opportunity. It is also important to act in a manner that inspires confidence. The founders have to be enthusiastic about the opportunity and be able to sell themselves. The key in communicating with investors, customers, partners, and potential employees is inspiring confidence in your knowledge about market challenges and your ability to meet those challenges.

Raj Atluru: Draper Fisher Jurvetson. Located in Redwood City, California, Draper Fisher Jurvetson is an early-stage venture capital firm that backed such successes as Hotmail, GoTo.com, Four11, Kana, Net Zero, and Tumbleweed. In particular, the firm is credited with creating the concept of viral marketing to rapidly penetrate an Internet market. This technique was instrumental in the success of Hotmail and Four11. Partner Raj Atluru stated that the firm generally funds companies with a potential market in excess of $1 billion, experienced management, and unique business models.

Atluru stated that the business model of the plan is most important. It should include a well-defined problem and indicate how the business will solve it. In addition, the founding team needs to be energetic, passionate, and experienced. He prefers receiving a clear and concise executive summary that details the problem in the market and how the problem will be solved.

David Cowan: Bessemer Venture Partners. Bessemer Venture Partners is a private venture capital firm founded in 1911, one of the longest-standing such firms in the country. David Cowan, the managing general partner, was one of the founders of VeriSign.

Cowan stated that the types of Internet businesses he is interested in investing in are those that aim to transform a legacy industry using the Internet as a platform for information exchange and market making, ultimately to rationalize the supply chain. This model would be most compelling for businesses with a fragmented or inefficient supply chain. Cowan also recommended the business plan be condensed into a series of slides that would enable them to be presented quickly to various financing sources.

Investment Bankers

Investment bankers sometimes pick up where venture capitalists leave off. They assist a growing company in raising funds at the middle and later stages of financing; these funds can be private or public equity and debt. Although investment bankers are commonly thought to be associated with public stock offerings, they are also involved in locating funds from such private sources as pension funds. Although most businesses are at a more mature stage before seeking investment bankers, it is never too early to think about the larger debt and equity markets that investment bankers have access to.

Investment bankers are generally interested in the same types of businesses that venture capitalists are—those that fulfill a compelling need in a large potential market. Unless your business has an outstanding profit potential, most investment bankers are not going to be interested. You also need to exercise caution in your dealings with investment bankers: although many are with large and reputable firms, others are with shady operations under the guise of investment banking. As with venture capitalists, be wary of those who want their fee up front to secure additional money for you. Many of the these "financing fees" have never been repaid or led to anything else.

One of the ways that investment bankers raise money for businesses is taking businesses public, a massive undertaking. A public offering is geared only for a company that is either mature or has demonstrated profit potential. In addition, a public offering can be a very expensive process requiring hundreds of thousands or even millions of dollars in up-front fees.

Venture Financing Incubators

Business incubators started as sleepy extensions of Small Business Development Centers, but in the new economy, they have become an important source of generating ideas in the marketplace. Incubators are popping up all over the country, particularly in the high-technology sector of the economy.

Incubators can perform a variety of functions for the start-up in addition to financing. They may provide reasonably priced office space as well as administrative support. The new economy has created certain bulked-up incubators that provide more than simply administrative support and that take an active role in helping businesses find seed capital. Venture financing firm Garage.com refers to this early stage of capital as "gapital" and links entrepreneurs seeking early funding with investors seeking early-stage opportunities.

Anila Fund. In some cases, the lines between incubators and venture capital firms are blurring, with firms such as Anila Fund offering venture capital funding as well as in-house professional services to its selected companies.

Venture capital firm Anila has two offices in Palo Alto as well as a core engineering facility in Minneapolis, Minnesota. Anila funds and supports early-stage optical and broadband communications and business-to-business Internet companies. Anila offers marketing, strategic planning, recruiting, and funding support to a few, highly select companies. Anila considers this a unique and innovative approach to venture funding. Its Venture Cyclotron, the trademarked process by which its start-ups rapidly accelerate through the corporate development cycle, is designed to jump-start, nurture, and complete a company's early-stage process, solidly preparing it for subsequent funding and growth. This unique environment fosters information sharing and support for all entrepreneurs who walk through the doors. As a result, interrelated deals and synergistic business relationships can be formed among resident start-ups before they leave Anila.

Anila was founded by Moses Joseph, an experienced executive, private investor, and entrepreneur, who took a number of companies public, including a major player in the embedded systems market. Joseph noted that the start-up experiences its greatest risk at the early stages and thus requires a degree of hand-holding. The goal of Anila's hands-on support is to take several years off the company's development and learning curve and enable the company to grow quickly by offering essential services.

Joseph claims that he knows very quickly if fledgling entrepreneurs are knowledgeable about their market, or in the vernacular "know their stuff." He can usually determine this by peppering the applicant with questions. He considers this comprehensive understanding more valuable than a full-blown business plan. Joseph is not an entrepreneur who minces words. A former brand manager for a major consumer company, Joseph referred to the e-tailing television blitz in late 1999 and early 2000 as "crap." He opined that effective brands are built up through a carefully integrated marketing program that includes proper targeting and positioning.

Garage.com. Another venture financing firm in Silicon Valley is Garage.com, which sometimes refers to itself as a virtual incubator. Garage.com was founded by individuals with a very high profile in the technology and venture capital community, including attorney Craig Johnson, the founder of the Venture Law Group, and Guy Kawasaki, a well-known Silicon Valley entrepreneur.

The primary function of Garage.com is matching entrepreneurs seeking funding with investors seeking early-stage growth companies. As its name suggests, Garage.com targets early-stage companies that are moving out of the garage and include ventures with a great idea or technology that needs to be completely flushed out. The purpose of Garage.com is to find promising companies, prepare them for investors, and then fund them.

The companies selected to participate in Garage.com receive a small up-front investment. In exchange for its services, Garage.com receives an up-front equity position, a co-investment fee, and a placement fee at the close of the funding. The value provided by Garage.com is compressing the time required to raise money for promising companies.

Veteran entrepreneur Bill Reichert, the president of Garage.com, stated that the five keys to success for the start-up today are as follows:

1. A compelling idea that offers a solution to a problem or opportunity
2. A strong team with a significant breadth of talent as well as passion and vision
3. Intense focus on its core purpose
4. Effective networking with customers, investors, employees, and affiliates
5. Financing

Reichert also cited the ability of the founders to motivate employees as important to the overall success of the venture.

Angels

Like venture capitalists, angels have had a tremendous impact on the new economy. The term *angel* was derived from Broadway and referred to the last-minute investors who "swooped in" and saved a particular production. Angels generally include wealthy and experienced businesspeople who invest in early-stage enterprises.

In many cases, angels are motivated by factors other than pure financial gain, although they are definitely sophisticated and shrewd investors. Unlike other financing sources, angels tend to take a more active, and even personal, interest in the businesses they fund. Although angels don't necessarily want to run a business, they want to take a more active role in helping to move it to the next level. The general funding at the angel level is under $1 million.

The primary function of the angel network is to serve as a bridge between an entrepreneur's personal funds and venture capitalist funds. The purposes of angel financing include (1) refining the business plan and business model, (2) hiring the necessary people, and (3) assembling the right resources for guiding the business to the next level.

The angel network has become more organized lately. Before the advent of the Internet, finding angels was based on some type of affinity. People who shared the same nationality, college, or other interests were the first targets of those seeking angel investors. The angel network has become an increasingly important part of the high-tech financing process. The advantage to entrepreneurs is that it allows them to build more value in their company before they seek venture capital financing, which allows them to relinquish a lesser share of their company. The terms of the angel network are usually not as stringent as terms of venture capitalists.

Finding angels is contingent on networking. Because you will be developing a personal relationship with the angels, they should be people you can work with. In addition, angels can provide more than simply funds. Like venture capitalists, angels can provide a mentoring service and help with business contacts and other referrals.

Angels come in many forms. Some already own and operate a highly successful business of their own but may be interested in other opportunities. Sometimes they are interested in a business related to their own so that they can diversify their investment portfolio. Other angels may be retired executives or entrepreneurs looking for something to do with their time and money; usually, this type of angel would take a more active part in the business. Some angels may be high-earning professionals who would consider investing in a business with a product or service that they have some connection with; they may use the product in their business or be aware of it. Finally, some angels just want to help worthy entrepreneurs. Perhaps you can come up with some type of social, ethnic, or educational affiliation with that type of angel.

The resource guide lists many types of angel investors.

Private Placements

Although the laws regulating the investment of funds differ around the world, private placements can generally be thought of as public offerings on a smaller scale. The private placement is less complicated than the public offering, but there are certain restrictions on the manner in which the offering can be advertised and investors solicited.

One site that serves as a depository for private investment is the Access to Capital Electronic Network (Ace-Net), which is a national securities offering service. The site is affiliated with the SBA (although the SBA disclaims any official connection) and can be linked from the SBA site. Ace-Net's site allows venture capitalists and institutional and individual accredited investors to find small, growing companies through a secure Internet database. The site operates under a "no-action letter" issued by the Securities and Exchange Commission.

The network can be accessed with an annual enrollment fee of a maximum of $450 for unlimited access to the service, which is managed by the University of New Hampshire. In addition to day-to-day management of the network, there are also entrepreneurial development centers in virtually every state to assist with all aspects of business development. The center also sponsors forums where entrepreneurs and investors can interact with each other.

Suppliers: Commercial Credit

The type of financing that you can obtain from your suppliers includes the traditional commercial credit account, which involves the vendors delivering goods and services before payment is received. A good cash management strategy is to request either credit terms or a discount for prompt payment. Remember your goal is to conserve your cash. Collect your money as quickly as you can, but take as long as possible to pay it back.

chapter 17

Exit Strategies for the Start-Up

The phrase *Begin with the end in mind* might seem out of place as the last thing you are thinking about when starting a business is getting out of it. But the name of the game is maximizing your return and that could be accomplished by a well-timed sale. In fact, many entrepreneurs are allergic to running mature companies and simply enjoy building a company and then selling it. This can be heartwarming as well as lucrative.

Another exit strategy is taking your company public. Although not as direct an exit strategy as the sale of a business, a public market provides an exit that assigns a market value to your shares. Private businesses are not liquid investments, and any exit strategy in this setting would inevitably involve the sale of the company. Going public grants a market value for your stock and provides for easy transferability.

Obviously, both of these strategies can be massive undertakings that are driven by valuation—Slide 10 of your e-plan.

SELLING THE BUSINESS

Several factors must be weighed when considering the sale of your business.

Timing is everything. All business owners need an exit strategy. All good things must come to an end and that includes your business. For owners who ultimately plan to sell their business, timing is very critical. The best time to sell may not be when you're ready to retire, because current market conditions could favor an immediate sale. Industry dynamics could be making your business particularly attractive. There could be more buyers than sellers and consequently a seller's market. Larger firms in the industry could be in an aggressive acquisition mode. The point is that the price offered today could be much higher than the one you could get next year or even ten years from now for your business. So consider serious offers carefully.

Protect yourself. Potential buyers are going to want to examine your business. Therefore, require anyone evaluating your business to execute a tightly drafted confidentiality agreement that protects you against unauthorized disclosures and misappropriation of information. You don't want to serve yourself up to a potential competitor on a platter. I often put substantial liquidated damage provisions in such agreements to give them teeth.

Maximize your price. Business owners need to think about obtaining a sufficient price to sustain their needs in what could end up to be a long retirement. Don't assume that because you have built one successful business you can take the sales proceeds and quickly build another. As you know, creating a successful business requires considerable effort. In addition, if the buyer is astute, you will probably be precluded from establishing a similar business in the area, which would require you to start over in a different area or in a different business. A better assumption is you don't plan to work again.

Tax structuring. Remember that it is the after-tax amount in the price that is most important. Generally, sellers whose business is a corporation prefer selling the stock rather than the assets to avoid the two levels of taxation, which is not as great a concern for S corporations or limited liability companies. In addition, taxes can be deferred through devices such as installment sales and like-kind exchanges. At a minimum, sellers should seek long-term capital gain treatment for the entire amount of the gain.

Done properly, the sale of your business can be an excellent exit strategy and provide perhaps an early payoff for your hard work in building the business. Although you may truly love your work, there are certainly other ways to fulfill yourself, especially during a well-funded early retirement. The key to obtaining the best price for your business is to do your homework, consider serious offers carefully, stay objective, and obtain the proper advice.

Valuing the Business

Valuation is one of the most fluid topics in the new economy. Internet stocks have experienced wild fluctuations in value and trying to find some consistency in valuation methods is like trying to hit a moving target. Initially, valuations were based on revenues, and companies with growing revenues were trading at lofty premiums despite the fact they were losing money. At that time, the market was not particularly worried about short-term losses. Instead, it was enamored with the long-term prospects of the Internet pioneers and allowed them to spill red ink in the name of building market share.

Then a bit of caution gripped the market and some stock analysts suggested that gross profits, which are revenues minus cost of goods sold, might be a more appropriate measurement. The difference between gross profits and net income or earnings is the administrative costs of the company. To simplify the income statement, net income or earnings equal revenues minus cost of goods sold minus administrative expenses. Consequently, gross profit would determine whether the fundamentals of your business model were sound—that is, you could offer your goods to the market at a price above their cost. While this might not cover all of your administrative expenses, the thought was that administrative expenses per unit sold would decrease as the process ratcheted up and economies of scale set in. Gross profit was considered a compromise between net income and revenues.

As this book went to press, the market started to become really antsy about profitability and began to focus more on net income. Companies with losses were hammered in the market, and even profitable companies saw their price multiples clipped.

There are two components to consider when valuing a company. The first is earnings or cash flow and the second is the earnings multiplier or multiple. The valuation of a company is calculated by multiplying earnings times the multiple. This is similar to the price-earnings, or PE, ratio for publicly traded stocks. In the case of public companies, the PE ratio is determined by comparing the market price of a company's shares with its earnings per share. In this case, the market has assigned a particular earnings multiple. In the case of valuing a private company, however, there are several considerations for assigning earnings multiples, which are as follows:

- The nature of the business and the history of the enterprise from its inception
- The economic outlook in general and the condition and outlook of the specific industry in particular
- The earning capacity of the company
- The dividend-paying capacity of the company
- The book value of the stock and the financial condition of the business
- Whether the enterprise has goodwill, is a going concern, or has other intangible values
- Other sales of stock and the size of the block to be valued
- The market price of publicly traded stocks of corporations engaged in the same or a similar line of business

For many businesses in the old economy, earnings multiples ranged between 5 and 15. Today, stocks often trade at earnings multiples in the 100s. Basing multiples on the factors above, most of the valuation of Internet businesses were driven by the excitement over the industry and its immense possibilities. Consequently, in times of such volatility the best way to make a case for value is to choose items from the list above that best support your case for value. If a public company similar to yours is trading at high multiples, isolate that factor and use its multiple for your earnings. If your industry is particularly promising, make that case. Valuation is still very fluid, and you can use the factors that best establish your case. Of course, this works best when the market is keen on your particular space or on new economy stocks in general.

Negotiating the Sale

The first step in the sale of your business is the preliminary negotiating process, whereby the buyer and the buyer's financial advisors need to review many of the company's financial records. Always require the buyer to execute a confidentiality agreement, which seeks to prevent the buyer from disclosing to everyone what is learned about the business from inside information. The confidentiality agreement should cover the kinds of information subject to the restrictions and provide for liquidated damages.

A sample confidentiality agreement appears in Figure 17.1.

FIGURE 17.1 Sample Confidentiality Agreement

(1) Dear _____: We are discussing with you the possibility of our company acquiring the X Corporation (the "Company"). In connection with this, you will be providing us with the financial statements and other information which is confidential and proprietary to the Company. The financial statements and other information provided to us are hereinafter referred to as the "Evaluation Materials."

(2) We acknowledge that the Evaluation Materials are confidential and that the fact that the sale of the Company is being considered is confidential. Intending to be legally bound, we agree that we will:

    (a) Maintain the confidentiality of the Evaluation Materials and of the fact that the sale of the Company is being considered.

    (b) Disclose the fact that the sale of the Company is being considered, and show the Evaluation Materials to only those individuals employed by us and any outside advisors retained by us if necessary to our determination of whether to make a proposal for the acquisition of the Company. In this regard, there shall be no disclosure to employees other than senior officers of the company nor to outside advisors unless and until approved in writing by the Company.

    (c) Prior to disclosing to any person the fact that a sale of the Company is being considered, require that such person agree to maintain the confidentiality of the possible sale and the Evaluation Materials.

    (d) Use the Evaluation Materials solely for the purpose of determining whether or not we wish to make a proposal for the acquisition of the Company and not in any way detrimental to the Company

    (e) Not make copies of any of the Evaluation Materials.

    (f) Return all of the Evaluation Materials to the Company and destroy all notes, reports, and other materials prepared by us if we or you decide to terminate our discussions.

    (g) Liquidated Damages: We understand that it is extremely important that we maintain the confidentiality of the fact that a sale is being considered and of the Evaluation Materials. We understand that the Company may suffer irreparable damage in the form of loss of customers and loss of profits if we or our employees or our advisors disclose in violation of this agreement the fact that the sale of the Company is being considered. We understand that our agreement to maintain confidentiality shall survive any termination of our evaluation of the Company. In the event of any such violation we agree in advance to be liable for liquidated damages in the sum of Twenty Thousand Dollars ($20,000).

The next step in the sale of the business is the execution of the letter of intent. Although the letter of intent can be very flexible, its purpose is to provide both the seller and the buyer assurances of rights in terms of the sale. Always obtain professional advice in the preparation of a letter of intent as it could bind both parties.

Finally, the agreement of sale should cover all material aspects regarding the sale of the business. A sample agreement of sale appears in Figure 17.2.

FIGURE 17.2   Sample Agreement of Sale

AGREEMENT MADE on this _____ day of _____, 20____, between _____ and _____

WHEREAS, Seller is the owner of Stock Certificate No. _____ and Stock Certificate No. _____, of _____ (the "Company"), representing _____ shares of the common stock of the Company, being all outstanding stock of the Company; and

WHEREAS, Seller desires to sell and Buyer desires to purchase _____ shares of such stock (the "Transfer Stock") of Seller; and

NOW THEREFORE, in consideration of the mutual benefits and covenants contained in this agreement, and for other good and valuable consideration, the receipt and sufficiency of which is hereby acknowledged, the parties do hereby mutually covenant, contract and agree as follows:

1. *Stock Transfer:* Seller does hereby sell, convey, transfer and assign to Buyer, all of Seller's right, title and interest in and to the Transfer Stock, being stock of _____ _____. The Stock Certificates, representing _____ shares of the common stock of said corporation, are hereby being canceled, new certificates being issued to evidence the Transfer canceled, new certificates being issued to evidence the Transfer Stock in the name of Buyer and the _____ shares of stock in the name of Seller.

Seller hereby releases, waives, and forever discharges any claim on account of any salary, consulting fee, loans, or any other advances made by Seller except for those provisions expressly provided for herein. It is the intention of the Buyer and Seller that Buyer is hereby acquiring a _____% ownership in the Company, including all assets of the Company. Seller acknowledges that after the date hereof, Buyer, as majority shareholder, shall have control of the affairs of the Company, including, but not limited to, changing the name of the Company.

2. *Excluded Assets.* It is agreed that the Company shall maintain ownership of all assets, including all accounts receivable of the Company arising prior to the date of this agreement. Seller has not in the last ninety (90) days, transferred to anyone any assets of the Company other than in the ordinary course of business. No assets of the Company have been transferred to Seller during the last ninety (90) days, other than the Seller's usual and ordinary salary.

3. *Non-Disclosure.* Seller agrees that it will not divulge nor disclose trade secrets and proprietary information of the Company relating to sales records, pricing methods, financial statements, profit margins and costs

FIGURE 17.2   Sample Agreement of Sale (continued)

associated with the operation of the Company except to Buyer, nor shall Seller reveal nor disclose to anyone except to Buyer the names, addresses and telephone numbers of customers of the Company.

4. *Selling Price.* The consideration for the transfer contained herein is the sum of _____ dollars per share paid contemporaneously herewith and in consideration of services previously rendered by Buyer to Seller and to the Company. Seller acknowledges that the Company currently has a significant negative net worth.

5. *Litigation.* There is no claim, cause of action, suit, action, arbitration or legal, administrative, or other proceeding, or governmental investigation pending or, to the best knowledge of Seller, threatened, affecting (i) Seller's ability to transfer the shares of stock or execute and deliver this agreement or consummate the transactions contemplated hereby, or (ii) the Company. Neither Seller, nor the Company, is in default with respect to any order, writ, injunction, or decree of any federal, state, local, or foreign court, department, agency, or instrumentality that would adversely affect the stock or the Company.

6. *Warranties and Representation.* Seller represents and warrants that:

a) *Owner.* Seller is the owner of the stock transferred hereby, that the stock is free from any liens, privileges, pledges, mortgages or other encumbrances of any nature whatsoever, and that Seller is not obligated to obtain any consent or approval in order to convey her interest in the stock not obtained. Seller agrees to not transfer to anyone without Buyer's consent, the shares of the Company retained by Seller.

b) *Organization.* The Company is a corporation duly organized, validly existing, and in good standing under the laws of the State of Louisiana, and has all necessary corporate power to own its properties and to carry on its business as now owned and being operated by it.

c) *Compliance with Laws.* Seller has complied, in all material respects, with, and is not in violation of, applicable federal, state, or local statutes, laws, and regulations affecting the operation of the Company.

d) *Taxes.* (i) All returns and reports relating to foreign, federal, state and local taxes, including income, profits, franchise, accumulated earnings, sales use payroll premium, occupancy, property, severance, excise, withholding, value added, customs, duties, unemployment, transfer, tangible, intangible, and other taxes (such taxes, including interest, additions to taxes, and penalties relating thereto, are referred to herein as "Taxes") required to be filed by, or with respect to, the Company have been filed on a timely basis with the appropriate governmental agencies in all jurisdictions in which such returns and reports are required to be filed, with all taxes due, except as set forth on Exhibit A, pursuant to such returns and reports having been paid, and all such returns and reports relating to the Taxes were true and correct in all material respects when filed. Seller shall be responsible for the payment of all taxes due by the Company for all business conducted by the Company for all prior years and for the portion of 20____ preceding this agreement, and shall hold Buyer harmless from any liability or responsibility for any such taxes.

e) *Debt.* The Company has no debts other than the debt for taxes as described on Exhibit A and obligations to _____.

f) *Employees.* The Company has no employees except as set forth on Exhibit B, with such salaries and benefits as described on Exhibit B.

(continued)

FIGURE 17.2 Sample Agreement of Sale (continued)

• •

g) *Type of Business.* The Company is a duly licensed _____, licensed to operate in the State of Louisiana.

7. *Interest and Affairs.* Upon execution of this agreement, Seller shall deliver all books, records, accounts, ledger cards, drawings, specifications, applications, permits, correspondence, licenses, or any other property of the Company of any nature whatsoever to Buyer. Seller hereby provides Buyer with the resignation of any other members of the board of directors of the Company.

8. *Parties.* Nothing in this agreement, whether expressed or implied, is intended to confer any rights or remedies under or by reason of this agreement on any persons other than the parties to this agreement and their respective successors and assigns, nor is anything in this agreement intended to relieve or discharge the obligation or liability of any third person to any party under this agreement, nor shall any provision give any third party any right of subrogation nor any action over or against any party to this agreement.

9. *Headings.* The subject headings of the sections of this agreement are included for the purposes of convenience only and shall not affect the construction or interpretation of its provisions.

10. *Invalidity.* In the event that any term or provision of this agreement is held to be illegal, invalid or unenforceable under the laws, regulations or ordinances of any federal, state or local government, the remaining terms and provisions shall remain unaffected thereby.

11. *Jurisdiction.* This agreement shall be construed in accordance with and shall be governed by the laws of the State of Louisiana.

12. *Broker Fees.* Each of the parties represents and warrants that it has dealt with no broker or finder in connection with any of the transactions contemplated by this agreement, and no broker or other person is entitled to any commission or finder's fee in connection with any of these transactions as a result of its actions. Seller and Buyer each agree to indemnify and hold harmless one another against any loss, liability, damage, cost, claim, or expense incurred by reason of any brokerage, commission, or finder's fee alleged to be payable because of any act, omission, or statement of the indemnifying party.

13. *Expenses.* Each of the parties shall pay all costs and expenses incurred or to be incurred by it in negotiation and preparation of this agreement and in closing and carrying out the transactions contemplated by this agreement, except as otherwise specified herein.

14. *Indemnification by Seller.* Seller shall indemnify and hold Buyer and its affiliates, and their respective officers, directors, employees, agents and representatives harmless from and against any and all claims, demands, liabilities, losses, damages and expenses (including, without limitation, reasonable attorneys' fees and costs of defense related thereto) arising from or related to (i) any breach or nonperformance of a representation, warranty, covenant or agreement contained in this agreement by Seller, (ii) Seller's operations of the Company and obligations (specifically including, but not limited to, any and all tax obligations) of the Company attributable to the period prior to the date of this agreement.

15. *General Provisions.* Seller and Buyer have read this Agreement and each warrants that each understands it, is executing this Agreement as their free and voluntary act, reflecting the terms negotiated by the parties, and has been given the opportunity to seek counsel.

• •

PUBLIC OFFERINGS

Much of the excitement around the companies in the new economy has been generated by their very successful public offerings. One of the first new economy companies to get out of the initial public offering (IPO) pipeline was Netscape. In its first day of trading its price shot up dramatically, making a billionaire out of founder Jim Clark. The Internet gold rush was underway.

Going public, however, is not automatic, and a company should carefully consider its options before making this bold step as it can represent a considerable drain on the resources of a company. If your company is in the very early stages of development, it may be better to seek loans from financial institutions or the Small Business Administration. Other alternatives include raising money by selling securities in transactions that are exempt from the registration process.

Some of the benefits of going public include:

- *Access to capital:* Once a company begins trading publicly, it obviously has access to many more potential investors. Without being publicly registered, the company can only be sold in a certain manner that leaves the bulk of the investing public out of the loop. Once public, the company has access to more investors and can therefore become more widely known.
- *Easier financing:* Not only do more people trade your stock, but once your stock is publicly issued, you can follow it with later issues of public debt or equity. In addition, subsequent registration requirements can be easier with the Securities and Exchange Commission (SEC).
- *Provision of an exit strategy:* As mentioned earlier, a public offering provides a partial or total exit strategy. Controlling shareholders, such as the company's officers or directors, may have a ready market for their shares, which means they can more easily sell their interests for retirement, for diversification, or for some other reason.
- *Attraction and retention of talent:* Once public, companies can use stock options to attract and retain more highly qualified personnel, because options and bonuses have a known market value.

- *Marketing benefits:* Not only does your company gain more credibility and attention in the marketplace when it is public, but a public company evokes an image of greater substantiality than does a private company.

Nevertheless, don't minimize the *disadvantages* of going public. Going public imposes a whole new set of obligations and responsibilities. Once your company becomes public, it is very difficult to again become private, and your life becomes generally much more complicated. Some of the disadvantages of going public include the following:

- *Reporting requirements:* All public companies have significant reporting requirements. Once public, you are now accountable to your shareholders for your actions, which must be reported to them. These reports require particular expertise as well as the attention of top management. For example, you must continue to keep shareholders informed about the company's business operations, financial condition, management, additional costs incurred, and new legal obligations.
- *Legal liability:* Under both the Securities Act of 1933 and the Securities Exchange Act of 1934, you are legally liable for failure to comply with your reporting obligations. In addition, you may lose some flexibility in managing your company's affairs, particularly when shareholders must approve your actions.
- *Time and expense:* A public offering is not an easy process. It generally begins with retaining an underwriter; and the underwriter and its counsel, because of the strict requirements of the Securities Act, go through a long and arduous process of due diligence to determined if any material parts of your business have not been explained adequately in the registration statement. Although you may be comfortable about your business, you still have to persuade outside auditors, investment bankers, and attorneys that you have nothing to hide.

Mechanics of the Public Offering Process

Public offering disclosure requirements are fulfilled by the registration statement, which the Securities Act requires you to file. Once filed, the registration statement is subject to review by the SEC. A company cannot issue securities until its statement is declared effective by the SEC.

The issuer must describe for the prospectus the important facts about its business operations, financial condition, and management. Everyone who buys the new issue, as well as anyone who is made an offer to purchase the securities, must have access to the prospectus.

Types of information about the company discussed in the prospectus include:

- Its business
- Its properties
- Its competition
- The identity of its officers and directors and their compensation
- Material transactions between the company and its officers and directors
- Material legal proceedings involving the company or its officers and directors
- The plan for distributing the securities and the intended use of the proceeds of the offering

Registration statements must also include financial statements audited by an independent certified public accountant. In addition to the information expressly required by the form, your company must also provide any other information that is necessary to make your disclosure complete and not misleading. You must also describe clearly and prominently any risks, usually at the beginning of the prospectus. Examples of risks are lack of an operating history; adverse economic conditions in your industry; lack of a market for the securities offered; and dependence on key personnel.

Small business issuers. An alternative process is available for a small business issuer that had less than $25 million in revenues in its last fiscal year and whose outstanding publicly held stock is worth no more than $25 million. If your company qualifies as a small business issuer, it can choose to file its registration statement on one of the simplified small business forms. Other simplified statements, such as Form SB-1—to raise $10 million or less—are also available.

Your company must file information after the registration process with the SEC about

- its operations;
- its officers, directors, and certain shareholders, including salary, various fringe benefits, and transactions between the company and management;
- the financial condition of the business, including financial statements audited by a national accounting firm; and
- its competitive position and material terms of contracts or lease agreements.

This information becomes publicly available when you file your reports with the SEC. As with Securities Act filings, small business issuers may use small business alternative forms for registration and reporting under the Securities Exchange Act.

To facilitate small business capital formation, the North American Securities Administrators Association, or NASAA, in conjunction with the American Bar Association, developed the Small Company Offering Registration, also known as SCOR. SCOR is a simplified question-and-answer registration form that companies may also use as the disclosure document for investors. SCOR was primarily designed for state registration of small business securities offerings conducted under the SEC's Rule 504 for the sale of securities up to $1 million. Currently, over 45 states recognize SCOR. To assist small business issuers in completing the SCOR form, NASAA has developed a detailed *Issuer's Manual*, which is available through NASAA's Web site at <www.nasaa.org>.

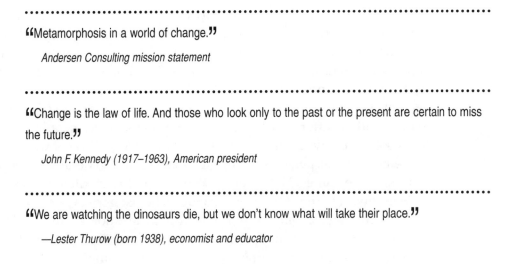

chapter 18

Turning from Bricks to Clicks

"Metamorphosis in a world of change."

Andersen Consulting mission statement

"Change is the law of life. And those who look only to the past or the present are certain to miss the future."

John F. Kennedy (1917–1963), American president

"We are watching the dinosaurs die, but we don't know what will take their place."

—Lester Thurow (born 1938), economist and educator

Many are predicting that in the next five years, no e-business or e-commerce distinction will exist. Businesses that don't integrate the Internet into their business models may end up going the route of the dinosaurs. The existing brick-and-mortar businesses face both challenges and opportunities in turning their businesses into what former Intel Chairman Andrew Grove called a "click-and-mortar" business.

There are tremendous opportunities in the new economy. Existing businesses already competing in a particular space have certain advantages, including knowledge of the industry and, more important, knowledge of its consumers. Much brick-and-mortar knowledge translates directly to the Internet, with existing insights and knowledge capable of being put to immediate use. However, this knowledge has to be refined for utilization in the new economy, requiring innovative thinking about how the Internet can transform a particular industry.

Such a requirement highlights one of the disadvantages of converting to click and mortar: loyalty to the status quo. In other words, your experience could bind you to the past. To be successful in the new economy, it is necessary to sever all ties with the past. Owners have to discard their previous business model and take a fresh look at their business through a consumer prism.

To reiterate, it is advisable to start from scratch and prepare an e-plan that fully exploits the potential opportunities in your industry. What could you do to put yourself out of business? In other words, how could you kill your own business with a better business? Although this question might seem sadistic, it describes the path that all great companies take. A good example is Microsoft. As soon as Microsoft owns a market, it tries to eliminate it with a better product. In its earlier days, many people referred to Microsoft as the house that DOS built because MS-DOS controlled nearly 90 percent of the personal computer market and generated most of the company's revenues. However, DOS was eventually killed off, of course, by Windows, another Microsoft product. The list goes on.

Similarly, how could you employ digital technology to replace your business with a better model? This is not necessarily a complicated question. It is based on attracting, serving, and retaining customers. Simply put, what could you do to improve the customer's experience and add more value to the product or service you offer? What do customers really value? How could you better benefit customers? Could you serve them faster and more efficiently? Could you provide valuable ancillary services? Could you be a one-stop shop for all of their needs in your industry or market? Is there any existing pain?

Another challenge for existing businesses is to build out the necessary IT architecture to support transformation to an e-business. This architecture could include technologies for customer relationship management (CRM), supply chain management, product distribution, and enterprise resource planning—possibly a monumental undertaking, particularly for larger businesses. Even more important than updating your business systems is working with your personnel, who may be wedded to the older model. In fact, it might be easier to reengineer business processes to accommodate the Internet than to reengineer management; at least the processes themselves are objective and not inherently resistant to change. The same might not be true for a company's managers.

Complications often arise when transforming a company to an e-business. One is cannibalization of existing customers. Is there any real benefit in converting existing customers into e-customers? Does it justify the cost of the IT architecture? The answer of course is a resounding YES! To begin with, the customers who gravitate to the online method of doing business could have easily been stolen by a competitor with online capabilities. In addition, the effective CRM technology could permit an even closer relationship with the customers. Naturally, the newer Internet start-ups are not going to have the same concerns, but then new businesses won't have some of the advantages of existing businesses.

Another aggravation for an existing business could be channel conflict. One of the advantages of the e-business is the ability to sidestep traditional distribution channels and deal directly with customers. However, this could lead to issues with existing distributors and become another challenge in transforming a business.

Before jumping to the conclusion that transforming your business is not worth the trouble, consider some of the advantages of the click-and-mortar business.

ADVANTAGES OF CLICK AND MORTAR

The business community is recognizing the tremendous advantages for the click-and-mortar business model, particularly in the highly competitive e-tailing space. It wasn't always this way. When Soon Yu was trying to fund Gazoontite.com for distributing nonprescription allergy products, he encountered resistance to his plans for retail stores. Many venture capital sources were skeptical about his desire to clutter up his business model with the traditional store. But through his research, Soon realized that many consumers were unfamiliar with allergy products, such as filters and air purifiers, and needed to be educated. In addition, Soon determined that retail stores could be a cost-effective way of marketing the overall business.

In fact, *Fortune* magazine referred to Gazoontite's use of retail stores as a truly innovative dot-com ad in contrast to companies spending "millions spraying the airwaves with goofy commercials." The retail store can be a self-sustaining and important part of the marketing equation to cross-promote a product. Implemented properly, the online and offline strategy could be synergistic with stores driving people to the site and vice versa. However, both online and offline marketing have to be closely coordinated in all aspects of the operation.

An example of an excellent online service with an offline counterpart is *The Wall Street Journal.* It began its online version several years ago, and its subscription base has been constantly growing. Its online version serves as a useful complement to the print publication.

A company that is making a significant error in integrating its operations is the giant bookseller Barnes & Noble. If you ever browse through one of their bookstores, the existence of barnesandnoble.com seems to be a secret. There is no mention of its Web presence anywhere in the store or in the Barnes & Noble newsletter. There are no terminals in the store where you can order books online and you cannot return books ordered online at the store. Such interaction between the store and site could be a clear advantage in how Barnes & Noble could distinguish itself from Amazon.com. It is missing a wonderful opportunity to cross-promote its site and bookstores.

The original business model of Gateway computers was to sell computers by mail order, primarily using phone orders. In 1996, Gateway began to open its country stores where customers could go to view products and order computers. Several financial commentators were openly skeptical of that move. After all, weren't the low-margin retail stores a vestige of the past? How could Gateway hope to compete with Dell in taking such a backward step? However, Gateway was paying more attention to customers as opposed to the financial press. It knew that a significant percentage of customers were not comfortable buying computers over the phone or online, but rather wanted the more traditional retail experience. This experience included viewing and sampling products as well as talking to sales representatives face-to-face. Gateway was able to provide the best of both worlds by providing the retail experience while still benefiting from economies of scale. Like Dell's online model, the computers were still manufactured to order and then shipped directly to the customer. Gateway was able to eliminate inventory and also provide for direct customer interaction. The country stores have been tremendously successful for Gateway.

Another example of a company successfully leveraging its brick-and-mortar competency to an online model is the Apollo Group, which owns the University of Phoenix. The University of Phoenix (UOP) is the largest university in the country with over 70,000 students. In addition, the university has been a leader in online education, having started using the Internet to offer courses in 1989. The market for online learning is growing rapidly, and that space is being quickly crowded by many start-ups and traditional educational institutions that are attracted to the enormous potential of the market. This potential stems from the ability to leverage technology to reach students without the physical operating costs of traditional educational institutions. Many companies have set up educational sites and are trying to attract students. The UOP has a decided advantage over many, particularly online universities, with its large number of existing campuses and its knowledge and experience with its core group of students. With 70,000 students, the university already knows how to get customers through the door and is applying this knowledge to its online division.

The core competency of the UOP is the adult learner. For many colleges and universities, their evening division or metropolitan college was often the stepchild of the institution. Adult students were often never completely integrated into the university experience. Enter the UOP, with an education model that caters specifically to the working adult student. It offers classes one night a week, and the courses last five to six weeks. Classes are generally small (13 to 14 students) and the students form study groups, which they remain in during their pursuit of a degree. Faculty members are required to have master's degrees and be employed in the area in which they instruct. Courses emphasize the application of theory to work situations, and many industry demographics are in their favor. For example, 40 percent of all people pursuing degrees are over the age of 40. In addition, the wage gap between those with a high school versus a college degree grew from 25 percent in 1980 to 89 percent in 1996.

According to Brian Mueller, vice president and chief operating officer of University of Phoenix Online, the online division is modeled after its brick-and-mortar campuses. The online division also caters to the working adult and uses many of the successful practices of the brick-and-mortar campuses. For example, the online model uses a discussion or cohort group composed of nine or ten students for each class. During the five- to six-week class period, students have to log on to their discussion group on five out of seven days. Students are graded on both the content and frequency of their online discussion. In addition, there is individual interaction between the instructor and the student in a separate and private chat room. In this private chat room, case studies, short papers, and long papers are submitted and evaluated. Finally, there are study groups of three or four that submit a team project. Like the brick-and-mortar campus, many in the study group as well as those in the cohort group go through the various curricula together. Although a bit cumbersome, these multiple chat forums provide the opportunity for considerable interaction and serve to replace the social experience of traditional education. Online education can be a very lonely experience and this collaboration helps to achieve a high retention rate.

The online program is currently growing at a 50 percent rate, adding 1,000 to 1,500 students a month. The UOP has a total of 13,500 students seeking online degrees, a faculty of 1,200, and a staff of 400. The IT infrastructure required to support such a large operation is considerable. The company is moving toward 24-hour, seven-day administrative support. In order to teach online, faculty members, besides meeting the regular faculty qualifications, must go through a four-week training period followed by a five- to six-week mentorship. Neither the mentorship nor the training is compensated, and 35 percent of the prospective faculty members who start the training complete it.

UOP Online derives a large portion of its students through referrals from existing online students. The next largest portion of students results from Internet advertising, which includes banner ads on related sites and premium positions on search engines. Finally, partnerships with educational portals are the next important source of students (e.g., Hungry Minds).

Another battleground where the click-and-mortar strategy is beginning to bear fruit is in the area of online brokerage. Although most traditional brokers were caught flatfooted by Internet brokers, such as E*Trade and Ameritrade, they have begun fighting back. Leveraging their customer service infrastructure, they have begun seriously challenging the pure e-brokers for the online market.

The main lessons from these click-and-mortar stories is that the melding of the old and new economy requires careful navigation. Traditional businesses, no matter what industry they are in, can only ignore the Internet at their peril. In addition, pure Internet businesses need to keep a watchful eye on the traditional models and infrastructure of the old economy. The businesses that successfully match the two will be the ones that thrive in the information age.

resource guide

Compiled with the Research Assistance of Information Matters, LLC

∙∙

There's no such thing as being too well informed when starting a business, much less starting an online company. Even though this book has shown you the steps needed to develop your plan, there's a lot of additional information you need to make decisions specific to your business. You need to use multiple methods for your research, including the telephone; you also need to use online research, both free and fee-based, much of which can be found in many different places on the Internet. So here is a fairly extensive list of sites and sources to provide you a variety of resources you can use to develop your strategies and write your e-plan.

(Disclaimer: The Web sites and their addresses listed below were operational as of the writing of this book—that is, during the first and second quarters of 2000. Because of the dynamic nature of the Web environment and the status of any given server along the network, the following URLs and the data under them may have changed.)

SITES OF START-UPS, IPOs, AND VENTURE CAPITALISTS

<www.ace.net.sr.unh.edu/pub>

Started by the U.S. government's Small Business Administration, this Internet-based service lists small companies looking for funds. It is a secure site where investors wanting to provide $250,000 to $5 million can become a member to learn about a proposed venture online before contact is made.

<www.angelatlanta.com>

A group of angel investors in search of early-stage technology companies in which it can invest wants to provide both capital and business expertise as well as being actively involved. Applicants are evaluated by the group, but individual angels pursue discussions with their specific selections.

<www.bcentral.com>

Microsoft's portal for small business provides headline information and has lots of links to lots of resources covering marketing online and offline, purchasing functions, and communities.

<www.businessfinance.com>

This business capital search engine seeks to match, through an auto-mated system, a database of small companies seeking financing with in-vestors who are searching for different niches in such companies. Funding sources must pay a fee to participate. The site also provides an expert cen-ter with a funding workbook you can download and links to Small Busi-ness Development Centers and the SBA's SCORE locations.

<www.edgar-online.com>

This site of the U.S. Securities and Exchange Commission for filings can be searched by company name or ticker symbol.

<www.entrepreneur.com>

A site designed for those just taking the leap into the risk/reward world of establishing a company and working to grow it provides information on starting a company and how to grow a business.

<www.garage.com>

This is a matchmaker site that facilitates pairing investors with science and technology start-ups for initial funding. Assistance in obtaining seed-level financing is its prime objective. It provides investors with screened, high-quality investment opportunities and hosts an investor community. Start-ups submit their business plans for screening and selection. The site also provides advice, research and reference materials, and forums.

<www.home3.americanexpress.com/smallbusiness>

This site, the Small Business Exchange, is a product of American Ex-press. It provides helpful information and articles on various aspects and stages of starting and running a business. Although it's also a vehicle to promote the American Express card, the value of the articles is worth a visit.

<www.ipodata.com>

This site specializes in reporting IPO news and data. It uses Edgar On-line and analyses to deliver tearsheets, datafeeds, and custom reporting.

<www.redherring.com>

Red Herring provides market information and insights on the technology industry as well as news about IPOs, investors, and start-ups. You will also find discussion groups.

<www.sba.gov>

This huge site has tons of information and advice from the Small Business Administration about starting, financing, and expanding a business; it also has local contacts and an answer desk. Interactive aspects include a gateway to such resources as SBA Net and procurement access.

<www.sba.gov/financing>

At this site you can learn about SBA loan and lender programs, download forms, and find workshops and other matters related to your financial functions.

<www.sba.gov/INV>

The Small Business Investment Companies Program was established by the SBA many years ago. Privately organized and managed investment firms have formed a partnership with government to provide equity capital, long-term loans, and expert management assistance.

<www.sba.gov/SBIR/sttr.html>

Here you can learn about the Small Business Technology Transfer program (STTR), which recognizes small business as the incubators where innovation and innovators are born and flourish. Because small business usually cannot financially afford the risk and expenses of research and development, the U.S. government, through the SBA, reserves a specific percentage of federal R&D funding to partner with small businesses and nonprofit research institutions. Its role is to foster innovations for the 21st century. States with the highest level of funding in 1998 were California with 67 awards totaling $14.6 million and Massachusetts with 49 awards for almost $10.5 million.

<www.startupzone.com>

StartupZone is a database of start-up technology companies for those seeking investment opportunities, acquisitions, partnerships, or jobs. The database is categorized by industry and profiles individual companies. You can register your start-up at the site so it's included in the database.

<www.tech-net.sba.gov>

This site is a source of technology transfer information as well as a database where a company can search for a technology partnership, licensing, and investment opportunities. It provides an opportunity for small businesses to expand by promoting their products and services.

<www.thecapitalnetwork.com>

This nonprofit economic development organization was developed to provide entrepreneurial ventures with training for selling their business concept to venture capital investors. It offers matchmaker services, software, seminars, conferences, and a pool of experts and advisors, including a 30-minute video it sells for coaching entrepreneurs in preparing presentations to potential investors.

<www.vcapital.com>

This home to venture capital firms with billions of assets, law firms, accounting firms, and other service providers provides information and resources for high-growth start-ups, including an e-mail newsletter and an online hardware and software retail outlet. It also hosts an idea exchange series in various parts of the country on educational and networking opportunities.

ONLINE PUBLICATIONS

<www.adage.com>

Advertising Age magazine covers all aspects of advertising, including Internet advertising. In partnership with Neilsen/NetRatings, it provides a weekly report on Web traffic and advertising, and shows a table of the most-viewed Internet banner ads for each week. You can also search its archive of articles.

<www.americandemographics.com>

At this site, you can search articles from back issues of this monthly magazine—*American Demographics*—that is geared for marketing professionals; and you can order other resources that will help you understand the American consumer.

<www.cyberatlas.internet.com>

This online magazine, or e-zine, site is chock-full of good articles and great data. Enter the above URL for the latest demographic trends, news stories, and research capsules.

<www.eiu.com>

The online home of the Economist Intelligence Unit is primarily a fee-based publisher of information for companies whose business crosses national borders, such as dot-coms. It analyzes and forecasts the political, economic, and business environments of most countries in the world.

<www.fastcompany.com>

This online e-zine spotlights leading-edge companies in changing businesses in the new economy. It is a community of people who believe and live in the business fast lane.

<www.platts.com>

Home of Standard & Poor's family of Platt's publications, it covers such industries as oil, petrochemicals, metals, shipping, power, and gas.

<www.venturewire.com>

Venture Wire is published by Technologic Partners, a company whose focus of its newsletters and conferences is high-tech companies. Through an e-mail subscription, it provides daily news flashes about privately held high-tech companies that cover new deals, new companies, new executives, market venture capital, high-tech CEOs, bankers, and high-tech specialist attorneys and accountants.

SITES FOR MARKETING RESEARCH AND MARKETING

<www.aiip.org>

This site is for an international association of owners of information research businesses. There are 1,800 such companies in 51 countries that conduct both primary and secondary research on a wide variety of subject areas. The site will help you locate the ones that meet your research needs and budget, and it can do it faster and better than you can do it yourself, leaving you more time to focus on planning and operations.

<www.ama.org>

The American Marketing Association (AMA) is an association of professional marketers and market researchers who practice and teach marketing. The AMA sponsors numerous events and programs around the United States each year. The site hosts special interest groups (SIGs) on business-to-business marketing, global marketing, consumer behavior, and the like.

<www.careerpath.com>

For information about your competitors, check out this site. It's for both job seekers and employers, but it provides insight into a competitor's strategies based on the kinds of positions posted.

<www.census.gov>

This is the U.S. Department of Commerce's Web site for demographic data, where you can get population estimates and projections, income distribution, and maps. It also provides business census data and a list of the new codes for the North American Industry Classification System (NAICS).

<www.corptech.com>

This site has a database of over 50,000 public and private high-tech companies searchable by name or ticker symbol. It can help discover information about competitors.

<www.dejanews.com>

This is a search engine that tracks online discussion groups. Postings for help wanted may also reveal competitors' strategies. Look for the Jobs archive under Search Discussions.

<www.glreach.com/globalstats>

The site has a table showing Internet usage by language and country.

<www.hoovers.com>

This site was founded by entrepreneur Gary Hoover, who developed the concept of the book superstore and the original *Hoover's Handbook* reference book series.

<www.infoUSA.com>

Business-to-business center for sales and marketing information on the Internet. Offers visitors access to exclusive database of 200 million customers and 12 million businesses.

<www.janal.com>

This is the site of Internet marketing guru Dan Janal. A highly respected speaker, author, University of California-Berkeley professor, and expert, Dan was on the PR team that launched AOL in 1982.

<www.nber.org>

The National Bureau of Economic Research is a nonprofit, nonpartisan research organization founded in 1920, whose site has high-level data on industries and consumers.

<www.nbia.org>

This Web site of the nonprofit National Business Incubation Association (NBIA), whose membership consists of the nation's business incubators, provides information about how an incubator works and what you can expect. It posts news and notices of conferences and also has an online bookstore specializing in business start-up and growth.

<www.nvca.org>

The National Venture Capital Association has a membership of more than 300 venture capital and private equity firms. One of the association's purposes is to help increase the flow of private risk equity capital to help young companies develop. Visit the site to learn how venture capitalists think.

<www.prnewswire.com>

This is an information outlet that publishes immediate and archived press releases of worldwide companies. Press releases are used by the media, business, financial communities, and individual investors. Keep in mind that because these are press releases, they generally report only what the company wants to show.

<www.scip.org>

This is the home of the Society of Competitive Intelligence (CI) Professionals, where you can understand how CI affects your business plan and everyday decision making. Here you can find a CI professional to whom to outsource your CI research.

<www.state.gov>

The U.S. Department of State's Web site provides information about countries' economic and trade policies and valuable links when considering the ramifications of global markets.

<www.survey.net>

This site provides demographic statistics about Web users and Internet use. Its surveys of business provide demographics on Net users, such as age, household income, frequency and purpose of use, and so on.

<www.websitez.com/zhub.shtml>

This site has a database of over 1 million Web addresses. You can search for a URL by entering a partial Web address or a company name, or you can search by category.

SITES RELATED TO OPERATING FUNCTIONS

<www.estamps.com>

This is a place to buy online postage.

<www.fcc.gov>

Here you can find out the Federal Communications Commission's policies and positions on such topics as broadband Internet access and other regulations that may affect your business.

<www.irs.ustreas.gov/bus_info/index.html>

This is the section of the IRS site dedicated to small business information and advice. It includes information about starting and operating a new small business, a tax calendar, and certain market-specific tax regulations.

<www.netnames.com>

This counterpart of Network Solutions for international domain name registration also provides links to related articles and information.

<www.nsol.com>

This is the site of Network Solutions, where you can find out if your preferred domain name is taken and also register your domain name. Also known as Internic, Network Solutions registered the ten millionth domain name in mid-April, 2000. Network Solutions was bought by Verisign in early 2000.

<www.smartbiz.com>

This resource site for business owners and managers to help them run their companies better contains many articles searchable by category or by searching. You can locate trade shows, check out special offers, or sub-scribe to the newsletter.

<www.verisign.com>

This is a provider of Internet trust services, which include authentica-tion, validation, and payment, needed by Web sites and e-commerce provid-ers to conduct trusted and secure electronic commerce and communications over Internet networks.

<www.usps.com>

This is the electronic home of the U.S. Postal Service. Even though you are a dot-com company, you will at some time send or receive items through the U.S. mail. That this site allows you to pay bills online tells you this is not your father's post office.

SEARCH ENGINES TO FIND MORE

If you haven't had enough, or if none of the above has the information you need, here is a list of search engines to help you try and locate even more information:

<www.altavista.com>
<www.google.com>
<http://home.miningco.com>
<www.lycos.com>
<www.northernlight.com>
<www.searchuk.com>
<www.webcrawler.com>
<www.yahoo.com>

The following are meta–search engines, which search multiple engines at one time:

<www.askjeeves.com>
<www.dogpile.com>
<www.find.com>

index